Discourse Particles in Asian Languages Volume I

This is the first of two volumes of research on discourse particles focusing exclusively on the languages of Asia from the perspective of formal as well as non-formal semantics and pragmatics.

Within linguistics, there has been a great deal of interest in discourse particles, especially within semantics and pragmatics. The term 'discourse particles' has been used to cover a broad range of phenomena, including such things as 'sentence-final particles,' 'discourse adverbs,' and other related phenomena. However, most research in the area (particularly within formal semantics and pragmatics) focuses on a restricted set of languages, and there is little consensus on the proper formal treatment of particles, partly due to the limited range of data available.

In recent years, there has been extensive development of the formal approach to discourse particles, which often treats these words as devices for marking information updates. It is also vital to extend this data to non-Western languages like Japanese, Korean, or Chinese. This edited volume includes chapters on Japanese, Mandarin, Tagalog, Kimaragang Dusun, Malay, Singlish, Thai, and Vietnamese. The chapters are informed by recent theoretical work in formal semantics and pragmatics relating to the meaning of particles. The collection contributes to our theoretical understanding of the meaning of discourse particles and to empirical knowledge of discourse particles in the languages of Asia. It will be of interest to postgraduate students and scholars of semantics and pragmatics.

Elin McCready is Professor in the Department of English Language and Literature at Aoyama Gakuin University, Japan.

Hiroki Nomoto is Associate Professor of Malay Language and Linguistics at Tokyo University of Foreign Studies, Japan.

Routledge Studies in Linguistics

For more information about this series, please visit: www.routledge.com/Routledge-Studies-in-Linguistics/book-series/SE0719

Discourse Particles in Asian Languages Volume I

East Asia

Edited by Elin McCready and
Hiroki Nomoto

Routledge
Taylor & Francis Group

LONDON AND NEW YORK

First published 2024
by Routledge
4 Park Square, Milton Park, Abingdon, Oxon OX14 4RN

and by Routledge
605 Third Avenue, New York, NY 10158

Routledge is an imprint of the Taylor & Francis Group, an informa business

© 2024 selection and editorial matter, Elin McCready and Hiroki Nomoto; individual chapters, the contributors

The right of Elin McCready and Hiroki Nomoto to be identified as the authors of the editorial material, and of the authors for their individual chapters, has been asserted in accordance with sections 77 and 78 of the Copyright, Designs and Patents Act 1988.

British Library Cataloguing-in-Publication Data
A catalogue record for this book is available from the British Library

ISBN: 978-1-138-48243-2 (hbk)
ISBN: 978-1-032-44839-8 (pbk)
ISBN: 978-1-351-05783-7 (ebk)

DOI: 10.4324/9781351057837

Typeset in Galliard
by Apex CoVantage, LLC

Contents

Figures

Tables

Contributors

Yurie Hara is an associate professor of linguistics at Hokkaido University. Her research interest is formal semantics and pragmatics.

Satomi Ito is a professor of Chinese linguistics at Ochanomizu University. Her research interests are formal semantics and Chinese grammar.

Regine Lai is an assistant professor at the Chinese University of Hong Kong. Her research interests are phonology and language acquisition.

Soo-Hwan Lee is a PhD student in linguistics at New York University. His research is on syntax and morphology. He focuses on discourse particles and case markers in Korean. He also focuses on evaluating language models on tasks related to linguistic phenomena, including control, anaphor binding, and presuppositions.

Zoe Pei-sui Luk is an assistant professor of linguistics at the Education University of Hong Kong. Her research interest is language acquisition and cognitive linguistics.

David Y. Oshima is an associate professor of linguistics at Nagoya University. His main research areas are semantics, pragmatics, and Japanese linguistics.

Lukas Rieser is a senior assistant professor of linguistics at Tokyo University of Agriculture and Technology. His research interest is (formal) analysis of pragmatic meaning.

Hooi Ling Soh is a professor of linguistics at the University of Minnesota. Her research interests include topics in syntax and semantics and how they interact, with focus on languages spoken in Southeast Asia. Her current research focuses on the syntax and semantics of discourse particles. She has worked on discourse particles in Mandarin Chinese, English, Malay, and Hmong.

Grégoire Winterstein is a professeur at Université du Québec à Montréal. His research interests cover formal semantics and pragmatics, as well as computational linguistics, with a focus on the argumentative side of language.

Introduction

Elin McCready and Hiroki Nomoto

In linguistics, especially in the subfield of discourse analysis, there has been substantial interest in 'discourse markers' since the introduction of the concept by such scholars as Schiffrin (1987) and Schourup (1985). For them, 'discourse markers' were restricted to interjections and conjunctives. The term 'discourse particles' has been used to cover a much broader range of phenomena, including such things as 'sentence-final particles,' 'discourse adverbs,' and other particles in addition to 'discourse markers' as defined earlier.

The meanings conveyed by discourse particles are extremely heterogeneous, leading to them also being called 'pragmatic particles' or 'modal particles.' They can indicate the information status of a sentence or part of a sentence, provide question meanings or mark politeness, or even indicate exclamation or surprise. Consequently, the best way to characterize their meanings remains controversial both from formal and informal perspectives.

Within the formal semantics and pragmatics literature, various approaches have been proposed to the meanings of particles, but no consensus is currently available. Existing resources for the semantics and pragmatics of discourse particles are collections of papers on the topic covering a somewhat-arbitrary selection of approaches and phenomena (Abraham 1991; Fischer 2006; Bayer & Struckmeier 2017). These books typically consider the meanings of particles in European languages, particularly German and English. The present volumes are the first to give an exclusive focus on discourse particles in non-European languages, more specifically East and Southeast Asian languages, which are well-known for their richness of discourse particles. This volume discusses four East Asian languages: Japanese, Mandarin Chinese, Cantonese, and Korean. Volume 2 discusses five Southeast Asian languages: Tagalog, Kimaragang Dusun, Malay, Thai, and Vietnamese.

The articles in these volumes offer descriptions and specific analyses of discourse particles in these languages. Considering data from these languages will deepen our empirical and theoretical understanding of discourse particles. First, it allows a characterization of the ingredients required for the general analysis of discourse particles. Second, one can deploy the resulting tools in the analysis of discourse particles from a range of diverse languages.

DOI: 10.4324/9781351057837-1

The present volumes consist of 16 chapters discussing nine languages in East and Southeast Asia. The chapters are ordered according to the areas in which the languages discussed are used. Some chapters are theoretical and are informed by recent theoretical work in formal semantics and pragmatics relating to the meaning of discourse particles. Others are more descriptive and present empirical facts that are quite unique in the literature and should be of great interest to researchers on both discourse particles and Asian languages in general.

The chapters in this volume consider several issues relating to particles in the languages of East Asia, specifically Japanese, Korean, and Chinese. The first two chapters discuss Japanese. In the first chapter, **David Y. Oshima** aims to provide an adequate semantic description of one of the major uses of the *no (da)* construction. The relevant use has been labeled as the 'discovery,' 'grasping,' or 'comprehension' use by Japanese grammarians and is exemplified by a sentence, such as *A, koko ni ita* **n da** 'Oh, there you are.' In light of the recent discussion of the notion of mirativity ('linguistic marking of an utterance as conveying information which is new or unexpected to the speaker,' DeLancey 2001) in the typological literature, Oshima argues that *no (da)* in its 'discovery' use can sensibly be regarded as a mirative marker. He further discusses some subtle aspects of its meaning that do not automatically follow from its being a mirative marker.

The second chapter, by **Lukas Rieser**, discusses the evidential particle *no* in Japanese, which has received considerable attention in the formal and descriptive literature. There is no consensus on how to distinguish it from and connect it to the homophonous complementizer typically occurring in the *no da* construction discussed in Oshima's chapter. Based on observations about various uses, Rieser argues that the particle *no* can be sharply distinguished from the complementizer *no* in the *no da* construction. He analyzes it as an utterance modifier introducing an evidence condition parallel to that on assertion but requiring mutually accessible evidence. On the background of comparison with *no da* construction counterparts in other languages, he proposes that evidential *no* has developed from the complementizer in bridging contexts of evidence-based inference.

The next two chapters are concerned with Mandarin Chinese. In the third chapter in the volume, **Hooi Ling Soh** presents new observations regarding discourse restrictions and interpretative effects of Mandarin Chinese sentence-final *de* in a bare *de* sentence and proposes an analysis of *de* as a discourse marker, marking 'private evidence.' She then considers distributional restrictions of *de* in yes/no questions and shows that they follow from the analysis, coupled with a specific proposal about the syntax of *de*, and certain standard assumptions about the syntax of yes/no questions and modal auxiliaries. Soh's analysis has implications for the syntax of modal auxiliaries, the relation between bare *de* sentences and *shi . . . de* sentences, and the syntax of discourse particles. It connects *de* with particles that mark the speaker's belief about whether the (evidence for the) asserted proposition is shared knowledge between the speaker and the hearer and whether it is 'verifiable on the spot.'

Satomi Ito, in the volume's fourth chapter, discusses the particle *ne* in Mandarin Chinese in light of partition semantics, according to which the meaning of an interrogative is represented as a partition on the set of possible worlds (Hamblin 1973; Karttunen 1977). Ito shows that the particle *ne* marks the contrast between the cells of the partition induced by an interrogative and that the contrastive use of the particle can be applied to declaratives and rhetorical questions. She further argues that the particle *ne* following nominals marks topic.

The next two chapters discuss another Chinese language, namely, Cantonese. The fifth chapter, by **Yurie Hara**, analyzes four kinds of polar questions, that is, *ho2*, *me1*, *aa4*, and A-not-A questions, in the framework of radical inquisitive semantics (Groenendijk & Roelofsen 2010; Aher 2012; Sano 2015). *Ho2*, *me1*, and A-not-A questions exhibit a multi-dimensional semantics. In addition to their primary speech act of questioning, *ho2* and *me1* interrogatives encode secondary assertive acts of positive and negative expectations, respectively, while A-not-A interrogatives conventionally encode lack of expectation, hence the neutrality requirement. In contrast, *aa4* interrogatives are semantically simplex question acts and so can be used in both biased and neutral contexts. The analysis is further supported by one forced-choice experiment and one naturalness rating experiment.

Grégoire Winterstein, Regine Lai, and Zoe Pei-sui Luk's chapter, the sixth in the present volume, examines the linguistic correlates of the notions of 'assertiveness' and 'softness' in Cantonese. Specifically, it focuses on a set of sentence-final particles often described as conveying these two values: the particles *aa3*, *ge3*, and *gaa3*. They argue that these elements do not directly encode assertiveness and softness but, rather, that these come as side effects of the conversational and dialogical nature of these particles. On one hand, they argue that *aa3* encodes an explicit call on the addressee to mirror the content of the conversational move of the speaker, while on the other hand, *ge3* indicates that the utterance of the speaker addresses (and is presented as solving) a salient decision problem in a way comparable to the Japanese particle *yo*. The particle *gaa3* combines the effects of *ge3* and *aa3*. It is then the competition between *ge3* and *gaa3* that explains the assertiveness attached to the former.

The last chapter in Volume 1 is a study on the Korean particle *yo* by **Soo-Hwan Lee**. The repeated use of expressives in general gives rise to a strengthening effect referred to as repeatability (Potts 2007). The notion of repeatability, however, requires further scrutiny. Unlike other formality-denoting expressives, medial *yo*s in Korean show an uncommon pattern of behavior: the more *yo*s you have, the less sense of formality you get. Adopting many of the concepts introduced in Potts (2005, 2007) and McCready (2019), Lee offers a formal analysis of how a repeated use of an expressive can weaken the expressive content. Further, medial *yo*s can only be realized in the presence of another formality marker, such as *(su)pni*. His findings suggest that there are predictable restrictions on expressives which have largely been understudied in the literature. Specifically, Lee argues that medial *yo*s are underspecified in terms of their expressive content and that they are dependent on a fully specified expressive elsewhere in the derivation.

The second volume discusses particles in several languages primarily spoken in Southeast Asia. The first two chapters in the second volume are concerned with Tagalog, an Austronesian language spoken in the Philippines. **Scott AnderBois** investigates the second-position particle *pala*. Similar to many descriptions of miratives cross-linguistically, Schachter and Otanes's (1972) classic descriptive grammar of Tagalog describes it as 'expressing mild surprise at new information, or an unexpected event or situation.' Drawing on recent work on mirativity in other languages, however, AnderBois shows that this characterization needs to be refined in two ways. First, while *pala* can be used in cases of surprise, *pala* itself merely encodes the speaker's sudden revelation with the counterexpectational nature of surprise arising pragmatically or from other aspects of the sentence, such as other particles and focus. Second, he presents data from imperatives and interrogatives, arguing that this revelation need not concern 'information' per se but rather the illocutionay update the sentence encodes. Finally, he explores the interactions between *pala* and other elements which express mirativity in some way and/or interact with the mirativity *pala* expresses.

Naonori Nagaya's chapter, the second chapter in Volume 2, provides an overview of discourse particles in Tagalog by observing naturalistic data produced by Tagalog speakers. In addition, Nagaya offers a case study of the sentence-final particle *e*, which is the most frequent sentence-final particle in his corpus. This particle has three different uses: as a marker of reason, a stance-justifying marker, and a marker of negative evaluation. It is suggested that a polysemy approach rather than a list or general-meaning approach can best account for the behavior of such a multifunctional particle.

Paul R. Kroeger, in Volume 2's third chapter, describes the particle *gima* in Kimaragang Dusun, an Austronesian language spoken in the northern part of Sabah, Malaysia. Its meaning and functions seem to be similar (but not identical) to those of German unstressed *ja*. The core descriptive meaning associated with *gima* seems to be that the propositional content of the utterance is uncontroversial and accessible to both speaker and addressee. In addition, this particle may convey expressive content, particularly in exclamatory utterances, conveying the speaker's surprise, annoyance, disapproval, etc.

In the fourth chapter in Volume 2, **Michael Yoshitaka Erlewine** investigates the syntax and semantics of Singlish (Colloquial Singapore English) sentence-final *already* and its development in the contact ecology of Singapore. Bao (2005) identifies the Mandarin Chinese perfective suffix *-le* and sentence-final particle *le* as two substrate sources for Singlish *already*. Erlewine argues instead that sentence-final *le* – together with its cognate *liao/laa* in other Chinese languages of Singapore – is the sole substrate source for the syntax and semantics of Singlish *already*. The various interpretational effects of *already* can be derived from a uniform semantics shared with its substrate cognate particles *le/liao/laa*, together with consideration of the telicity of the predicate. He furthermore shows that the syntax of *already* differs subtly from that of its substrate cognates. Singlish sentence-final *already* unambiguously scopes over the entire clause, whereas its substrate cognate particles *le/liau/ laa* are in a clause-medial position. It is proposed that this difference can be explained through a process of reanalysis forced by the interaction of a syntactic universal, the final-over-final constraint, together with independent differences between Singlish and its substrate Chinese languages.

The next chapter, by **Hooi Ling Soh**, is also about 'already,' but in Malay: *dah* in Colloquial Malay spoken in Peninsular Malaysia and *sudah* in Standard Formal Malay and Sabah Malay. Presenting new empirical facts, Soh argues that two uses of *dah* must be distinguished: one as an aspectual marker, and one as a discourse marker whose use indicates that the speaker holds a certain belief about the common ground. The two uses differ in their syntactic positioning. Soh also compares the use of *dah* with *sudah* in Sabah Malay. While *sudah* has been noted to exhibit a preference to appear post-verbally in Sabah Malay (Hoogervorst 2011), she shows that post-verbal *sudah* patterns like sentence-final *sudah* and unlike preverbal *sudah*. The results have implications on the cross-linguistic properties distinguishing 'already' from perfect aspect (Vander Klok & Matthewson 2015). Furthermore, Soh connects Colloquial Malay *dah* and Sabah Malay *sudah* with Mandarin Chinese particle *le*, which is known to have an aspectual or a discourse function, depending on its syntactic positioning, whether post-verbally or sentence-finally (Li & Thompson 1981). As the aspectual and discourse *le* have been analyzed as sharing a core meaning, with different semantic effects arising from their distinct syntactic positions (e.g. Huang & Davis 1989; Soh 2008), Soh's chapter adds two varieties of Malay to the group of languages that are fruitful to consider when determining how the syntactic positioning of a grammatical item may affect its meaning.

Hiroki Nomoto's chapter is also on Malay. Nomoto discusses the particle *pun* in Standard Malay, which is polyfunctional. Besides the simple additive (≈ *too, also*), scalar additive (≈ *even*), and final particle uses, it has another use that has been described as expressing a temporal meaning in the literature. He offers formal analyses of these uses, with a primary focus on the last kind, namely, the so-called 'event-sequence' *pun*. He shows that this use is in fact more general and is not restricted to temporal relations between events. He argues that it is essentially a type of additive: 'propositional additive.' Propositional additive differs from the ordinary 'individual additive' in that the alternative propositions share a discourse-structural property (= properties of propositions) rather than properties concerning individuals. Specifically, they answer the same immediate question under discussion (QUD). The temporal meaning is not encoded by the *pun* itself but arises pragmatically when the QUD is 'What happened to X?'

Upsorn Tawilapakul and Elin McCready also utilize the QUD model and analyze discourse particles in Thai, in the seventh chapter in Volume 2. Taking the status of information in the common ground and information management by the speaker into account, they propose an approach which incorporates the mechanism of QUD. They connect QUD-based approaches with other non-officially QUD-based particle analyses and exemplify its application with new analyses of the particles in Central Thai. The relation between particles and intonation is briefly discussed through the analysis of the particle *ná*.

Kiyoko Takahashi presents a data-driven analysis of spoken uses of the Thai pragmatic particle /kˆOO/. Drawing on an examination of instances in dialogic discourse, Takahashi's chapter identifies several speech-act types related to uses of /kˆOO/ and reveals that /kˆOO/ interpersonally functions as a reaction marker when the speaker uses it turn-initially and takes into consideration the interlocutor's previous utterance as a communicatively given presupposition. A fine classification of the instances enables us to see the plausibility of /kˆOO/ having broadened past its original, text-procedural function to a logical and modal one, and further to an interpersonal one.

The last two chapters deal with Vietnamese. **Anne Nguyen** documents the usage and distribution of the Vietnamese sentence-final particle *cơ* in the ninth chapter in Volume 2. The particle is found in different sentence types and seemingly used for various purposes. Nguyen argues that those uses attributed to the particle can be unified and proposes that *cơ* is a scalar particle, reflecting a conflict between speaker belief and expectations that arise from the preceding conversation. The proposition marked by *cơ* is required to be stronger than its contrasting alternatives on a given scale.

Thuan Tran's chapter is concerned with the interface between information structure and syntax in Vietnamese; this is the final chapter in Volume 2. Tran argues that left dislocation in Vietnamese is triggered by contrast, an information structural category as autonomous as topic and focus. However, contrast differs from topic and focus in a fundamental way. While the former is semantic in nature and is syntactically operative, the latter are pragmatic and syntactically inert.

We believe that with these chapters collected in one place, the present volumes will contribute to our theoretical understanding of the meaning of discourse particles and to empirical knowledge of discourse particles in the languages of Asia and beyond.

We would like to express our gratitude to Christopher Davis, Henrison Hsieh, Wataru Okubo, Jozina Vander Klok, and Mengxi Yuan, who read some of the chapters and offered insightful comments to improve them. We would also like to thank Yukinori Takubo, who was originally part of the editorial team. It was Yuki who first proposed putting together the research on discourse particles on Asian languages into a volume. Without his initial initiative and encouragement, this volume would not have been possible. Lastly, we would like to note that many of the contributors of this volume were members of the joint project 'Semantics of Discourse Particles in East and Southeast Asian Languages' at the Research Institute for Languages and Cultures of Asia and Africa, Tokyo University of Foreign Studies. This project played an important role of gathering researchers of various Asian languages to discuss the same topic and learn from each other, which finally resulted in this volume.

References

Abraham, Werner (ed.). 1991. *Discourse particles: Descriptive and theoretical investigations on the logical, syntactic and pragmatic properties of discourse particles in German*. Amsterdam: John Benjamins. doi:10.1075/pbns.12.

Aher, Martin. 2012. Free choice in deontic inquisitive semantics. In Maria Aloni, Vadim Kimmelman, Floris Roelofsen, Galit W. Sassoon, Katrin Schulz & Matthijs Westera (eds.), *Logic, language and meaning, 18th Amsterdam Colloquium, Amsterdam*, 22–31. Berlin, Heidelberg: Springer. doi:10.1007/978-3-642-31482-7_3. Lecture Notes in Computer Science.

Bao, Zhiming. 2005. The aspectual system of Singapore English and the systemic substratist explanation. *Journal of Linguistics* 41. 237–267. doi:10.1017/S0022226705003269.

Bayer, Josef & Volker Struckmeier (eds.). 2017. *Discourse particles: Formal approaches to their syntax and semantics*. Berlin: Walter de Gruyter. doi:10.1515/9783110497151.

DeLancey, Scott. 2001. The mirative and evidentiality. *Journal of Pragmatics* 33. 369–382. doi:10.1016/S0378-2166(01)80001-1.

Fischer, Kerstin (ed.). 2006. *Approaches to discourse particles*. Leiden: Brill. doi:10.1163/9780080461588.

Groenendijk, Jeroen & Floris Roelofsen. 2010. Radical inquisitive semantics. https://projects.illc.uva.nl/inquisitivesemantics/assets/files/papers/GroenendijkRoelofsen2010_CLC.pdf.

Hamblin, Charles L. 1973. Questions in Montague English. *Foundations of Language* 10(1). 41–53. www.jstor.org/stable/25000703.

Hoogervorst, Tom G. 2011. Some introductory notes on the development and characteristics of Sabah Malay. *Wacana* 13. 50–77. doi:10.17510/wjhi.v13i1.9.

Huang, Lillian Meei Jin & Philip W Davis. 1989. An aspectual system in Mandarin Chinese. *Journal of Chinese Linguistics* 17. 128–166. www.jstor.org/stable/23757128.

Karttunen, Lauri. 1977. Syntax and semantics of questions. *Linguistics and Philosophy* 1(1). 3–44. doi:10.1007/BF00351935.

Li, Charles N. & Sandra A. Thompson. 1981. *Mandarin Chinese: A functional reference grammar*. Berkeley, CA: University of California Press.

McCready, Elin. 2019. *The semantics and pragmatics of honorification: Register and social meaning*. Oxford: Oxford University Press.

Potts, Christopher. 2005. *The logic of conventional implicatures*. Oxford: Oxford University Press.

Potts, Christopher. 2007. The expressive dimension. *Theoretical Linguistics* 33(2). 165–197. doi:10.1515/TL.2007.011.

Sano, Katsuhiko. 2015. Avoiding impossibility theorems in radical inquisitive semantics. In Shier Ju, Hu Liu & Hiroakira Ono (eds.), *Modality, semantics and interpretations*, Berlin, Heidelberg: Springer. doi:10.1007/978-3-662-47197-5_6.

Schachter, Paul & Fe T. Otanes. 1972. *Tagalog reference grammar*. Berkeley, CA: University of California Press.

Schiffrin, Deborah. 1987. *Discourse markers*. Cambridge: Cambridge University Press.

Schourup, Lawrence C. 1985. *Common discourse particles in English conversation*. London: Routledge.

Soh, Hooi Ling. 2008. The syntax and semantics of change/transition: Evidence from Mandarin Chinese. In Susan Rothstein (ed.), *Theoretical and cross-linguistic approaches to the semantics of aspect*, 387–419. Philadelphia: John Benjamins.

Vander Klok, Jozina & Lisa Matthewson. 2015. Distinguishing *already* from perfect aspect: A case study of Javanese *wis*. *Oceanic Linguistics* 54(1). 172–205. doi: 10.1353/ol.2015.0007.

1 On the mirative use of the *no* (*da*) construction in Japanese

David Y. Oshima

1 Introduction[1]

It has been widely acknowledged that the auxiliary NO (DA)[2] in Japanese, commonly characterized as an auxiliary of "explanation" (Alfonso 1966; Kuno 1973; Teramura 1984, among many others), has a wide range of uses. This work aims to provide an adequate semantic description of one of the major uses of NO (DA), which has been labeled as the "discovery," "grasping," or "comprehension" use by Japanese grammarians (Okuda 1990; Noda 1997; Yoshida 1988, 2000; Miyazaki *et al.* 2002; Najima 2007, among others), in light of the recent discussion of the notion of mirativity in typologically oriented works.

The discovery use of NO (DA) is illustrated in (1); here, as is highly common in informal speech, NO is phonetically reduced to the moraic nasal [n] (a phonetic realization of the special phoneme /N/; Vance 2008) and is incorporated to the preceding syllable.[3]

(1) **Situation:** Ken and Mari are graduate students at Nagoya University. Mari has been away for fieldwork in a distant location, and Ken thinks that Mari will not be back until next week. When Ken comes to the department, he unexpectedly sees Mari and says:)
A, modotteta **n da**.
oh return.NPFV.PST *no* COP.PRS
'Oh, you're back.'

While some scholars treat NO DA as an unsegmentable auxiliary predicate (with the same inflection pattern as the copula DA), I consider NO to be an "auxiliary noun" that (i) selects for a finite clause, (ii) is typically followed by a copula,[4] and (iii) forms a natural class along with HAZU 'must,' YOO 'seem,' etc. (see Saji 1991, Wrona 2011, and references therein for relevant discussions).

2 The functional diversity of NO (DA)

2.1 *Existing classifications*

In past studies, there have been various attempts to identify and classify the uses/senses of NO, as well as various proposals as to how the different uses of

DOI: 10.4324/9781351057837-2

NO may be related to each other (see Najima 2007 and Ijima 2010 for literature reviews). It is beyond the reach of the current work to do justice to all existing proposals; here, I aim only to provide a brief overview.

Classifications put forth by different authors can be plotted on the axis of "splittting" vs. "lumping" approaches. Toward the end of "lumpers," Noda (1997) proposes a five-way classification which involves one "scope(-marking)" use and four "mood (of explanation)" uses.

(2) Noda's (1997) classification:
a. *sukoopu* [scope]
b. *muudo* [mood], *haaku (taiji-teki)* [grasping (proposition-oriented)], *kankeizuke* [relational]
c. *muudo* [mood], *haaku (taiji-teki)* [grasping (proposition-oriented)], *hi-kankeizuke* [non-relational]
d. *muudo* [mood], *teiji (taijin-teki)* [presentation (hearer-oriented)], *kankeizuke* [relational]
e. *muudo* [mood], *teiji (taijin-teki)* [presentation (hearer-oriented)], *hi-kankeizuke* [non-relational]

On the end of "splitters," Yoshida (1988) and Okuda (1990) respectively list 11 and 14 uses of present-tensed NO DA occurring at the end of a declarative clause.

(3) Yoshida's (1988) classification:
(biclausal)
iikae [paraphrasing]
(monoclausal, hearer-oriented)
kokuhaku [confession], *kyooji* [instruction], *kyoochoo* [emphasis], *ketsui* [resolution], *meirei* [order]
(monoclausal, speaker-oriented)
hakken [discovery], *sai-ninshiki* [recollection], *kakunin* [confirmation]
(monoclausal, other)
seichoo [stylistic adjustment], *kyakutaika* [objectification]

(4) Okuda's (1990) classification:
(Group I: *tsuketashi-teki setsumei* 'supplementary explanation')
gen'in [cause], *riyuu* [reason], *dooki* [motivation], *kyoochoo* [emphasis], *gensen* [source], *handan no konkyo* [basis of judgment]
(Group II: *hikidashi-teki setsumei* 'derived explanation')
gen'in no kekka [consequence of a cause], *riyuu no kekka* [consequence of a reason], *hakken-teki na handan* [judgment based on discovery], *hitsuzen no handan* [judgment of necessity], *hyooka-teki na handan* [evaluative judgment], *ippan-ka no handan* [judgment of generalization]

(Group III: other)
gutai-ka/seimitsu-ka/iikae [concretization/elaboration/paraphrasing],
shikoo no taishoo-teki na naiyoo [the objectified content of thought],
igizuke [rationalization]

For the purpose of the current work, I posit seven uses, including the ⟨mirative⟩ use[5] (to be discussed in detail in Section 4), of NO occurring at the end of a declarative clause, from a descriptive viewpoint and largely putting aside the issue of how they are related to each other. For what it is worth, I am inclined to believe that the connection between these uses is best explained in terms of clustering based on family resemblance (see Section 7 for some discussion) rather than the postulation of one (or some small number) of conceptual core(s), or proto-meaning(s), from which more specific uses are derived.

The listed uses are not meant to be exhaustive but rather to cover the most extensively discussed types of usage.

2.2 *The seven major uses of* NO (DA)

2.2.1 *The ⟨information structure⟩ use*

The ⟨information structure⟩ use partially corresponds to Noda's (1997) "scope" use, and also to Yoshida's (1988) and Okuda's (1990) "emphasis" use. I suggest that NO in this use puts additional emphasis on the information-structural focus. For example, in (5), in conjunction with tonal features, NO emphasizes that the focus is the meaning of the lexical content of the (transitive) verb, rather than the positive polarity, as in (6), or the meanings of the verb and its direct object, as in (7).

(5) (in reply to: "Did Ken make a cake?")
Ie, (tsukutta   n   ja   nakute)   katta   **n**   desu.
no   make.PST   *no* COP.INF NEGAUX.GER   buy.PST   *no*   COP.PRS.PLT
'No, he bought(, rather than made,) one.'
focus = 'buy,' *ground* = 'Ken did *X* to a cake'

(6) (in reply to: "Did Ken buy a cake?")
Hai,   kaimashita.
yes   buy.PST.PLT
'Yes, he bought it.'

(7) (in reply to: "What did Ken do?")
Keeki   o   kaimashita.
cake   ACC   buy.PST.PLT
'He bought a cake.'

(8) is an additional example.

(8) Kore   wa   (Osaka   ja   nakute)   Kobe   de   katta
this   TOP   O.   COP.INF   NEGAUX.GER   K.   LOC   buy.PST
n   da.
no   COP. PRS
'I bought this in Kobe (not in Osaka).'
focus = 'Kobe,' *ground* = 'I bought this in *X*'

I further suggest that emphasis of the positive or negative polarity by NO may bring out the effect of conveying S's (= the speaker's) want for convincing H (= the hearer) of the propositional content. (9) is an example to illustrate this point.

(9) Uso   ja   nai   **n   desu.**   Hontoo   ni   mita
lie   COP.INF   NEGAUX.PRS   *no*   COP.PRS.PLT   real   ADV   see.PST
n   desu.
no   cop.prs.plt
'I am *not* lying. I really *did* see it.'

2.2.2   The ⟨inferential relation⟩ use

NODA in its ⟨inferential relation⟩ use, which partially corresponds to Yoshida's (1988) "paraphrasing" use and Okuda's (1990) "concretization/elaboration/ paraphrasing" use, signals that the proposition *p* represented by the prejacent, in context, allows to infer (or even entails), or can be inferred from (or even is entailed by), another proposition *q* (the "antecedent" proposition) represented by a preceding discourse segment. When *p* allows to infer *q* but not vice versa, the sentence with NO can be characterized as a "summary" of the relevant preceding discourse segment. When (i) *p* can be inferred from *q* but not vice versa, and (ii) *p* and *q* allow inference of each other, the sentence with NO can be characterized as an "elaboration" and as a "paraphrase," respectively. Examples of the three patterns are provided in the following:

(10) (*p* is a summary)
Ken   wa,   kore   made   Minami-Amerika,   Chuutoo,   Chuugoku
K.   TOP   this   until   South-America   Middle.East   China
de,   gookei   juuni-nen-kan   chuuzai   shiteiru.   (Yoosuruni,)
LOC   in.total   12-year-for   reside   do.NPFV.PRS   in.short
kaigai-keiken   ga   hoofu   na   **no   da.**
overseas-experience   NOM   abundant   COP.ATTR   *no*   COP.PRS
'Ken has been posted to offices in South America, Middle East, and China for 12 years in total. (In short,) he is very much experienced in life in overseas countries.'

(11) (*p* is an elaboration)
Ken   wa,   kaigai-keiken   ga   hoofu   da.   Kore
K.   TOP   overseas-experience   NOM   abundant   COP.PRS   this
made   Minami-Amerika,   Chuutoo,   Chuugoku   de,   gookei
until   South-America   Middle.East   China   LOC   in.total

juuni-nen-kan	chuuzai	shiteiru	**no**	**da**.
12-year-for	reside	do.NPFV.PRS	*no*	COP.PRS

'Ken is very much experienced in life in overseas countries. He has been posted to offices in America, Middle East, and China for 12 years in total.'

(12) (*p* is a paraphrase)

Juunana	no	yakusuu	wa	ichi	to	sore	jishin	dake	da.
17	GEN	divisor	TOP	1	and	that	self	only	COP.PRS

(Tsumari)	sosuu		na	**no**	**da**.
that.is	prime.number		COP.ATTR	*no*	COP.PRS

'17 is divisible only by 1 and itself. (That is,) it is a prime number.'

2.2.3 *The ⟨reason⟩ use*

NODA, in its ⟨reason⟩ use, which covers what Okuda (1990) calls the "reason" and "cause" uses, indicates that the proposition *p*, represented by the prejacent, is the reason of some contextually prominent proposition *q*.

(13)

Heya	ni	hikari	ga	sashikonda.	Ken	ga	kaaten	o
room	DAT	light	NOM	come.in.PST	K.	NOM	curtain	ACC

aketa	**no**	**da**.
open.PST	*no*	cop.prs

'Light came into the room. (That is because) Ken opened the curtains.'

(14) (**Situation**: S and H have an appointment. S shows up 15 minutes late and says:)

Gomen,	gomen.	Basu	ga	juutai	ni
sorry	sorry	bus	NOM	congestion	DAT

makikomareteshimatta	**n**	**da**.
involve.PSV.end.up.PST	*no*	cop.prs

'My apologies. The bus was caught in traffic.'

2.2.4 *The ⟨revelation⟩ use*

The ⟨revelation⟩ use roughly corresponds to Yoshida's (1988) "confession" and "instruction" uses. I suggest that NODA in this use indicates that the propositional content *p* is a matter within a domain where S claims "informational dominance." Typical instances of such domains are one's privacy and fields of expertise.

(15) (**Situation**: S is speaking to a colleague at his workplace.)

Jitsu-wa	boku,	mukashi		wa	keiba		no	kishu
actually	I	a.long.time.ago		TOP	horse.race		GEN	jockey

o	mezashiteita	**n**	**desu**.
ACC	aim.NPFV.PST	*no*	COP.PRS.PLT

'Actually, I used to want to become a jockey.'

(16) (**Situation**: S is an anthropologist and speaking to a non-anthropologist friend.)
Dentoo-teki   na   Ainu   no   bunka   de   wa,   doobutsu
traditional   COP.ATTR   Ainu   GEN   culture   LOC   TOP   animal
wa   kami   no   keshin   to   minasareteita   **n**   **da**.
TOP   deity   GEN   incarnation   as   consider.PSV.NPFV.PST   *no*   COP.PRS
'In the traditional Ainu culture, animals were considered to be incarnations of deities.'

(17) (**Situation**: S has lived in the city of Nagoya for a long time, and H has never lived there.)
Nagoya   de   wa,   dooiuwakeka   minna   yoru   ga
N.   LOC   Top   for.some.reason   everyone   night   NOM
hayai   **n**   **da**.
early.PRS   *no*   cop.prs
'In Nagoya, for some reason, people go to bed early.'

2.2.5   The ⟨order⟩ use

NODA, in its ⟨order⟩ use, indicates that the utterance has the illocutionary force of order or request.

(18) (A police officer to a suspicious person.)
Te   o   agete,   yukkuri   kocchi   o   muku   **n**   **da**.
hand   ACC   raise.GER   slowly   this.way   ACC   turn.PRS   *no*   COP.PRS
'Put your hands up and turn around slowly.'

2.2.6   The ⟨resolution⟩ use

NODA, in its ⟨resolution⟩ use, indicates that S intends to express his resolution (determination) to achieve the described action.

(19) Ore   wa   nantoshitemo   aitsu   ni   katsu   **n**   **da**.
I   TOP   no.matter.what   that.person   DAT   win.PRS   *no*   COP.PRS
'I will beat that guy, no matter what it takes.'

3   Mirativity: marking of new and unassimilated knowledge for the speaker

The linguistic notion of mirativity (or admirativity) had received relatively scarce attention before the seminal paper by DeLancey (1997), and there is no clear consensus yet about its exact definition and extent. DeLancey (2001:370) defines *mirativity* quite broadly, as "linguistic marking of an utterance as conveying information which is new or unexpected to the speaker." In a more recent work, he states:

[T]he question of whether there is such a phenomenon as mirativity or the mirative is in fact two separate questions: whether there is a semantic category of new or unassimilated information, which can manifest itself in one way or another in linguistic expression, and, if so, whether this semantic category is one which regularly finds expression in languages as a grammatical category. I will use the term *mirativity* to refer to the semantic category in the first question, and *mirative* to refer to the crosslinguistic grammatical phenomenon addressed in the second.

(Delancey 2012:533; emphasis added)

Aikhenvald (2004, 2012), on the other hand, emphasizes that mirativity is *grammatical* marking of a new and/or unexpected status of the propositional content, and that not all lexical items and constructions that convey such information are to be called mirative markers, in the same way as not all expressions with temporal meaning are to be called tense or aspect markers. In Aikhenvald (2012), she argues that there is a good deal of variation within mirativity (mirative systems) across languages, and sometimes mirativity makes reference to the knowledge of an individual other than the speaker; more specifically, she proposes that individual mirative markers may have one or several of the semantic values (15 in total), listed in (20):

(20) i. Sudden discovery, sudden revelation or realization (a) by the speaker, (b) by the audience (or addressee), or (c) by the main character.
  ii. *Surprise (a) of the speaker, (b) of the audience (or addressee), or (c) of the main character.*
  iii. Unprepared mind (a) of the speaker, (b) of the audience (or addressee), or (c) of the main character.
  iv. Counterexpectation (a) to the speaker, (b) to the addressee, or (c) to the main character.
  v. Information new (a) to the speaker, (b) to the addressee, or (c) to the main character.

(Aikhenvald 2012:437)

For the present purpose, I adopt the broader understanding of mirativity in line with DeLancey (2012). It is not clear whether NO, which I take to be an auxiliary (noun), is to be regarded as a "grammatical" marker of anything or not. Japanese auxiliary predicates selecting for a finite clause do form a closed grammatical class and express such semantic notions as modality (e.g., HAZU, BEKI) and evidentiality (e.g., YOO, RASHII) (Masuoka & Takubo 1992; Nihongo Kijutsu Bunpoo Kenkyuukai 2003); it seems thus not unreasonable to regard NO as a grammatical expression. My concerns in this chapter, however, are about the semantic characterization of the "discovery" use of NO, and I leave open the question of whether it counts as a grammatical mirative marker.

Mirative markers in a broad sense – grammatical mirative markers plus what Aikhenvald (2004, 2012) calls "mirative strategies" – can be classified into several types, based on their relation with other grammatical categories. First, a mirative marker oftentimes has a distinct use as an evidential marker (in a broad sense, again) that encodes the "non-firsthand," "inferred," or less frequently, "reported" status of the information (note that "non-firsthand" semantically subsumes "inferred" and "reported"). Second, a mirative marker may be an extension of some grammatical category other than evidentiality, such as tense, aspect, mood, and disjunct person-marking (Aikhenvald 2004:210–211). Finally, in some languages, mirativity is "a category in its own right" (Aikhenvald 2004:207), and there are "mirative-only" markers whose sole or main meaning/function is to encode mirativity.

NO is by no means a "mirative-only" expression. It has numerous other uses, as we have seen earlier. None of them can be properly characterized as an evidential marker; it is worth noting that Japanese has several evidentiality markers – if not strictly grammatical ones – which include the auxiliary nouns YOO, MITAI, and SOO and the auxiliary adjective RASHII (see, for example, Teramura 1984; Aoki 1986; Masuoka & Takubo 1992; Nihongo Kijutsu Bunpoo Kenkyuukai 2003).

4 No (DA) as a mirative marker

NO has a major use that has been labeled as the "discovery" (*hakken*), "grasping" (*haaku*), or "comprehension" (*tokushin*) use (Okuda 1990; Noda 1997; Yoshida 1988, 2000; Miyazaki *et al.* 2002; Najima 2007, among others). I suggest that NO in this use, exemplified in (21) (repeated from (1)) through (26) in the following, is a marker of mirativity and conveys, as a conventional implicature, that the propositional content became part of the speaker's beliefs "on the spot," in the discourse situation.

(21) (**Situation**: Ken and Mari are graduate students at Nagoya University. Mari has been away for fieldwork in a distant location, and Ken thinks that Mari will not be back until next week. When Ken comes to the department, he unexpectedly sees Mari and says:)
A,   modotteta   **n**   **da**.
oh   return.NPFV.PST   *no*   COP.PRS
'Oh, you're back.'

(22) (**Situation**: A husband says to his wife that they ran out of coffee, and they agree that they need to buy some later. After a while, the wife sees the husband drinking coffee. She says:)
Koohii   atta   **n**   **da**.
coffee   exist.PST   *no*   COP.PRS
'We had some coffee.'

(23) (**Situation**: Entering her office, S notices that a colleague is looking out of the window with a worried look. Wondering why, she approaches to the window and figures out the reason.)

Wa, konbini ni kyuukyuusha ga tsukkonjatta
wow convenience.store DAT ambulance NOM run.into.end.up.PST
n da.
no cop.prs
'Wow, an ambulance ran into the convenience store.'

(24) (**Situation**: A husband, looking at a news website, learns that the Hanshin Tigers, a professional baseball team, won today. He says to his wife, who is a Tigers fan:)

A, Taigassu katta **n da**.
oh T. win.PST *no* COP.PRS
'Oh, the Tigers won.'

(25) (**Situation**: S peels a fruit that is not familiar to her or H:)

Naka wa shiroi **n da**.
inside TOP white.PRS *no* COP.PRS
'It's white inside.'

(26) (**Situation**: In a furniture shop, S looks at the price tag of a sofa that looks quite expensive and says:)

Yappari, kekkoo takai **n da**.
as.suspected fairly expensive.Prs *no* Cop.Prs
'It is quite expensive, as we suspected.'

If the speaker of (21) reports the return of Mari to somebody else in the department, say, one hour after realizing that Mari is back, the use of mirative NO would be unnatural, the propositional content being not "hot news" for her anymore.

(27) (**Situation**: S learned that Mari was back from her fieldwork trip one hour ago.)

H: *Mari wa itsu kaettekuru no kana.*
   M. TOP when return.come.PRS *no* DP
   'I wonder when Mari will come back.'
S: Moo modottekiteru {yo /?∅}.
   already return.come.NPFV.PRS DP
   'She's already back.'
S': #Moo modottekiteru **n da** (yo).
   already return.come.NPFV.PST *no* COP.PRS DP
   'She's already back.'

To give further illustration, utterance (24) would be infelicitous, or insincere, if the husband had come to know the result of the baseball game, say, 15 minutes ago. (If this were the case, he would be *pretending* that he just learned the news.)

The absence of mirative NO sometimes leads to unnaturalness. For example, without *n da*, (21)–(23) would sound unnatural. On the other hand, (24)–(26) would be fine without *n da*. The factor accounting for this contrast is whether the speaker assumes that the propositional content is already known to the hearer. In (21), for instance, it is contextually impossible for the hearer, Mari, not to be aware that she is back from her trip. With (24), on the other hand, it is plausible that the speaker utters it with an intention to inform the hearer of the outcome of the baseball game, expecting her not to know it yet. I will come back to this matter in Section 7.

One remaining question here is whether NO conveys unexpectedness, surprise, or at least some sort of heightened emotion on the part of the speaker as conventionalized meaning, or they can be used in emotionally neutral statements. Aikhenvald (2012) suggests that most reported instances of mirative markers encode unexpectedness or surprise, and it is worth asking whether mirative NO, too, has such a property. Example (26) previously, where NO co-occurs with the adverb *yappari* 'as suspected,' indicates that for felicitous use of NO, the propositional content need not be a total surprise for the speaker. Observe also that (28) in the following can be uttered with an indifferent tone and is compatible with the contextual assumption that convenience stores starting and closing their businesses is a totally commonplace, everyday affair in the area.

(28) (**Situation**: S and H are walking on a busy street in their neighborhood. Passing by a building recently renovated, they realize that it is going to be a convenience store.)
Mata   konbini   ga   dekiru   **n**   da.
again   convenience.store   NOM   come.into.existence.PRS   *no*   COP.PRS
'There's going to be another convenience store.'

Such observations are, however, not incompatible with the supposition, adopted in such works as Noda (1997:87) and Ikarashi (2015), that NO in the relevant use conventionally conveys that the speaker has an (at least slightly) heightened emotion. Arguably, the English interjection *oh* is conventionally associated with a heightened emotion, yet it is not unnatural to say something like, "Oh, there's going to be another convenience store" in situation (28), with an indifferent tone. Thus, it will be hasty to conclude, from data like (26) and (28), that NO does not have any emotive (expressive) meaning. The question of what kind and level of emotion (expressivity), if any, NO conveys appears to be a matter that waits for further investigations.

5 Discourse-configurational constraints on mirative NO (DA)

5.1 The ban on the "all-focus" configuration

The "hot news for the speaker" status of the propositional content does not guarantee the felicity of the use of mirative NO. Examples (29) and (30) illustrate this point.

(29) (**Situation:** S and H enter a hotel room where they are going to stay. S opens the door of the bathroom and notices that there is a dead cockroach on the floor.)
A, gokiburi ga shinderu (#n da).
oh cockroach NOM die.NPFV.PRS *no* COP.PRS
'Oh, there's a dead cockroach.' (lit. 'Oh, a cockroach is dead.')
(adapted from Noda 1997:81)

(30) (**Situation:** S and H are government agents on a secret mission. They are sitting on the back seat of a taxi. S realizes that they are being tailed by the car behind them.)
Ushiro no kuruma ni tsukerareteru (#n da).
back GEN car DAT tail.PSV.NPFV.PRS *no* COP.PRS
'We are being tailed by the car behind us.'

To account for such data, Noda (1997) suggests that the use of NO (in the relevant use) is subject to the constraint such that the propositional content of its prejacent cannot be something that is "totally beyond the speaker's expectations." This generalization cannot be maintained, however, in view of the felicity of an utterance like (23), where the propositional content cannot be sensibly regarded something that is more probable/predictable than finding a dead cockroach in a bathroom.

I instead suggest that mirative NO must satisfy constraint (31).

(31) *The ban on the "all-focus" configuration*
The informational content (the explicature in the relevance theoretical sense) of an utterance with NO in its mirative use must involve some ground (non-focus) component, which may or may not be explicitly coded.

This amounts to saying that, for an utterance with mirative NO to be felicitous, there must be a non-trivial (i.e., relatively specific) immediate question-under-discussion (QUD; Roberts 1996/2012), as opposed to a trivial one along the lines of 'What's up?' Table 1.1 illustrates the approximate focus/ground partition and QUD plausible for utterances (21)–(26) and (28)–(30).

Table 1.1 The ground/focus configurations in (21)–(26) and (28)–(30)

	Ground	Focus	(Accommodated) approximate immediate QUD
(21)	$\lambda x[\textbf{at}(\textbf{mari}, x)]$	**nagoya**	Is Mari back to Nagoya yet? / Where is Mari now?
(22)	$\lambda P_{<t,t>}[P(\textbf{exist}(\textbf{coffee}))]$	$\lambda t[t]$	Is there any coffee?
(23)	$\lambda p_{<s,t>}[\textbf{because}$ ($^\wedge$**look-out-the-window** (**the-colleague**), p)]	$^\wedge[\textbf{a}(\textbf{ambulance},$ $\lambda x[\textbf{run-into}(x, \textbf{the-convenience.store})])]$	Why is the colleague looking out the window?
(24)	$\lambda P_{<e,t>}[P(\textbf{tigers})]$	**win**	Did the Tigers win or lose?
(25)	$\lambda P_{<e,t>}[P(\textbf{the-inside-of}(\textbf{the-fruit}))]$	**white**	What color is the inside of the fruit?
(26)	$\lambda P_{<e,t>}[P(\textbf{the-cost}(\textbf{the-sofa}))]$	**expensive**	How much does the sofa cost?
(28)	$\lambda P_{<e,t>}[P(\textbf{the-renovated-building})]$	**convenience.store**	What is the renovated building going to be?
(29)	(none)	$\textbf{a}(\lambda x[\textbf{cockroach}(x)\ \&\ \textbf{dead}(x)], \lambda x[\textbf{in}(x, \textbf{the-bathroom})])$	(What's up?)
(30)	(none)	$\textbf{be.tailing}(\textbf{the-car}, \textbf{S}\oplus\textbf{H})$	(What's up?)

The relevant ground component or QUD does not need to be explicitly coded (mentioned) but only needs to be contextually recoverable (accommodatable); (32) is a case in point.

(32) (**Situation:** S and H walk out of a building.)
   A,   ame   futteru   **n**   da.
   oh   rain   fall.NPFV.PRS   *no*   COP.PRS
   'Oh, it's raining.'
   Immediate QUD: 'What's the weather like?'

The supposition that utterance (32) involves an implicit ground component can be justified by the observation that it can be appropriately reported as in (33), which implies that in the discourse context of (32), 'What's the weather like?' is a plausible (accommodatable) QUD.

(33) S {mentioned/commented on} what the weather was like.

Crucially, (29) and (30) are not amenable to a similar way of reporting.

(34) a. ??S {mentioned/commented on} what the bathroom was like.
    b. ??S {mentioned/commented on} where there is a dead cockroach.

c. ??S {mentioned/commented on} whether there is a dead cockroach in the bathroom.

(35) ??S {mentioned/commented on} what the car behind them was doing.

5.2 *The "establishedness" requirement*

The ban on the "all-focus" configuration, formulated in (31), is not quite sufficient to account for data like (36).

(36) (**Siuation**: S and H run at full speed to catch a train but miss it just in the nick of time.)
Aa, maniawanakatta (#n da).
oh make.it.NEG.PST *no* COP.PRS

(adapted from Noda 1997:81)

Note that here it is plausible that S has been wondering about the question of whether S and H will manage to catch the train or not; thus, the ban on the "all-focus" configuration cannot be held responsible for the infelicity of (36).

Noda (1997) suggests that an utterance with NO (in the relevant use) cannot be felicitously used in an utterance that describes that "takes place in the utterance situation." Elaborating this idea, I posit (37) as a further constraint that mirative NO must satisfy.

(37) The "establishedness" requirement.
The propositional character (in Kaplan's 1989 sense) of a sentence with NO in its mirative use must be such that not only does it yield a true proposition with respect to the actual time of utterance t but also with respect to t' that precedes t by a significant margin.

Notice that at the utterance time of (36) (= right after the moment the train doors closed), the propositional character of 'We did not make it' is evaluated as true, whereas, say, at one minute before the utterance time of (36), it is *not* evaluated as true. (38) is a felicitous utterance with a comparable content but satisfies the "establishedness" requirement; the obligatoriness of the *n da* here has to do with the propositional content being (assumed to be) known to the hearer (Sections 4, 7).

(38) (**Situation**: H wants to catch the last train of the day, which leaves in 10 minutes. It is likely that he will not make it, but he gives it a try anyway. After some 30 minutes, H comes back with a disappointed look. S, who was wondering about the outcome of H's attempt, says:)
Yappari, maniawanakatta #(n da).
as.suspected make.it.NEG.PST *no* COP.PRS
'You did not make it, after all.'

6   The "soliloquy-orientation" of mirative no (da)

Japanese has several sentence-final expressions that are characteristic to, although not confined in, soliloquy (monologue), including the discourse particle NA accompanied by the "insisting rise" intonation (which corresponds to H% in Venditti 2005 and is annotated with "↑" here), and the question markers KANA accompanied a "rise-fall" intonation (corresponding to LH% in Venditti 2005 and annotated with "↑↓" here) and DAROOKA (with a flat intonation typical of a declarative sentence; "↘").[6]

(39)   "Okashii   na↑"   to   omotta.
       strange.PRS *na*   QUOT   think.PST
       'I thought (to myself), "This is strange."'

(40)   "Aitsu   wa   kuru   kana↑↓"   to   kangaeta.
       that.guy TOP   come.PRS   *kana*   QUOT   think.PST
       '(I) wondered, "Will he come?"'

(41)   "Dare   ga   kuru   darooka↘"   to   omotta.
       who   NOM   come.PRS   *darooka*   QUOT   think.PST
       '(I) wondered, "Who will come?"'

Sentences with such a soliloquy-oriented expression can be used in what Miyazaki *et al.* (2002:282) call "pseudo-soliloquy (*giji dokuwa*)," that is, utterances that constitute part of a dialogic conversation but nevertheless are presented *as if* they were self-talk. The utterance (42S$_2$) is an example.

(42)   (**Situation**: S is looking for a place to have lunch with H and spots a restaurant.)
       S$_1$: Koko   de   tabemashoo.
              here   LOC   eat.VOL.PLT
              'Let's eat here.'
       S$_2$: Demo,   suwareru   kana↑↓
              but   sit.POT.PRS *kana*.
              'But, I wonder if there are any seats available.'
       S$_3$: A,   daijoobu   desu.   Ano   teeburu   ga   aitemasu.
              oh   good   COP.PRS   that   table   NOM   open.NPFV.PRS.PLT
              'Oh, no problem. That table is available.'

Unlike in the preceding and subsequent parts (i.e., (42S$_{1,3}$)), the predicate in (42S$_2$) is in the plain, rather than polite, form. This does not make this segment "impolite," because with *kana*, it is presented *as if* it were not addressed to the hearer. It is not genuine soliloquy, but rather pseudo-soliloquy, in that the speaker intends to convey a message – something along the lines of, "Please wait, as I am trying to figure out whether there are available seats" – to the hearer with it and also assumes that the hearer is aware of this communicative intention. If the predicate (42S₂) is turned into a polite form (which is "anti-monologic"), oddity arises.[7]

(43) #Demo, suwaremasu **kana↑↓**
 but   sit.POT.PRS.PLT *kana*.

Note that, in the context of (42), it would be odd for the speaker to ask the hearer about the availability of seats (since he cannot be expected to know that answer); thus, (44), a question with no soliloquy-like feature, is likewise inappropriate in the context of (42S₂).

(44) #Demo, suwaremasu ka?
 but   sit.pot.prs.plt dp
 'But, are there any seats available?'

Let us now turn to NO. Authors such as Yoshida (1988:51, 2000:20) and Noda (1997:80 *et passim*) remark that statements with mirative NO are generally soliloquy-like. The observation that mirative NO cannot be followed by a polite copula form – a sort of audience-oriented honorific (Oshima 2019) – endorses this claim (Noda 1997:63).

(45) (**Situation**: as in (21).)
 #A, modotteta **n** **desu**.
 oh   return.NPFV.PST *no* COP.PRS.PLT
 (Oh, you're back.)

(46) (**Situation**: as in (25))
 #Naka wa shiroi **n** **desu**.
 inside TOP white.PRS *no* COP.PRS.PLT
 (It's white inside.)

Interestingly, however, when the sentence is followed by the discourse particle NE in its "shared information" use (typically associated with the insisting-rise intonation; Oshima 2014, 2016), which conveys that the speaker assumes that the hearer already knows the propositional content, NO can be combined with a polite copula form, as well as with a plain one.

(47) (**Situation**: as in (21).)
 A, modotteta **n** {**da/desu**} **ne↑**
 oh return.NPFV.PST *no* {COP.PRS/COP.PRS.PLT} *ne*
 'Oh, you're back, aren't you.'

(48) (**Situation**: as in (23).)
 Wa, konbini ni kyuukyuusha ga tsukkonjatta
 wow convenience.store DAT ambulance NOM run.into.end.up.PST

> n   {da/desu}   ne↑
> *no*   {COP.PRS/COP.PRS.PLT}   *ne*
> 'Wow, an ambulance ran into the convenience store, didn't it.'

This shows that the soliloquy-orientation of mirative NO can be overridden with attachment of NE; it is not clear to me why this is the case.

7   The obligatoriness of no (da) and the "already known to the hearer" status of the proposition

In Section 5 earlier, I examined discourse conditions under which the use of mirative NO is allowed. A related but distinct question is whether the use of mirative NO is obligatory when these conditions are met.

Mirative NO seems to be generally omissible when the propositional content is new, or unknown, information for the hearer; (49) ($\approx$ (25)) illustrates this point.

(49) (**Situation**: S peels a fruit that is not familiar to her or H. H does not know and cannot see what the fruit looks like inside.)
>   O,   naka   wa   shiroi   {a. **n   da**   /b. ∅}.
>   oh   inside TOP white.PRS   *no* COP.PRS
>   'It's white inside.'

On the other hand, when it is contextually established that the propositional content is already known to the hearer, as in (50) ($\approx$ (21)), the absence of NO leads to oddity.

(50) (**Situation**: Ken and Mari are graduate students at Nagoya University. Mari has been away for fieldwork in a distant location, and Ken thinks that Mari will not be back until next week. When Ken comes to the department, he unexpectedly sees Mari and says:)
>   A,   modotteta   {a. **n   da**   /b. ??∅}.
>   oh   return.NPFV.PST   *no* COP.PRS.PLT
>   'Oh, you're back.'

It is tempting to attribute the unnaturalness of (50b) to the general principle shown in (51), which Japanese discourse has been pointed out to be generally subject to (Kimura & Moriyama 1997):

(51) Explicit marking of the "old news" status of a statement.
     (As a rule) a statement such that it is contextually established that its content is already known to the hearer must be explicitly coded as such (e.g., with a discourse particle).

Canonically, a statement is made (a declarative sentence is uttered) in purpose to inform the hearer of its propositional content. (51) amounts to saying that, when the speaker makes an "uninformative" statement for whatever pragmatic reason, she (as a rule) must make it clear that she is doing so purposefully – by means of, for example, using the discourse partible NE. The contrast between (52a) and (52b), and that between (53a) and (53b), illustrates the effect of principle (51).

(52) (**Situation**: S and H are walking on a street on a very sunny, hot, and humid day.)
    Kyoo   wa   atsui   {a. **ne↑** /b. ??∅.}
    today TOP hot.PRS   *ne*
    'It's hot today(, isn't it).'

(53) (**Situation**: Ken and Mari are friends. Seeing Mari for the first time in two weeks, Ken notices that Mari, who had long hair two weeks ago, now has a bob cut.)
    A,   kamigata   kaeta   {a. **ne↑** /b. ??∅.}
    oh   hair.style change.PST   *ne*
    'Oh, you changed your hairstyle(, didn't you).'

Going back to (50a, b), the two utterances both appear to violate principle (51). I suggest that what makes (50a) acceptable is the soliloquy-orientation of NO; being "soliloquy-like," utterances like (50a) are exempt from discourse principle (51), which is dialogic in nature – in a way analogous to how (42S$_2$) is exempt from the pragmatic norm such that one should consistently use polite forms when talking to a person who is socially superior or distant.

Is the unnaturalness of (50b), now, simply due to the violation of (51) (and the lack of a feature that makes it soliloquy-like)? This cannot be the whole story, because addition of NE does not improve (and actually worsens) its acceptability, as is shown in (54b).

(54) (**Situation**: the same as in (50).)
    a. *A,   modotteta*   **n**   **da**   (**ne↑**)
       oh   return.NPFV.PST *no* COP.PRS *ne*
       'Oh, you're back(, aren't you).'
    b. A,   modotteta   {i. ??∅. /ii. **#ne↑**}
       oh   return.NPFV.PST   *ne*
       (Oh, you're back.)

The conditions under which mirative NO is obligatory and optional can be summarized as follows.

(55) Let *p* be the prejacent-proposition, and suppose that the speaker has just learned *p* and that the (other) discourse-configurational constraints on mirative NO are all met. Then:
    i. The use of mirative NO is obligatory when it is contextually established that p is already known to the hearer; the discourse particle NE, too, may be used, but this is optional.

ii. The use of mirative NO is optional when *p* is taken to be new information for the hearer.

Statements whose propositional contents are already known to the hearer are pragmatically marked, and it seems reasonable to suppose that such "uninformative" statements are generally motivated and expected to involve richer conventional implicature than regular, informative ones. This appears to be a rationale behind (though presumably not a full account of) the pattern presented in (55).

One caveat here is that in some discourse situations, either a relatively specific QUD or a trivial QUD is plausible, so that the discourse constraints on mirative NO can be taken to be either met or violated. Observe the following discourse, where the propositional content is obviously already known to the speaker and yet the use of mirative NO is optional.

(56) (**Situation**: Ken and Mari are friends. Seeing Mari for the first time in two weeks, Ken notices that Mari, who had long hair two weeks ago, now has a bob cut.)

   a. A, kamigata kaeta   **n** **da**   (ne↑)
       oh hair.style change.PST *no* COP.PRS *ne*
       'Oh, you changed your hairstyle(, didn't you).'

   b. A, kamigata kaeta   {i. ne↑ /ii. ??∅.}
       oh hair.style change.PST   *ne*
       'Oh, you changed your hairstyle(, didn't you).'

I suggest that in the situation described here, the speaker may either be addressing a relatively specific QUD along the lines of 'What is noteworthy about Mary's appearance today?' or 'Why does Mary look different?' or a trivial one along the lines of 'What's new?' When the former is the case, the appropriate choice, called for by (55), is (56a). When the latter is the case, the appropriate choice is (56b), mirative NO being unavailable due to the ban on the "all-focus" configuration. (56) thus does not constitute an exception to or evidence against (55). The same account can be applied to the apparent optionality of mirative NO in (57), where the speaker may or may not have in mind a relatively specific QUD, such as "What's the garden like?"

(57) (**Situation**: S was invited to H's home for the first time. Looking out on the garden, S notices that there is a pine tree.)

   a. Matsu-no-ki ga   aru   **n** **desu**   ne↑
       pine.tree   NOM exist.PRS *no* COP.PRS.PLT *ne*
       'You have a pine tree, don't you.'

   b. Matsu-no-ki ga   arimasu   ne↑
       pine.tree   NOM exist.PRS.PLT *ne*
       'You have a pine tree, don't you.'

8 Mirativity and interrogatives with no

NO occurs in (polar and constituent) interrogatives too. NO in interrogatives has multiple functions, though probably fewer than NO in declaratives does (Yoshida 1994; Ijima 1995; Noda 1997:117–134). Notably, one of these functions can be seen as a counterpart of the mirative use of NO in declaratives. NO in this use – which I label as the "epistemic bias" use – occurs in a polar interrogative and conveys that the speaker expects the prejacent-proposition to hold, that is, is epistemically biased toward the positive answer, and furthermore, that this expectation (epistemic bias) was formed on the information newly acquired in the discourse situation.

(58S) is an example of NO in its epistemic bias use; in the described situation, (58S') without NO is less natural. (59), on the other hand, illustrates a situation where the licensing condition of NO in this use is not satisfied.

(58) (**Situation**: S and H are walking downtown, looking for a place to have lunch. H points to a ramen noodle restaurant and says, "How about that place?" S asks H:)

S: Raamen,   suki na   n   desu   ka?
   ramen.noodle fond COP.ATTR *no* COP.PRS.PLT   DP
   '(So,) do you like ramen noodles?'

S': ??Raamen,   suki desu   ka?
    ramen.noodle fond COP.ATTR   DP
    'Do you like ramen noodles?'

(59) (**Situation**: S and H are walking downtown, looking for a place to have lunch. S spots a ramen noodle restaurant, which looks good to him. S asks H:)

S: #Raamen,   suki na   n   desu   ka?
   ramen.noodle fond COP.ATTR *no* COP.PRS.PLT   DP
   '(So,) do you like ramen noodles?'

S': Raamen,   suki desu   ka?
    ramen.noodle fond COP.ATTR   DP
    'Do you like ramen noodles?'

9 The relation between the ⟨mirative⟩ and ⟨reason⟩ uses

There is conspicuous affinity, and perhaps continuity, between the ⟨mirative⟩ and ⟨reason⟩ uses of NO. As has been argued, the felicitous use of mirative NO requires a relatively specific immediate QUD; this QUD can be a *why*-question, as in (60) (≈ (23)), or of a different type, as in (61) (≈ (25)).

(60) (**Situation**: Matsui, an office worker, enters her office and notices that her colleague Takeda is looking out of the window with a worried look.

Wondering why, Matsui approaches to the window and figures out the reason.)

Wa,	konbini		ni	kyuukyuusha	ga	
wow	convenience.store		DAT	ambulance	NOM	

tsukkonjatta		**n**	**da**.
run.into.end.up.PST		*no*	cop.prs

'Wow, an ambulance ran into the convenience store.'
Immediate QUD: 'Why is Takeda looking out of the window?'

(61) (**Situation**: S peels a fruit that is not familiar to her or H.)

Naka	wa	shiroi	**n**	**da**.
inside	TOP	white.PRS	*no*	COP.PRS

'It's white inside.'
Immediate QUD: 'What color is the inside of the fruit?'

Suppose that, two minutes after the utterance in (60), another colleague, called Umeno, enters the office and shows a puzzled look upon noticing that his two colleagues, Matsui and Takeda, are standing by the window. Matsui or Takeda may utter (62) to Umeno, to explain why they are doing so.

(62)

Konbini		ni	kyuukyuusha	ga	tsukkonjatta
convenience.store	DAT	ambulance	NOM	run.into.end.up.PST	

n	**desu**.
no	cop.prs.plt

'An ambulance ran into the convenience store. (That's why.)'
Immediate QUD: 'Why are Matsui and Takeda looking out of the window?'

In both (60) and (62), the presence of an implicit *why*-question is part of the reason that the use of NO is felicitous. A case can be made, indeed, in the case of (60), that NO plays a dual role, indicating both the "hot news" status of the propositional content and the causality between the propositional content and another proposition. It is plausible that cases like (60) have served as a "pivot" through which the ⟨mirative⟩ use diachronically arose from the ⟨reason⟩ use. Accordingly, the constraint on mirative NO such that it requires a specific QUD (i.e., the ban on the "all-focus" configuration) might be a property residually inherited from its origin, that is, NO as a causal-relation marker, which generally occurs in a statement serving to answer a contextually prominent (*why*-)question.

10   Conclusion

This work discussed that the Japanese discourse auxiliary noun NO can be used as a marker of mirativity, which conveys that the propositional content of the prejacent is something that the speaker has just learned in the discourse situation. It was argued that the use of mirative NO is subject to two constraints that do not automatically follow from its being a mirative marker: (i) the ban on the "all-focus" configuration and (ii) the "establishedness" requirement. It was also discussed that mirative NO has soliloquy-orientation, but this feature may be overridden when the utterance involves a discourse particle like NE.

Abbreviations

ATTR	first person	COP	copula
DAT	dative	DP	discourse particle
GEN	genitive	GER	gerund
INF	infinitive	LOC	locative
NEG	negative	NEGAUX	negative auxiliary
NOM	nominative	NPFV	nonperfective
PLT	polite	PRS	present
PST	past	PSV	passive
QUOT	quotative particle	TOP	topic-marker
VOL	volitional		

Notes

1 **Acknowledgments:** I am grateful to Elin McCready, Christopher Tancredi, and the other members of ILCAA Joint Research Project "Semantics of Discourse Particles in East and Southeast Asian Languages" for helpful feedbacks and discussions.
2 Throughout the chapter, lexemes are referred to in small capitals (e.g., GO), and word forms are referred to in italics (e.g., *go, goes*).
3 What is referred to as PRS (present) in glosses is equivalent to what is referred as "non-past" in some works.
4 A copula is left out in certain configurations, for example, in interrogatives.

   (i) a. Kimi ga   yaru   **no** (ka)?
        you   NOM do.PRS *no* DP
        '(So,) are you going to do (it)?'
      b. *Kimi ga   yaru   **no** da   (ka)?
         you   NOM do.PRS *no* COP.PRS DP

Occurrence of the copula after NO patterns the same as that after a regular noun; observe the parallelism between (i) and (ii).

   (ii) a. Kimi   ga   hannin (ka)?
         you   NOM   culprit DP
  'Are you the culprit?'
      b. *Kimi ga   hannin da   (ka)?
         you   NOM   culprit COP.PRS DP

In some grammatical configurations (e.g., before the discourse particle *yo*), omission of the copula, after NO as well as a regular noun, is observed only in certain register (stereo)typically connected to female speech.

(iii) a. Ken   ga   yatta   {**n**   da   /   **%no**   Ø}   yo.
     K.   NOM   do.PRS   *no*   COP.PRS   *no*   DP
     '(It is) Ken (who) did it.'
   b. Ken   ga   hannin   {da   /   %Ø}   yo.
     K.   NOM   culprit   COP.PRS   DP
     '(It is) Ken (who) is the culprit.'

5 I use angle brackets to refer to the (total of the seven) uses of NO occurring at the end of a declarative clause that I acknowledge, each of which may or may not correspond straightforwardly to the uses acknowledged in other works.
6 Littell *et al.* (2010) discuss questions markers with similar properties from some North American indigenous languages, labeling them as "conjectural question markers."
7 The combination of a polite predicate and *kana*↑↓ is not possible in the speech of typical contemporary speakers. Even if the combination is possible for the speaker of (42), (43) would still be unacceptable in the slot of (42S$_2$), in the same way as (44) would be.

References

Aikhenvald, Alexandra Y. 2004. *Evidentiality*. Oxford: Oxford University Press.

Aikhenvald, Alexandra Y. 2012. The essence of mirativity. *Linguistic Typology* 16. 434–485.

Alfonso, Anthony. 1966. *Japanese language patterns: A structural approach*. Tokyo: Sophia University.

Aoki, Haruo. 1986. Evidentials in Japanese. In Wallace Chafe & Johanna Nichols (eds.), *Evidentiality: The linguistic coding of epistemology*, 223–238. Norwood, NJ: Ablex.

DeLancey, Scott. 1997. Mirativity: The grammatical marking of unexpected information. *Linguistic Typology* 1. 33–52.

DeLancey, Scott. 2001. The mirative and evidentiality. *Journal of Pragmatics* 33. 369–382.

DeLancey, Scott. 2012. Still mirative after all these years. *Linguistic Typology* 16. 529–564.

Ijima, Masahiro. 1995. Gimonbun no tasooteki bunseki [A multi-dimensional analysis of interrogatives]. *Bulletin of the Faculty of Humanities, Seikei University* 30. 1–62.

Ijima, Masahiro. 2010. Nodabun no kinoo to koozoo [The function and structure of the *noda*-sentences]. *Nihongogaku Ronshuu* 6. 75–117.

Ikarashi, Keita. 2015. The Japanese sentence-final particle *no* and mirativity. *Tsukuba English Studies* 34. 79–98.

Kaplan, David. 1989. Demonstratives. In Joseph Almog, John Perry & Howard Wettstein (eds.), *Themes from Kaplan*, 481–563. Oxford: Oxford University Press.

Kimura, Hideki & Takuro Moriyama. 1997. Kikite joohoo hairyo to bunmatsu keishiki [Consideration of hearer-information and sentence-final forms]. In Yasunori Okochi (ed.) *Nihongo to chuugokugo no taishoo kennkyuu ronbunshuu [Papers on Comparative Studies of Japanese and Chinese]*, 235–275. Tokyo: Kurosio Publishers.

Kuno, Susumu. 1973. *The structure of the Japanese language*. Cambridge, MA: The MIT Press.

Littell, Patrick, Lisa Matthewson & Tyler Peterson. 2010. On the semantics of conjectural questions. In *Evidence from Evidentials*, vol. 28, 89–104. Tyler Peterson and Uli Sauerland, eds., University of British Columbia Working Papers in Linguistics.

Masuoka, Takashi & Yukinori Takubo. 1992. *Kiso nihongo bunpoo [Basic Japanese grammar]*, revised edition. Tokyo: Kuroshio Publishers.

Miyazaki, Kazuhito, Taro Adachi, Harumi Noda & Shino Takanashi. 2002. *Modaritii [Modality]*. Tokyo: Kurosio Publishers.

Najima, Yoshinao. 2007. *Noda no imi/kinoo: Kanrensei riron no kanten kara [The meaning and function of* noda*: From the perspective of Relevance Theory]*. Tokyo: Kurosio Publishers.

Nihongo Kijutsu Bunpoo Kenkyuukai. 2003. *Gendai nihongo bunpoo 4 [Contemporary Japanese grammar 4]*. Tokyo: Kurosio Publishers.

Noda, Harumi. 1997. *No(da) no kinoo [The functions of* no(da)*]*. Tokyo: Kurosio Publishers.

Okuda, Yasuo. 1990. Setsumei (sono 1): Noda, nodearu, nodesu [Explanation (Part 1): *Noda, nodearu, nodesu*]. In Gengogaku Kenkyuukai (ed.), *Kotoba no kagaku [Science of Language]*, vol. 4, 173–216. Tokyo: Mugi Shobo.

Oshima, David Y. 2014. On the functional differences between the discourse particles *ne* and *yone* in Japanese. In *Proceedings of Pacific Asia Conference on Language, Information and Computation (PACLIC)*, vol. 28, 442–451. Bangkok: Chulalongkorn University.

Oshima, David Y. 2016. On the polysemy of the Japanese discourse particle *ne*: A study with special reference to intonation. *Forum of International Development Studies* 47(3). 1–17.

Oshima, David Y. 2019. The logical principles of honorification and dishonorification in Japanese. In Kazuhiro Kojima, Maki Sakamoto, Koji Mineshima & Ken Satoh (eds.), *New Frontiers in Artificial Intelligence: JSAI-isAI 2018 Workshops, JURISIN, AI-Biz, SKL, LENLS, IDAA, Yokohama, Japan, November 12–14, 2018, Revised Selected Papers*, 325–340. Heidelberg: Springer.Roberts, Craige. 1996/2012. Information structure in discourse: Towards an integrated formal theory of pragmatics. *OSU Working Papers in Linguistics* 49. 91–136. Reprinted in *Semantics and Pragmatics* 5(6). 1–69.

Saji, Keizo. 1991. *Nihongo no bunpoo no kenkyuu [A study of the Japanese grammar]*. Tokyo: Hituzi Shobo.

Teramura, Hideo. 1984. *Nihongo no shintakusu to imi [The syntax and meaning of Japanese]*, Vol. 2. Tokyo: Kurosio Publishers.

Vance, Timothy. 2008. *The sounds of Japanese*. Cambridge: Cambridge University Press.

Venditti, Jennifer J. 2005. The J_ToBI model of Japanese intonation. In Sun-Ah Jun (ed.), *Prosodic Typology: The Phonology of Intonation and Phrasing*, 172–200. Oxford: Oxford University Press.

Wrona, Janick. 2011. A case of non-derived stand-alone nominalization: Evidence from Japanese. In Foong Ha Yap, Karen Grunow-Hårsta & Janick Wrona (eds.), *Nominalization in Asian languages: Diachronic and typological perspectives*, 423–452. Amsterdam: John Benjamins.

Yoshida, Shigeaki. 1988. Noda keishiki no koozoo to hyoogen kooka [The structure and expressive effects of the form *noda*]. *Kokubun Ronso: The Journal of Japanese Language and Literature* 15. 41–51.

Yoshida, Shigeaki. 1994. Gimonbun no shoruikei to sono bunmatsu keishiki: Nodes-uka/masuka-gata gimonbun no yoohoo o megutte [Varieties of interrogatives and their sentence-final forms: On the uses of interrogatives of the *nodesuka-* and *masuka*-types]. *Shimadai kokubun* 22. 1–13.

Yoshida, Shigeaki. 2000. "Noda" no hyoogen naiyoo to gosei ni tsuite: Noda wa set-sumei no jodooshi ka [On the expressed content and lexical status of *noda*: Is *noda* an auxiliary verb of explanation?]. *Yamanobe no michi: Kokubungaku kenkyuushi* 44. 7–31.

2 Evidentiality, inference, conclusion

Japanese *no* as a particle and complementizer

Lukas Rieser

Overview

Sections 1 and 2 summarize extant observations on *no*'s evidential properties and on COMP-COP constructions, defending my claim that the pragmatic particle *no* (henceforth no_2) and the homophonous complementizer (henceforth no_1)[1] can be sharply distinguished in all cases but bridging contexts for the development of no_2 from no_1, and the gray zones discussed in Section 3. Section 4 offers a formal analysis of no_2 as an utterance modifier, and Section 5 sketches a pragmaticalization path $no_1 > no_2$, followed by conclusion and outlook in Section 6.

1 The evidential particle no_2

The evidential properties of no_2 become apparent to varying degrees in different utterance types. In what follows I discuss data showing the effect of adding no_2 in descending order of perceived impact: falling interrogatives (1.1), assertions with the conjecture marker *daroo* (1.2), utterances with final rising intonation (1.3), and finally, plain assertion (1.4), where the effect of adding no_2 is arguably the most subtle. In the analysis, I seek to account for these observations by modeling how no_2 modifies the original felicity condition of each utterance type.

1.1 *Falling interrogatives*

Interrogatives with falling final intonation,[2] henceforth falling interrogatives (FIs), are a particularly productive class of utterances in Japanese. As there is no syntactic distinction between interrogative and declarative sentence types in Japanese, interrogative-marking with *ka* is mandatory in FIs, thus alternatively labeled "(*no-*)*ka* constructions,"

Observations on the evidential properties of no_2 in FIs, as those summarized in the following, show some of the clearest contrasts out of all utterance types no_2 occurs in. On my view, this is because FIs, in contrast to some rising utterances and assertions, come without evidence conditions on their own, providing a clearer view on additional conditions introduced by no_2.

DOI: 10.4324/9781351057837-3

1.1.1   Expressions of doubt vs. exclamations

Davis (2011) provides example (1) of an FI[3] alongside the scenarios in (2) to bring out readings salient with and without no_2. The underlined translation approximates the reading forced by no_2, which is salient under scenario 2.

(1) S: *Tori-ga   konna tokoro-ni sumeru   (<u>no</u>) ka.*
        birds-NOM such_a place-in live.POT.NPST no_2 INT
        {'Can birds live in a place like this?'/<u>'Ah, so birds can live here after all.'</u>}
(2) a. Scenario 1: S believes that birds cannot live here. S's friend A says something that suggests they do. S utters (1), thereby indicating that A is mistaken, and that it should be obvious birds cannot live here.
     b. Scenario 2: S is biased toward it being the case that birds cannot live here but, looking out the window, is surprised to discover that, in fact, they do. S utters (1) to indicate his surprise.

While both scenarios in (2) set up negative epistemic bias w.r.t. the prejacent φ = "birds can live in a place like this," that is, a pre-existing speaker belief $\neg\varphi$, they differ in at least two relevant points. First, only scenario 2 indicates revision of this speaker bias. I thus label this interpretation the "revision" reading, as opposed to the "rejection" reading scenario 1 describes. Second, only in scenario 2 is contextual evidence sufficient grounds for belief revision. On my view, no_2 functions to mark the presence of such evidence, thus forcing the revision reading.

1.1.2   Positive vs. negative bias in exclamations

Expanding on Davis's observation that the sentence-final particle *yo* excludes a rejection reading,[4] Taniguchi (2016) observes a more subtle interpretational nuance, differentiating between the revision reading of FIs and third interpretation as in (3) I label "doubt" reading, on which belief revision is considered but bias is sustained.

(3) Scenario: S observes someone about to eat something not usually expected to be eaten.
     Sonna   mono   taberu   (no)   ka yo.
     such_a   thing   eat.NPST no_2 INT SFP
     {'What the hell! He isn't going to eat that!'/<u>'Holy shit! He's going to eat that!'</u>}

Note that the translations corresponding to the doubt and revision readings are both exclamations, in contrast to Davis's (rhetorical) interrogative translation approximating the rejection reading. This is because *yo* excludes outright rejection, making the doubt reading on which the speaker considers revision, but retains the negative bias salient for plain (3). Adding no_2 brings out the revision reading, approximated by the underlined translation, on which the speaker is (at least) strongly inclined to revise their bias and accept the prejacent.[5]

1.1.3 *Evidence in FIs and* no$_2$

Addition of *no$_2$* can disambiguate readings of FIs, as summarized in Table 2.1. (Contextual) evidence is necessary to license *no$_2$*, but it is only added when the speaker considers this evidence strong enough to revise negative epistemic bias.[6]

Table 2.1 Readings of FIs, *no*, and contextual evidence

	No evidence	*Contextual evidence*
ka(-yo)	rejection (1)	doubt (3)
no-ka(-yo)	–	revision (1), (3)

To account for this pattern, an analysis of *no$_2$* needs to capture not only presence or absence of contextual evidence but also subjective evaluation of its strength by the speaker. What *no$_2$* marks in FIs is that the speaker judges contextual evidence strong enough to warrant revision of a negative bias, which is based on potentially stronger (private) evidence.

Furthermore, *no$_2$* interacts not only with interrogative force but also with the sentence-final particle *yo* to narrate the speaker's belief revision process. This supports my view that both are non-propositional utterance modifiers, with the difference that the contribution of *no$_2$* is evidential, that of *yo* epistemic, that is, the latter introduces belief rather than evidence conditions.

1.2 No$_2$ *in conjecture utterances*

Analyzing *no$_2$* as an utterance modifier also links it to the conjecture marker *daroo*.[7] Utterances with *daroo* are another stage on which *no$_2$* yields clear contrasts, not least because contextual, verifiable evidence is important information to evaluate results of conjecture. When such evidence is available, *no$_2$* is mandatory in *daroo*-utterances.[8]

1.2.1 *Evidence-sensitive and conjecture*

Hara (2006) provides (4), adapted from Izvorski's (1997) study of Bulgarian evidentials, illustrating the evidence-sensitivity of *daroo* in assertions.

(4) *John-wa   kinoo   wain-o   takusan nonda   (no)   daroo.*
     John-TOP   yesterday wine-ACC   a_lot drink.PST   *no$_2$*   CONJ
     'I bet John had a lot of wine yesterday.'
(5) a. Scenario 1: The speaker sees there are some empty wine bottles in John's room.
     b. Scenario 2: The speaker knows that John likes wine a lot.

The plain version of (4) is only acceptable in scenario 2, where the speaker is merely guessing, whereas no_2 is mandatory in scenario 1, where there is indirect visual evidence for the prejacent. Hara (2006) accounts for this by analyzing *daroo* as an epistemic modal quantifying prejacent likelihood at >50%, with an evidential meaning component requiring the absence, rather than presence, of contextual evidence. Revising this view, Hara and Davis (2013) propose *daroo* lowers the Gricean quality threshold and explain the incompatibility of plain *daroo* with evidence by optimality constraints. Neither analysis discusses the role of no_2 in any detail.

1.2.2   *Types of inference and* no

Takubo (2009) argues that *no* (as a complementizer) differentiates types of inference in *daroo*-utterances, citing example (6) due to Morimoto (1994).

(6) Scenario: S looks at the newly published alumni newsletter and finds that one of his classmates changed her surname.
Kanojo-wa   kekkon-shi-ta   #(no)   daroo.
she-TOP   get_married-PST   *no*   CONJ
'I bet she got married.'

The claim is that *no* is mandatory in *daroo*-utterances conveying the result of abductive rather than the standard deductive inference. Deduction corresponds to inference by *modus ponens*, as schematized in (7), whereas abduction is a form of defeasible reasoning, here written as, which is used to speculate about reasons or causes, as shown in (7b).

(7) a. **Deduction:** $[(\psi \rightarrow \varphi) \wedge \psi] \rightarrow \varphi$
     b. **Abduction:** $[(\varphi \rightarrow \psi) \wedge \psi] \rightsquigarrow \varphi$

Resolving φ to "she got married," ψ to "her name has changed," (7b), but not (7a), applies, so that (6) is an instance of abduction. Takubo proposes that *daroo*, like negation (*cf.* Section 2.1), takes narrow scope – when attaching to a biclausal construction "Her name changed because she got married" ($\varphi \rightarrow \psi$), *daroo* can only target the consequent ψ (or the entire clause) but requires *no* to target the possible explanation φ. This property of the complementizer is taken to carry over to cases like (6), where *no* occurs in a monoclausal, stand-alone utterance.

1.2.3   *Conjecture, evidence, and type of inference*

Table 2.2 summarizes the interaction of *no* and types of evidence and inference in conjecture utterances. With contextual evidence/abductive inference, no_2 is mandatory, in contrast to its optionality for evidence-marking in FIs.

Table 2.2 Readings of *daroo*-utterances, *no*, and contextual evidence

	Evidence	Inference
daroo	private	deductive
no-daroo	contextual	abductive

In Section 5, I return to how these observations connect no_1 to no_2. Discussing data from Takubo (2009) in more detail, I propose that *daroo*-utterances of evidence-based inference are a bridging context for the development from no_1 to no_2, making some functional overlap expected. While scope-adjusting (in the biclausal case) and discourse-connection (in the case of two separate utterances) are functions of the complementizer no_1 (*cf.* Section 2) that can serve to mark abductive inference, I maintain that monoclausal, stand-alone utterances like (4) and (6) are instances of no_2 externally anchoring results of inference, which here happens to be abductive in nature. This function of no_2 has generalized to other uses where no inference is involved.

1.3 No$_2$ *in final rising utterances*

Final rising utterances have received attention as a background on which no_2's evidential properties become apparent, mainly based on comparison with bias patterns of English polar questions, in particular the role of negation. As Japanese rising interrogatives and declaratives are not easily distinguishable, both possibilities need to be taken into account.

1.3.1 *Evidential bias and* no$_2$

Sudo (2013) provides (8) along with two scenarios in (9) to illustrate the interaction between no_2 and bias in final rising utterances without negation.[9]

(8) *John-wa   hidarikiki   (na   no)?*
    John-TOP left_handed COP.ADN no$_2$
    'Is John a lefty?/John is a lefty?'
(9) Scenario: Looking for a left-handed person (for instance for an experiment) . . .
    a. Scenario 1: S is wondering about John, who is not around.
    b. Scenario 2: S sees John writing with his left hand.

Scenario 1 is constructed as evidentially neutral, whereas scenario 2 is positively biased toward φ = "John is a lefty," in which case no_2 is preferred, straightforwardly connecting it to extralinguistic evidence – on Sudo's terminology, no_2 introduces evidential bias.

1.3.2   Interaction of no_2 and negation

Ito and Oshima's (2014) observations on example (10) under the scenarios in (11) illustrate how negation results in more complex bias patterns with no_2.[10]

(10)   *Amakunai   (no)?*
     sweet.NEG no_2
     '[Is it] not sweet?/[It's] not sweet?'
(11)   a.   Scenario 1: S is looking for sweet sake. A points out two bottles that are not sweet. S is asking about another bottle.
      b.   Scenario 2: A eats a piece of orange and makes a grimace.

Scenario 1 is constructed as evidentially neutral but makes the negated prejacent salient – the addressee's pointing out non-sweet sake makes proffering $\neg\varphi$ in (10) less, or at least not more, marked than proffering φ. Under this scenario, bare (10) is perfectly felicitous, and adding no_2 introduces evidential bias, parallel to non-negated examples like (8).[11]

In scenario 2, the positive alternative φ = "[This orange] is sweet" is salient for lack of priming with $\neg\varphi$. Proffering $\neg\varphi$ then leads to polarity mismatch, which in turn gives rise to negative evidential bias. Under evidential bias, no_2 adds epistemic bias, so that (10) with no_2 obligatorily conveys a speaker expectation that the orange be sweet, contrary to evidence.

1.3.3   Evidential and epistemic bias and polarity

The effect of adding no_2 to final rising utterances is summarized in Table 2.3, where "evidential" indicates bias of prejacent polarity, "epistemic" of opposite polarity, as observed in the preceding examples.

Table 2.3 Final rising utterances, *no*, and types of bias

	Match	*Mismatch*
plain rising	–	evidential
no rising	evidential	evidential, epistemic

There are thus two sources for evidential bias: the addition of no_2 and polarity mismatch. I assume that the latter is due to convention, as the presence of according evidence is the most plausible reason for choosing to proffer the prejacent in non-salient polarity.

On the background of extant evidential bias, no_2 marks not the presence of evidence but, as in the FIs discussed in 1.1, that the speaker deems it sufficient to revise a belief to the contrary. The examples of rising utterances discussed here, in contrast to the examples of FIs discussed earlier, do not, by default, convey there is such a belief. Adding no_2 on the background of evidential bias indicates that revision is on the table, thereby presupposing the existence of a pre-existing belief contrary to evidence and giving rise to epistemic bias.

1.3.4 The nature of no₂-marked evidence

In case of matching polarity, *no₂* in final rising utterances is purely evidence-marking, providing a window on the nature of the evidence it makes required across utterance types. Büring and Gunlogson (2000)[12] provide a definition of what they label compelling contextual evidence (CCE), sensitivity to which determines evidential bias in English polar questions, on the following lines.

(12) a. Contextual evidence "has just become mutually available to the participants in the current discourse situation."
  b. Evidence for φ is compelling "if, considered in isolation, . . . would allow the participants to assume [φ]."

Previewing the analysis I propose in Section 4, mutual availability as defined in (12a) is reflected in *no₂* requiring evidence available to all participants, rather than evidence private to the speaker as sufficient for assertion. The requirement on CCE just having become available, on the other hand, is limited to utterances narrating the speaker's belief formation or revision process and is absent from some uses of *no₂* assertions (*cf.* Section 1.4).

The requirement that CEE allow participants to assume φ when considered in isolation, as defined in (12b), is reflected in *no₂* marking φ as assertable by requiring evidence in principle adequate to assert φ in absence of (potentially private) conflicting evidence. I adopt Gricean terminology of quality requiring "adequate" evidence, parallel to "compelling" in (12b).

1.4 No₂ in assertions: perspective shifting and exasperated uses

If *no₂* indeed adds an assertion-like evidence requirement, the comparably less-pronounced contrasts in falling declaratives (i.e., assertions) are expected. In what follows I discuss three, in my view, unambiguous instances of *no₂* in assertions functioning as what I label an "external anchor."

1.4.1 Perspective shifting

Japanese subjective predicates, here defined as adjectival predicates[13] describing psychological states, evaluations, or perceptions like temperature or taste, have their perspective center fixed to the speaker in assertions which convey the speaker's perspective by default. One way to shift perspective to the grammatical subject is adding *no₂*, as (13) illustrates.

(13) *Kare-wa   tanoshii   (n   da).*
  he-TOP   be_fun   *no₂* COP
  {'He's fun.'/'He's having fun.'}

On the default reading of bare (13), the perspective center is the speaker, who perceives the grammatical subject *kare* 'he' as fun, yielding the reading "He's fun." Only when *no₂* is added does a reading "He's having fun," where perspective is shifted to *kare* 'he,' become (readily) available. This links *no₂* to other evidential expressions, such as *-soo*, which indicates that the speaker has indirect, often perceptual, evidence supporting the prejacent, as in (14).

(14) *Kare-wa   tanoshi-soo   da.*
       he-TOP   be_fun-EVID   COP
       {'He seems fun.'/'He seems to be having fun.'}

Parallel to (13) with *no₂*, both paraphrased readings are available for (14), with the difference that *soo* requires perceptual evidence while *no₂* is not specified for type of evidence.

Crucially, however, *no₂* differs from other Japanese evidentials in that it can take scope over any of them, yielding, for instance, narrative soliloquy or exasperated/convincing readings, which are discussed in the following. This supports my view that *no₂* is a non-propositional utterance modifier not changing what is asserted, in contrast to propositional evidentials like *-soo*.

1.4.2   Narrative soliloquy

Utterances I label "narrative soliloquy" are core examples for external anchoring by *no₂*. The prejacent of (15) denotes a state of affairs observed at utterance time,[14] and *no₂* marks that assertion is grounded in external evidence rather than private beliefs.

Scenario: S is having a beer after work.

(15) *Soo, kore-ga   (yappari/sasugani) umai ??(n   da).*
        SO   DEM-NOM   tasty   *no₂*   COP
        'Yeah, this sure is tasty.'

On the intended soliloquous reading of (15), *no₂* is strongly preferred. In contrast to exclamatives, which have a similar contextual evidence requirement, narrative soliloquy does not necessarily carry mirative meaning or convey surprise. In (15), for instance, the adverbs *yappari/sasuga* 'as expected'[15] indicate that the observation only confirms speaker expectations.

The requirement for immediately available evidence in the utterance situation distinguished narrative soliloquy from the perspective-switching use of *no₂* in (13), where evidence can be private and no longer accessible in the context, as long as it is sufficient to allow the speaker to evaluate the subject's psychological state. On both uses of *no₂*-assertions discussed so far, evidence must, in one way or another, be external to the speaker's epistemic state.

1.4.3   Exasperated/convincing use

On the use of no_2 in assertions I label "exasperated/convincing," immediate contextual evidence is not only optional but also typically absent. This use is the most clearly addressee-oriented, as it seeks to present the prejacent as an established fact[16] within the discourse, often absent not only of immediate evidence in the utterance situation but also of the consensus the speaker desires to establish.

To relate this use to no_2 in narrative soliloquy, (16) shows a non-soliloquous variant of (15) with the particle *yo*.[17] Here, no_2 is used to convey that the speaker deems the prejacent to be obvious to the point of going without saying. That is, no_2 does not (necessarily) indicate the presence of external grounds in the current utterance situation, but that such grounds exists within the discourse, that is, the addressee is also in a position to assert the prejacent.

(16) *Mochiron   umai   (n   da)   yo!*
      of_course tasty no_2 COP   SFP
      'Duh, of course it's tasty!'

This example could, for instance, be uttered in reply to a question of whether or not something is delicious. The non-soliloquous reading is forced by the sentence-final particle *yo* familiar from the FI examples, and the adverb *mochiron* conveys that the prejacent is expected, or a matter of course, to the speaker. What no_2 adds is a nuance of exasperation, signaling that the addressee should already be aware of and has grounds to believe the prejacent, thereby answering their question while simultaneously marking, or dismissing, it as superfluous.

1.4.4   No$_2$ as an external anchor

The effect of no_2 in declaratives I subsume under "external anchoring" differs by type of prejacent, as summarized in Table 2.4. With subjective predicates, no_2 can shift the perspective center from the speaker, with an observed state of affairs it makes a soliloquous reading salient, elsewhere it gives rise to an exasperated or convincing reading.

Table 2.4 Declaratives, *no*, and types of prejacents

	Subjective	*Observation*	*Other*
assertion	speaker-centered	conveying	standard
no_2-assertion	shifted	soliloquous	exasperated/convincing

2   The complementizer no_1

In this section, I discuss the scope-adjusting and discourse-structuring (explanation and elaboration) uses of no_1, with some comparison to uses of

COMP-COP[18] constructions in other languages. I conclude that the productivity of no_1 in COMP-COP constructions is comparatively high, which has likely contributed to the development of no_2.

2.1 No₁ *as a scope-adjuster*

In what follows I summarize how no_1 adjusts the scope of negation and focus and argue that the availability of an equivalent cleft is a test for no_1 (as opposed to no_2) in *no-da* constructions.

2.1.1 *Adjusting the scope of negation*

Adjusting the scope of negation is a particularly productive use of no_1 in Japanese,[19] where negation occurs on the predicate regardless of the constituent it targets. In (17), adapted from Kuno (1986), no_1 intervenes between predicate and negation, which occurs on an additional copula and targets a constituent other than the predicate.

(17) *Kore-wa Pari-de {??kawa-na-katta/ kat-ta n ja-nai }*
     this-TOP Paris-LOC   buy-NEG-PST   buy-PST no_1 COP-neg
     'I didn't buy this in **Paris**.'

German is an example where rather than complementizer constructions, positioning of the negation morpheme is the dominant strategy to encode the scope of negation, as in (18), a translation of (17), where the position of *nicht* NEG marked with # is infelicitous on the intended reading.

(18) *Ich habe das {nicht} in Paris {#nicht} gekauft.*
     I   have this NEG   in Paris NEG   bought
     'I didn't buy this in **Paris**.'

2.1.2 *Adjusting the scope of focus*

When no_1 adjusts the scope of focus in positive assertions, the lack of intervention between negation and predicate makes it harder to distinguish between particle and complementizer. In this case, availability of a corresponding cleft is a possible diagnostic to identify no_1 on its scope-adjusting use. Hiraiwa and Ishihara (2012)[20] propose a transformational link between scope-adjusting COMP-COP constructions (their label: "*noda in-situ* focus constructions") and clefts, as illustrated in their examples (19) and (20).[21]

(19) *Naoya-ga ringo-o mittsu tabeta no da.*
     Naoya-NOM apple-ACC three   ate no_1 COP
     'It's three apples that Naoya ate.'

(20) *Naoya-ga   tabeta   no-wa   mochiron ringo-o   mittsu*
      Naoya-NOM   ate no_1-TOP   of_course   apple-ACC   three
      na   n   da   yo.
      COP.ADN no_2 COP   SFP
      'Duh, it's three apples that Naoya ate!'

Hiraiwa and Ishihara claim that clefts like (20) are derived by focus movement and subsequent remnant CP-topicalization[22] from COMP-COP constructions, like (19), so that the same instance of no_1 occurs in different positions in both examples. Based on this, availability of a derived cleft is a diagnostic for a scope-adjusting COMP-COP construction and hence for no_1.

The contribution of the additional instance of *no* in (20), together with *yo* (both added by me), is parallel to no_2 in exasperation/confirmation use, as in example (16). I take this as support for my assumption that no_1 and no_2 are distinct lexical items. A confounding factor is that adding no_2 to (19) would result in merger, where one instance of *no* has the functions of both particle and complementizer, as I argue in Section 3.2.

2.2 Discourse-structuring no_1: explanation and elaboration

On its discourse-structuring, connective use, no_1 is closer to no_2 in that it does not serve to internally structure the utterance but can be distinguished by its lack of evidential meaning. In contrast to no_2, connective complementizers can be observed in languages other than Japanese. In the following I discuss two types of relations no_1 marks: explanation and elaboration.

2.2.1 Explanation and no_1

In a number of languages, COMP-COP constructions function as explanation markers to provide a reason for a salient proposition. (21) provides a paraphrase where φ is the COMP-COP prejacent, ψ the salient antecedent, and $\leadsto$ represents defeasible entailment.[23]

(21) **Explanation:** proffering[24] φ conveys: $\exists \psi$ such that $\varphi \leadsto \psi$.

Explanation thus conveys that, given the circumstances, ψ is normally a consequence of φ; hence, φ explains ψ. The English example (22) illustrates this, where assertion of ψ = "John isn't coming" is immediately followed by an explaining assertion of φ = "[John]'s got a cold."

(22) *John isn't coming. He's got a cold.*

When assertion of φ in (22) is interpreted as an explanation, the relation $\varphi \leadsto \psi$ is understood – when one has a cold, one usually does not come. Crucially, there is no converse relation $\psi \rightsquigarrow \varphi$, differentiating explanation from elaboration, which will be discussed shortly. Note the absence of an explanation marker, typical for English, in (22). In (23), a parallel Japanese example, on the other hand, no_1 overtly connects the explanation to the antecedent utterance.

(23) *Taro-wa   konai.   Kaze-o   hiiteru   n   da.*
     PN-TOP   come.NEG   cold-ACC   get.RES no_1 COP

It should be noted that the explanation use of *no-da* constructions is salient enough to have inspired the label *setsumei no modariti* 'modality of explanation' in the descriptive literature, suggesting pragmatic meaning closer to no_2 than to scope-adjusting no_1. As *no* in explanations has an information-structuring function on the discourse level parallel to that of no_1 within the clause and lacks the obligatory evidential meaning of no_2, I maintain it is best analyzed as no_1.

2.2.2   *Explanation in other languages*

Further support for viewing explanation as a function of no_1 comes from COMP-COP explanation being observable in other languages. As an example for romance,[25] consider Brazilian Portuguese (24), parallel to English (22) and Japanese (23).

(24) *O   João não   vem.   É   que   'tá   resfriado.*
     DET   PN   NEG   come   COP   COMP   is   sick_with_cold
     'João isn't coming. [It's that] he's got a cold.'

While the English translation shows that COMP-COP explanation is not unacceptable in English, it is the dominant strategy in both Portuguese and Japanese, where *é que* in (24) and *no-da* in (23) are clearly preferred. In English, COMP-COP explanation is only productive where negation excludes alternatives or possible objections are brought up, as in these examples.

(25) a. It's not that John doesn't want to go; it's just that he's got a cold.
     b. [Yeah, we could do it tomorrow. . . .] It's just that John's got a cold.

Portuguese and Japanese have similar contrastive uses of COMP-COP constructions, in the case of Japanese often with *wake* (lit. 'reason'), a complementizer specialized for explanations, reasons, and the like, as the following examples parallel to English (25a) and (25b) illustrate.

(26) a. *Não   que   o   João não   queira   ir,   é*
      NEG   COMP   DET   PN   NEG   want.SUBV   go   COP
      só   que   ele está resfriado.
      just   COMP   he is   sick_with_cold

b. *[Yeah, we could do it tomorrow . . .]*   *só*   *que*   *o*
                                             just COMP DET
    João *está* *resfriado.*
    PN   is   sick_with_cold

(27) a. *Taro-wa* *ikitakunai* *wake* *janai* *kedo,*
      PN-TOP   go.VOL.NEG COMP COP.NEG but
      kaze-wo *hiiteru* *n*   *da.*
      cold-ACC get.RES COMP COP

b. *[Yeah, we could do it tomorrow . . .]* *tada, Taro-wa*
                                                 just pn-top
    kaze-wo *hiiteru* *n*   *da.*
    cold-ACC get.RES COMP COP

Other than supporting my claim that explanation is a use of no_1 rather than no_2, these observations on COMP-COP explanations across languages point toward a hierarchy from utterance to discourse-structuring uses (German has neither) and contrastive to non-contrastive uses in explanations (only the former are productive in English), which I propose culminates in elaborations unique to Japanese within the small sample discussed here.

2.2.3 *Elaboration and* no_1

Elaboration is a discourse-structuring use of COMP-COP constructions defined as the mirror-image of explanation, as schematized in (28).

(28) **Elaboration:** proffering φ conveys: $\exists \psi$ such that $\psi \rightsquigarrow \varphi$.

(29) shows an elaboration variant of the explanation example (23). The entailment relation in the background is the same, but the consequent, rather than the antecedent, is proffered.

(29) *Taro-wa* *kaze-o* *hii-ta* *yo.* *Ko-nai* *n* *da.*
     PN-TOP   cold-ACC pull-PST SFP come-NEG *no* COP
    'He got a cold. [It's that he's] not coming.'

Out of the languages compared here, only in Japanese do plain COMP-COP constructions have a fully productive elaboration use as in (29). Elsewhere, specialized constructions, like English "That is (to say), . . .," Portuguese *Isto é* 'That is,' and *Quer dizer (que)* . . . 'Wants to say (that) . . .,' as well as German *Das heißt* . . . 'That means . . .' take over this role. In Japanese, adverbial markers with similar meanings co-occur with no_1, as the examples in (30) illustrate.

(30) John was born in NY. . . .
    a. . . . *(Tsumari,) Amerikajin-ni* *umareta n-da.*
            That_is   American-DAT born   COMP-COP

    b. ... *{#É que /   Quer dizer} ele já   nasceu Americano.*
           COP COMP want say he already born American
    c. ... *{#Es   ist   so, / Das heißt,} dass er von   Geburt*
           EXPL COP so   that means that he from birth
         an Amerikaner war.
         on American   was
    'John was born in NY. That is (to say), he was born American.'

The strictly right-headed syntax of Japanese likely supports the high productivity of plain COMP-COP constructions, including elaborations, as Portuguese and German (EXPL) COP-COMP share a syntactic slot with the specialized elaboration markers, while corresponding Japanese adverbials occur sentence-internally, making co-occurrence with *no-da* COMP-COP possible.

    From the observations on discourse-connective COMP-COP summarized in Table 2.5, I tentatively conclude that (contrastive) explanation is more basic than elaboration, limited to Japanese. In Section 5, I argue elaboration has contributed to the development of fully productive no_2.

Table 2.5 Explanation, elaboration, and complementizers across languages

	German	*English*	*Portuguese*	*Japanese*
explanation	#	(contrastive)	✓	✓
elaboration	(	specialized	forms)	✓

3   Gray zones: COMP-exclamatives and conflation of no_1 and no_2

In this section, I discuss two reasons for which distinguishing no_2 from no_1 can be difficult: (apparent) functional overlap in exclamatives and exclamations and merger into a single instance.

3.1   No *in exclamatives*

Distinguishing between functionally similar no_1 exclamatives from exclamations – I claim that the former correspond to COMP exclamatives, a speech-act type distinct from assertion, thereby excluding apparent counterexamples to generalizations on no_2.

3.1.1   No *in* wh-*exclamatives*

In Japanese *wh*-exclamatives, *no* is mandatory, as in the degree exclamative (31) taken from Ono (2006), who discusses this class of utterances in detail.

(31) *John wa   nante ookina pizza-o   tabeta *(no) da(roo)!*
      John TOP EXCL big   pizza-ACC ate   *no*   COP CONJ
      'What a big pizza John ate!'

As *no* in (31) has neither an apparent sentence- nor discourse-structuring function and the utterance narrates contextual evidence, one might conclude that it is an instance of no_2. However, exclamatives are a speech-act type that comes with a direct evidence requirement (*cf.* Rett 2011) similar to no_2's external anchoring function. Furthermore, as (COMP-)exclamatives are syntactically distinct from assertions in many languages, it is plausible that *no* in (31) fulfills a purely syntactical role as part of an exclamative construction and is hence an instance of no_1.

3.1.2   *(Apparent) limits of external anchoring:* COMP-*exclamatives*

While the distinction between no_1 and no_2 in degree-exclamatives has no obvious ramifications for the analysis of no_2, examples of what I take to be non-degree no_1-exclamatives have been discussed as problematic for generalizations on no_2. Building on counterexamples to her own generalization that no_2[26] encodes "settledness" (*kiteisei*) observed by Noda (1997), Najima (2007) provides (32), where *no-da* can be made felicitous by modifying the utterance situation in terms of epistemic bias.

(32) Scenario: S discovers there is a dead dog on the street.

    A! Inu-ga   shinderu (#n-da).
    oh dog-NOM   die.RES COMP-COP
    'Oh! There's a dead dog!'

The badness of *no* in (32) is puzzling when taken as an instance of no_2 encoding "settledness" or, as I propose, external (evidential) anchoring, in particular considering how close (32) seems to no_2 in narrative soliloquy. Noting that *no* in (32) becomes acceptable when the speaker, sometime after having initially observed that "there is a dead dog," notices this is still the case against an expectation that the carcass has been removed, Najima proposes that not "settledness" but the presence of an expectation w.r.t. the observed state of affairs licenses *no*.

    On my view, these apparent counterexamples are in fact uses of no_1 rather than no_2, the badness of (32) stemming from the felicity conditions on exclamatives. Support for this comes from (33), adapted from (32) into German, where COMP-exclamatives are similarly productive.[27]

(33) *Dass da   ??(immer noch) ein toter Hund liegt!*
    that there still   yet a   dead dog lies
    'That there's (still) a dead dog there!'

To make the relevant contrast clearer, I have added *immer noch* 'still'/'even now,' without which the COMP-exclamative is degraded. This is to say that the utterance is infelicitous when the observation made is completely out of the blue, parallel to Najima's example. This is not to say that no_2-assertions cannot have mirative overtones, as the no_2-exclamation (34) shows. However, (34) involves evidence-based inference, distinguishing it from the exclamations (31) and (32), which only convey a speaker attitude w.r.t. an observed state of affairs.

(34)   Seeing that a colleague's stuff is gone:

   A, moo   kaetta   ??(n da)!
   oh already return.pst no_2 COP
   'Oh, he already went home!'

In sum, the line between no_1 and no_2 can be somewhat blurry in exclamations and exclamatives due to their similar function. I defend that taking no_1 to occur in exclamatives, but no_2 in exclamations, explains apparent counterexamples like (32) as COMP-exclamatives, parallel to German (33), an utterance type with felicity conditions distinct from soliloquous no_2-assertions.

3.2   Merger of no_2 and no_1

Another complication for distinguishing no_2 and no_1 are utterances in which a single instance of *no* appears to function as both particle and scope-adjusting complementizer. Merger of two instances of *no* occurs when an additional instance would yield a string *no-na-$n(o)$ (no COP.ADN-no).[28] (35), adapted from example (17) for scope-adjusting no_1, shows separate instances of no_1 and no_2 merging, in absence of negation, to a single instance of *no*, which both adjusts the scope of focus and conveys pragmatic meaning.

(35)   *Kore-wa Pari-de   { kat-ta   n   ja-nai   / kat-ta } n   da   yo.*
   this-TOP Paris-LOC buy-PST no_1 COP-neg buy-PST no COP SFP
   'I didn't buy this in Paris!'

That a string *no-na-no (COMP-COP.ADN-PRT) is unavailable whereas *no-janai-no* (COMP-COP.NEG-PRT) is perfectly fine makes it likely that morphotactic or phonological constraints lead to merger of no_2 and no_1. Thus, one instance of *no* can function as both a scope adjuster and an evidence marker (and/or have a connective function). This shows that morphologically, no_2 remains a nominal element, differing from no_1 only in meaning and function.

4   No$_2$ as a speech-act level evidence marker

This section outlines a formal analysis implementing two core claims. First, no_2 is a particle with evidential meaning distinct from the complementizer no_1, which has structuring function but no lexical meaning. Second, the pragmatic meaning no_2 lets it function as an external anchor. To account for this, I model no_2 as an utterance modifier adding an evidence condition parallel to assertion, with an additional mutual-availability requirement.[29]

4.1 Speech-act meaning and no₂

My analysis is based on a Gricean view on utterance felicity, in particular the maxim of quality. While adding an addressee variable to an according evidence condition on assertion is but one (quite possibly not ideal) alternative of formally implementing the notion of external anchoring, I maintain that no_2 operates on the speech-act level of meaning and introduces a variant of a condition on felicitous assertion[30] to any utterance type it attaches to.

Extant proposals for an evidence-based analysis of no_2 do not necessarily take it to be operating as a modifier of utterance felicity, as for instance the presuppositional analysis with which Davis (2011) accounts for its effect in FIs. The analysis I propose has the advantage of differentiating no_2 from other, propositional evidentials and of directly modeling its interaction with different utterance types (declaratives and interrogatives with final rising and falling intonation), as well as with other utterance modifiers like *daroo*.

4.1.1 Speech-act level meaning and the evidence condition

Defining and formalizing evidence required by evidentials is generally complex, and Japanese is no exception (*cf.* McCready & Ogata 2007; McCready 2014). I propose that there is a simpler solution for no_2, as it does not require evidence of a specific source or modality (such as sensory, hearsay, etc.). Rather, it requires evidence "adequate" for felicitous assertion of the prejacent as defined in the first specific maxim of quality (cf. Grice 1975), paraphrased in (36).

(36) Do not say anything for which you lack adequate evidence.

For my analysis, on which no_2 requires this evidence to be mutually available, the agent to whom evidence is accessible is crucial. I therefore write evidence sufficient for assertion of prejacent φ by speaker S as $E_S\varphi$.

While individual speakers (and addressees) arguably have an intuition as to whether or not $E_S\varphi$ is fulfilled, there is significant interpersonal variation in such judgments – disagreement on whether or not one "can say something" is often essentially a debate on whether or not the evidence condition is met. My analysis only makes claims on how the contribution of no_2 relates to Gricean "adequate" evidence, without discussing its nature in much detail.

4.1.1.1 AN EVIDENCE CONDITION FROM NO₂

The central premise of my analysis of no_2 is that for felicitous assertion, adequate evidence needs to be accessible to the speaker, but not necessarily the addressee, whereas no_2 requires the same evidence to be accessible to all participants. I simplify this as accessibility to both participants S and A, written as $E_{S,A}\varphi$. (37) shows a paraphrase for this condition based on the first Gricean maxim and Büring and Gunlogson's (2000) definition of "compelling contextual evidence" (CCE) as discussed in Section 1.3, without their requirement for evidence just having become available in the utterance situation.

(37) Evidence condition added by no_2:
   "There is evidence adequate, if considered in isolation, to support assertion of the prejacent proposition φ accessible to all discourse participants in the utterance situation."

In order to compositionally derive the modified meaning of utterances with no_2, I take *utterance meaning* to be defined by the set of its felicity conditions. While the effect that an utterance has on the context, that is, what the utterance does to the context rather than what it requires from it, ultimately needs to be considered as well, I restrict the formal notation to context requirements, as these are what I defend no_2 modifies.

The lexical meaning of no_2 as an utterance modifier introducing the condition $E_{S,A}\varphi$, paraphrased in (37), is shown in (38). $\rightsquigarrow$ represents the meaning of an utterance $\mathcal{U}$ with the prejacent φ as the set of felicity conditions it imposes on the context.

(38) $[\![no]\!] = \lambda \mathcal{U} \lambda \varphi \cdot \mathcal{U}(\varphi) \cup E_{S,A}\varphi$

This is to say that no_2 is a function mapping the set of felicity conditions of a given utterance to a set enriched with a mutually available evidence condition, constituting external anchoring.

Other than no_2, the contents of $\mathcal{U}$ depend on the illocutionary type of the utterance at hand and the presence of other utterance modifiers such as *daroo* or sentence-final particles. Felicity conditions can broadly be classified into evidence conditions, as that introduced by no_2, and belief conditions, as those introduced by epistemic particles. In order to account for the effect of no_2 in different utterance types, their original felicity conditions need to be captured first.

4.1.1.2   UTTERANCE TYPES BY FORCE AND ORIENTATION

To cover the data discussed here, I differentiate utterance types on two dimensions: declarative *vs.* interrogative force, and final falling *vs.* final rising intonation.[31] What I label declarative (DEC) and interrogative (INT) force can also be labeled sentence type, as their characteristic sets of felicity conditions may involve participant variables. These are resolved to speaker or addressee by sentence-final intonation, yielding what is more conventionally labeled illocutionary force.

4.1.2   *Felicity conditions by utterance type*

This section defines the felicity conditions for each utterance types from Section 1. Evidence conditions are given in the same format as those from assertion and *no*$_2$ defined earlier, where $E_x\varphi$ indicates participant x has access to adequate evidence for φ. In addition to this, belief conditions are required to capture utterance meanings.

4.1.2.1   ASSERTIONS

The basis for defining the evidence condition from *no*$_2$, but also for the derivation of interrogative felicity conditions are assertions. Having defined $E_S\varphi$ earlier, I follow the first specific maxim of quality from Grice (1975), as paraphrased in (39), to define the belief condition on assertion as in (40), where $E_x\varphi$ stands for "participant x believes φ to be true."

(39) Do not say anything you believe to be false.
(40) Condition on felicitous assertion of φ by S: $\neg B_S\neg\varphi$.

Together with the evidence condition $E_S\varphi$ from the second maxim of quality, the belief condition $\neg B_S\neg\varphi$ forms the characteristic set $\mathcal{U}(\varphi)$ for assertion of φ. I take this set to be equivalent to utterance meaning; hence, the denotation of assertion is shown in (41), where declarative force is written as DEC, final falling intonation encoding speaker orientation as $\downarrow$.

(41) $[\![\mathrm{DEC}(\varphi)\downarrow]\!] = \{\neg B_S\neg\varphi, E_S\varphi\}$

Note that $\neg B_S\neg\varphi$ only excludes cases in which the speaker S believes the prejacent to be false ($\neg B_S\neg\varphi$) but is weaker than, for instance, a Searlean sincerity condition that S believe the prejacent to be true ($E_S\varphi$, *cf.* Searle 1969). This is intended, as, for instance, in externally anchored exclamations, there is not necessarily such a pre-existing belief.

   Furthermore, while I do not formalize speaker commitment arising from assertion, that is, the change assertion imposes on the context, this can be derived from satisfaction of the conditions in (41) – if $E_S\varphi$ and $\neg B_S\neg\varphi$ hold, an observer of felicitous assertion can conclude $E_S\varphi$, which corresponds to a private speaker belief made public by assertion of φ.

4.1.2.2   INTERROGATIVES

I propose that the belief conditions of interrogatives are the mirror image of declaratives, but that they come without evidence conditions of their own. Formulating a maxim for (falling) interrogatives as in (42) yields a characteristic set as in (43).

(42) Do not doubt anything you believe to be true.

(43) $\llbracket \mathrm{INT}(\varphi) \downarrow \rrbracket = \{\neg B_S \varphi\}$.

It might not be necessary to formulate a separate maxim, however. As noted regarding assertion, an observer can conclude $E_S \varphi$ from assertion of j by S. Considering a (falling) interrogative an utterance that forgoes assertion (i.e., uttering of a falling declarative), an observer of an FI can conclude that $\neg B_S \varphi$ holds; otherwise, an assertion would have been chosen. Such implicatures from forgone alternatives play an even larger role in final rising utterances.

4.1.2.3   FINAL RISING UTTERANCES

As there is no obvious way to distinguish between rising interrogatives and declaratives in Japanese, the bias patterns of both need to be formalized. Starting with the latter, I build on Gunlogson's (2003) proposal for English RDs, on which final intonation resolves a participant variable within utterance meaning. (44) shows the according set of underspecified declarative felicity conditions. The notation $E_y B_x \varphi$ indicates that evidence can support not only a prejacent (in which case y and x are resolved to the same participant) but also higher-order belief, that is, assumptions about others' beliefs (where y and x are distinct).

(44) $\llbracket \mathrm{DEC}(\varphi) \rrbracket = \{B_S \neg B_x \neg \varphi, E_S B_x \varphi\}$ (where $\downarrow$ resolves x to S, $\uparrow$ to A).

With a final fall, this results in the utterance meaning repeated in (45) from (41), assuming that $B_S \neg B_S \neg \varphi$ is reducible to $\neg B_S \neg \varphi$, $E_S B_S \varphi$ due to epistemic privilege, whereas with a final rise, an utterance meaning as in (46) results from $\uparrow$ resolving x to A.

(45) $\llbracket \mathrm{DEC}(\varphi) \downarrow \rrbracket = \{\neg B_S \neg \varphi, E_S \varphi\}$
(46) $\llbracket \mathrm{DEC}(\varphi) \uparrow \rrbracket = \{B_S \neg B_A \neg \varphi, E_S B_A \varphi\}$

I propose that rising interrogatives (canonical questions) forgo both their rising and their falling declarative counterparts. While the condition arising from forgone assertion can alternatively be thought of as a result of the interrogative maxim (42), it should be obvious that when there is evidence regarding addressee belief available to the speaker, an RD should be chosen over a question, in parallel to preference of assertion over an FI in case the speaker believes the prejacent to hold. This results in the following enriched set of felicity conditions for RIs.

(47) $\llbracket \mathrm{INT}(\varphi) \uparrow \rrbracket = \{\neg B_S \varphi, \neg B_S B_A \varphi\}$

Note that the condition from forgoing an RD could also be an inherent property of questions, like the Searlean sincerity condition that S not assume the addressee to believe the prejacent (*cf.* Searle 1969), with the same result. However, I find it preferable to derive as much of utterance meaning as possible from the basic meaning of declaratives, as it better illustrates connections between utterance types.

Finally, it is possible to assume that rising declaratives forgo falling declaratives on the grounds that addressee orientation is generally more marked than speaker orientation. While this may not be plausible for English, I assume that this is the case in Japanese, where rising declaratives are of the same form as rising interrogatives and, in the examples discussed here, are used in the same contexts. Thus, for the purposes of the following discussion, I add condition $\neg B_S\varphi$, shared with all other utterance types but assertions, to (46).

4.1.2.4 DERIVING THE MEANING OF NO_2-UTTERANCES

Table 2.6 shows characteristic sets of falling and rising declaratives as well as interrogatives and the effect of modification with no_2.

Table 2.6 Characteristic sets of falling and rising (*no-*)declaratives and interrogatives

$\mathscr{U}(\varphi)$	$[\![\mathscr{U}(\varphi)]\!]$	$[\![no_2(\mathscr{U}(\varphi))]\!]$
$\text{DEC}(\varphi)\downarrow$	$\{\ \neg B_S\neg\varphi, E_S\varphi\ \}$	$\{\neg B_S\neg\varphi,\quad\quad E_S\varphi,\quad E_{S,A}\varphi\}$
$\text{DEC}(\varphi)\uparrow$	$\{\ \neg B_S\varphi, B_S\neg B_A\neg\varphi, E_SB_A\varphi\}$	$\{\neg B_S\varphi, B_S\neg B_A\neg\varphi, E_SB_A\varphi, E_{S,A}\varphi\}$
$\text{INT}(\varphi)\downarrow$	$\{\ \neg B_S\varphi\quad\quad\quad\quad\quad\}$	$\{\neg B_S\varphi,\quad\quad\quad\quad\quad E_{S,A}\varphi\}$
$\text{INT}(\varphi)\uparrow$	$\{\ \neg B_S\varphi, \neg B_SB_A\varphi\quad\quad\}$	$\{\neg B_S\varphi, \neg B_SB_A\varphi\quad\quad E_{S,A}\varphi\}$

With these sets of (pragmatically enriched) felicity conditions, I seek to account for no_2's function of "external anchoring." In the remainder of this section, I revisit examples from Section 1 to demonstrate how the analysis outlined earlier can account for them.

4.2 Accounting for the uses of no₂

The view of no_2 as an utterance modifier has the advantage of placing it on the same level of meaning as elements like the illocutionary force marker *ka*, the sentence-final particle *yo*, and the conjecture marker *daroo*, with which it conspires to convey information regarding the speaker's belief revision and formation process in the light of mutually available evidence. In this way, accounting for all different uses of no_2 not only straightforwardly reflects intuitions on its evidence-marking function but also makes the difference between a complementizer without lexical meaning like no_1 and the evidential particle no_2 explicit.

4.2.1 No₂ in falling interrogative utterances

The lack of evidence conditions in (falling) interrogatives predicts the strong perceived impact of no_2. The contrast between the positive evidence indicated by no_2

and lack of speaker belief indicated by the interrogative marker *ka* is a suitable strategy for narrative processes of evidence-based belief revision, as in (48) repeated from (1), where *no₂* disambiguates between a rejection and a revision reading.

(48) S: *Tori-ga   konna   tokoro-ni   sumeru   (no)   ka.*
         birds-NOM   such_a   place-in   live.POT.NPST   *no₂*   INT
      {'Can birds live in a place like this?'/'Ah, so birds can live here after all.'}

The two scenarios given by Davis for (48) are differentiated by the presence or absence of contextual evidence, directly reflected in felicity conditions with or without a condition $E_{S,A}\varphi$ as introduced by *no₂*.

Example (49), repeated from (3), is more subtle, as *no₂* disambiguates between a revision and a sustained doubt reading on a scenario where there is contextual evidence.

(49) *Sonna   mono   taberu   (no)   ka   yo.*
      such_a   thing eat.NPST   *no₂*   INT   SFP
      {'What the hell! He isn't going to eat that!'/'Holy shit! He's going to eat that!'}

The "positive bias" that is introduced by *no₂* in this example according to Taniguchi (2016) is parallel to the belief revision reading of (48). As marking of evidence with *no₂* is not mandatory, its absence can indicate that the speaker does not consider the available evidence to be "adequate" in the sense of making the prejacent in principle assertable. The particle *yo*, formalizing the contribution of which I have to forgo due to space,[32] excludes a rejection reading of (49). With or without *yo*, adding *no₂* makes falling interrogatives more assertion-like, as the comparison that follows illustrates.

(50) a. $\llbracket \text{INT}(\varphi) \downarrow \rrbracket = \{ \neg B_S \varphi \}$

     b. $\llbracket \text{DEC}(\varphi) \downarrow \rrbracket = \{ \neg B_S \neg \varphi \wedge E_S \varphi \}$

     c. $\llbracket no(\text{INT}(\varphi)) \downarrow \rrbracket = \{ \neg B_S \varphi \wedge E_{S,A} \varphi \}$

Whereas the polarity of the belief condition is in favor of non-commitment to the prejacent in the FIs, the additional evidence condition in (50c) approximates the plain FI (50a) to the declarative in (50b), with the crucial difference that if commitment to j ensues from (50c), this necessarily involves belief revision, or at least revision of negative epistemic bias.

4.2.2   No₂ *in conjecture utterances*

No₂'s evidential meaning makes a bigger impact in *daroo*-assertions than in their plain counterparts, mandatorily marking evidence-based inference as in (51), repeated from (6).

(51) *Kanojo-wa kekkon-shi-ta   (no) daroo.*
    she-TOP   get_married-PST *no_2* CONJ
    'I bet she got married.'

When there is contextual evidence for the prejacent, (51) is degraded without *no_2*. As mentioned in Section 1.2, I assume external anchoring is mandatory in such cases because of the importance to convey difference between mere guesswork and evidence-based conjecture.

To account for the effect of *no_2* in conjecture utterances, (52) shows the meaning of (51) on the assumption that *daroo* lowers the strength of the assertion; thus, weaker evidence is adequate. I write $E_x^{>50\%}\varphi$ for a modified evidence condition requiring evidence that is sufficient grounds for committing to j being more probable than $\neg\varphi$, but not for asserting φ.[33]

(52) $\left[\!\left[no(\text{daroo}(\text{DEC}(\varphi))) \downarrow \right]\!\right] = \left\{ \neg B_S \neg\varphi, E_{S,\underline{A}}^{>50\%}\varphi \right\}$

The underlined index A indicates the contribution of *no_2*. While this appears to be a minute difference, on the background of weakened commitment arising from a *daroo-* as opposed to a plain assertion, mutually accessible evidence amounts distinguished a subjective from an objective evaluation under uncertainty. While without *no_2*, all that is required for felicitous utterance is a slight epistemic bias on part of the speaker, the availability of external evidence verifiable to the addressee, as indicated by *no_2*, gives much more weight to the conjecture.

An additional contributing factor is the status of *daroo-*utterances as a likely bridging context, as propose in Section 5. Where *no_1* marks explanation in *daroo-*utterances, connecting prejacent to antecedent like *no_2* connects it to external evidence, it is mandatory. Remnant ambiguity potential influences the acceptability of *daroo-*utterances without *no_2*.

4.2.3 No$_2$ in assertions

When there is no lowering of the commitment threshold by *daroo*, the contribution of *no_2* to assertions is less pronounced. Plain assertion does, however, provide a clear view on external anchoring in its most basic form, in particular, in cases of perspective switching and narrative soliloquy, where grounds for assertion are external to the speaker's epistemic state and addition of *no_2* is strongly preferred.

In (53), repeated from (13), the psychological state of a third person can hardly be judged from evidence private to the speaker, whereas in (54), repeated from (15), the speaker happens to be epistemically bias, for which there are plausibly grounds in form of private evidence, but the utterance is made in reaction to external evidence confirming this bias.

(53) *Kare-wa tanoshii ??(n da).*
    he-TOP be_fun *no_2* COP
    Intended reading: 'He is having fun.'

(54) *Soo, kore-ga*   *(yappari/sasugani) umai ??(n da)*.
     SO   DEM-NOM   as_expected   tasty *no₂* COP
     'Yeah, this sure is tasty.'

In either case, evidence for the respective prejacent is available to the speaker (so that the condition on assertion $E_S \varphi$ is, in principle, satisfied), but marking this evidence as external ($E_{S,A} \varphi$ on my analysis) is preferred, presumably due to a requirement to be optimally informative, even if not on the propositional level of meaning.[34] While it is not clear whether involving an addressee variable here is the ideal solution, considering that at least (54) is felicitous in soliloquy and addressee accessibility in (53) is questionable, I maintain that a modified version of grounds for assertion best accounts for the data.

In contrast to the preceding cases, the exasperated or convincing use of *no₂*-assertions is clearly addressee-oriented, making the proposed analysis a more straightforward fit. Contextual evidence supporting the prejacent is not necessary, as in example (55), repeated from (16).

(55) *Mochiron umai (n da)   yo!*
     of_course tasty *no₂* COP SFP
     'Of course it's tasty!'

In absence of contextual evidence, (55) indicates that the speaker considers the prejacent φ = "it is delicious" to be a shared belief, or common ground, between participants, meaning, it can be assumed that all participants have access to (potentially private) evidence for φ, satisfying $E_{S,A} \varphi$. When mutual, private availability of adequate evidence is indicated, the speaker seeks the addressee to accept the prejacent, often against obvious reluctance.

4.2.4 No₂ in rising utterances

Addition of *no₂* to a rising utterance the polarity of which matches the salient polarity in the context marks the presence or absence of evidence, as in (56), repeated from (8).

(56) *John-wa   hidarikiki   (na   no)?*
     John-TOP left_handed COP.ADN no
     'Is John a lefty?/John is a lefty?'

Adding *no* is preferred when there is evidence for the prejacent, such as John using the left hand to perform some action. This can be accounted for by taking (56) to be an example of a rising interrogative without evidence conditions, with the felicity conditions in (57a).

(57) a. $\llbracket \text{INT}(\varphi) \uparrow \rrbracket = \{ \neg B_S \varphi, \neg B_S B_A \varphi \}$

b. $[\![no(\text{INT}(\varphi)) \uparrow]\!] = \{ \neg B_S \varphi, \neg B_S B_A \varphi, \underline{E_{S,A} \varphi} \}$

Negation can result in more complex bias patterns. This is, however, a context-dependent phenomenon, as (58), repeated from (10), on its reading under scenario (59) illustrates.

(58) *Amakunai (no)?*
   sweet.NEG   *no*$_2$
   {'[Is it] not sweet?/[It's] not sweet?'}

(59) Scenario 2: A eats a piece of orange and makes a grimace.

As discussed in Section 1, not negation as such, but polarity mismatch, complicates bias patterns. This is the case under (59), where the positive alternative is salient, and evidential bias arises from plain (58). Here, adding *no*$_2$ gives rise to epistemic bias (reflecting, for instance, an expectation that oranges are sweet), similar to its effect in FIs.

  Recall that there is no distinction in form between declaratives and interrogatives in Japanese. Thus, in particular, where complex bias patterns are involved, the possibility of looking at rising declaratives needs to be taken into account. (60) shows the meaning of rising declaratives enriched under the assumption that they forgo assertion, in a plain version and with *no*$_2$.

(60) a. $[\![\text{DEC}(\neg\varphi) \uparrow]\!] = \{ \neg B_S \neg \varphi, B_S \neg B_A \varphi, E_S B_A \neg \varphi \}$

   b. $[\![no(\text{DEC}(\neg\varphi)) \uparrow]\!] = \{ \neg B_S \neg \varphi, B_S \neg B_A \varphi, E_S B_A \neg \varphi, \underline{E_{S,A} \neg \varphi} \}$

Taking (58) to be a rising declarative under the scenario in (59), the condition $E_S B_A \neg \varphi$ accounts straightforwardly for evidential bias. The subjective predicate with the perspective center switched to the addressee by final rising intonation makes it rather plausible on the given scenario that the utterance is motivated by addressee-centered evidence. In contrast to the rising interrogative, the declarative indicates a misalignment of bias: the speaker remains skeptical in the light of evidence to assume the addressee believes $\neg\varphi$.

  As for epistemic bias, the condition $\neg B_S \neg \varphi$ is derived from forgoing assertion whether (58) is a rising declarative or interrogative. When the positive alternative φ is salient, this (conventionally) indicates that the choice of proffering $\neg\varphi$ is motivated in contextual evidence, giving rise to evidential bias. It is on this background that addition of *no*$_2$, marking evidence for $\neg\varphi$ strong enough to warrant belief revision, triggers a revision reading together with $\neg B_S \neg \varphi$, thus giving rise to epistemic bias (strengthening of $\neg B_S \neg \varphi$ to $B_S \varphi$).

5 The path to evidentiality: from *no*$_1$ to *no*$_2$

I assume that *no*$_2$ is the result of a pragmaticalization[35] process *no*$_1$ > *no*$_2$. At least three factors have likely contributed to this process: strict right-headedness, therefore sentence-final occurrence of both complementizers and utterance-modifiers, the use of no_2 in COMP-exclamatives, and most importantly, the full productivity of no_1's discourse-connective use.

5.1   *Right-headedness, exclamatives, and external anchoring*

In Section 2.2, I have argued that the syntactic structure of Japanese has presumably contributed to the productivity of no_1 in connective use, in particular elaboration marking, as sentential adverbials signaling elaboration occur sentence-initially, but discourse-structuring COMP-COP invariably remains in a sentence-final position, not competing with more specialized markers. In addition to this, the proximity of no_1 to other utterance modifiers and force markers has presumably facilitated a switching of lexical category to a pragmatic particle.

Right-headedness also connects to COMP-exclamatives, where no_1 occurs sentence-finally and functionally overlaps with no_2-assertions on their narrative soliloquy use, in particular when they are used as exclamations conveying an emotive attitude, as discussed in Section 3.1. As speech acts conveying a speaker attitude toward a (just) observed state of affairs, exclamatives require direct evidence in the utterance situation, similar to the (somewhat-broader) evidence requirement no_2 imposes on its host utterance. As COMP-exclamatives are cross-linguistically attested and productive in Japanese, they are a likely source for the fully productive external anchoring function of no_2 as an evidential particle.

5.2   *Connective* no$_1$ *and inference*

I propose that utterances conveying results of evidence-based inference with connective no_1 are a bridging context for $no_1 > no_2$. This can be linked to no_1 as a scope-adjuster in biclausal *daroo*-utterances conveying abductive inference, in turn linking to no_1 as an explanation marker when the clauses are separately uttered, where ambiguity with no_2 arises when contextual evidence replaces the linguistic antecedent.

First, consider (61), a biclausal utterance narrating evidence-based inference, with which Takubo (2009) illustrates the scope-adjusting function of *no* in *daroo*-utterances.

(61) *Kouteibuai-ga   sagatta   kara   keiki-ga*
      interest_rates-NOM   drop.PST   because economy-NOM
      yokunatta   #(no) daroo.
      improve.PST   *no*   CON9
      'The economy must have improved, because the interest rate dropped.'

Assuming a relation $\varphi \rightarrow \psi$ between φ = "the interest rates dropped" and ψ = "the economy improved," inference on the intended reading of (61) is abductive inference, as in (62).

(62) **Abduction:** $[(\varphi \rightarrow \psi) \wedge \psi] \rightsquigarrow \varphi$

As discussed in 1.2, Takubo argues that *no* serves as a scope-adjuster, allowing *daroo* to target the constituent φ, which availability of the corresponding cleft (63) confirms.

(63) *Keiki-ga*   *yokunatta*   *no-wa*   *kouteibuai-ga*
economy-NOM   improve.PST no_1-TOP   interest_rates-NOM
sagatta   *kara*   *daroo*
drop.PST   because   CONJ
'That the economy improved must be because the interest rate dropped.'

The following additional example from Takubo (2009) shows the same reasoning process across separate utterances. Here, *no* functions as an explanation marker rather than a scope-adjuster, and that between no_1 and no_2 are only distinguished by the presence of a linguistic antecedent.

(64) a.   A: *Keiki-ga*   *yokunatta*   *yo.*
         economy-NOM   improve.PST   SFP
         'The economy improved.'
   b.   S: *Ja, kootei-buai-ga*   *sagatta*   *#(no) daroo.*
         then   interest_rate-NOM   drop.PST   *no*   CONJ
         'Then the interest rates must have dropped.'

In (64), no_1 functions to mark explanation, as defined in (65), but not as a scope-adjuster, as in (61) and (63). Note the parallel background entailments behind explanation and abduction.

(65) **Explanation**: proffering φ conveys: $\exists \psi$ such that $\varphi \rightsquigarrow \psi$

Note that when instead of a linguistic antecedent like (64a), (64b) explains contextual evidence, *no* here must be considered an instance of no_2. In this way, conjecture utterances are a plausible environment for a process from utterance- to discourse-structuring no_1, and cases where no_1 serves as an explanation marker, a likely bridging context for $no_1 > no_2$.

5.3 *Elaboration on contextual evidence*

The external anchoring function of no_2 is by no means limited to abductive inference but links the prejacent to, in many cases, unmistakable external evidence. I propose that the elaboration function of no_1 is crucial in the development of external anchoring. Consider the following example from Mieda (2003) of two separate utterances where hearsay evidence as stated in the first utterance is the grounds for inference.

(66) *Kare-wa kono shigoto kotowat-ta   soo   da.*
    he-TOP   this job   decline-PST EVID   COP
    Kono shigoto-wa kare-ni-wa   muzukashii no daroo.
    this   job-TOP   he-DAT-CTOP   difficult   *no* CONJ
    'I hear he's declined this job. I bet it's [too] hard for him.'

The hearsay marker *soo*[36] indicates that only indirect evidence is available to the speaker, the second assertion being an inference based on this evidence. While this appears to be a clear case of abductive reasoning, the example can felicitously be reversed:

(67) *Kono shigoto-wa kare-ni-wa muzukashii soo da. Kotowa-ru no daroo.*
    'I hear this job is too hard for him. I bet he'll decline it.'

With this reversal, the relation between ψ = "this job is too hard for him" and φ = "he'll decline it" is as shown in (68) and (69), that is, connective no_1 in (67) serves as an elaboration, rather than an explanation marker, and inference is deductive, rather than abductive, in nature.

(68) **Elaboration**: proffering φ conveys: $\exists \psi$ such that $\psi \rightsquigarrow \varphi$

(69) **Deduction**: $[(\psi \rightarrow \varphi) \wedge \psi] \rightarrow \varphi$

Without a linguistic antecedent, the second utterance in (67) has to be considered an instance of no_2, with a stronger connection between evidence and conclusion than in the case of abduction, where the result of inference is but one of the possible reasons for, rather than an expected consequence of, the premise. I propose that it is in contexts like this that no_1 as an elaboration marker is most likely to detach from its original structuring functions and developed into a fully flexible external anchor.

5.4 Pragmaticalization from COMP to PRT

Summing up, I propose that no_2 has likely developed from no_1 in a process where the structuring function of the latter has given way to the evidential meaning of the former, aided by the independent use of no_1 in exclamatives, which have an evidence requirement as speech acts.

Table 2.7 summarizes the stages I suggest for the development of no_2 in utterances of evidence-based (abductive) inference. In the first stage, no_1 adjusts the scope of the conjecture marker *daroo* in a biclausal structure, which is equivalent to explanation-marking in the bridging context, where the two propositions involved occur in separate utterances. Finally, when contextual evidence replaces the linguistic antecedent, no_2 serves as an external anchor.

Table 2.7 Development of evidential *no* in evidence-based inference contexts

	Function/meaning	Structure
COMP	scope-adjusting	biclausal
bridging	discourse-structuring	separate utterances
PRT	evidential	stand-alone utterance

This external anchoring function of no_2 outside of uses close to the aforementioned bridging context not only has likely required a productive elaboration function of the complementizer to license cases where the connection between antecedent/evidence and conclusion is more immediate but was also aided by analogy with COMP-exclamations.

As shown in Table 2.8, I assume that the external anchoring function of no_2 in assertions is likely connected to the sentence-final use of *no-da* in exclamatives, which by illocutionary force come with an evidence condition closely related to external anchoring but are more limited in their use.

Table 2.8 Development of external anchoring from *no* in exclamatives

	Speech act	Evidence condition
COMP	exclamative	speech act
PRT	assertion	external anchoring

If these contributing factors to the development of no_2 are on the right track, the emergence of evidential meaning from complementizers is likely in languages with similar environments. Horie (2008), providing Korean examples of a connective complementizer[37] with evidential overtones, notes that Korean COMP-COP constructions have uses similar to sentence-final *no-da* in Japanese, but that evidential meaning is more conventionalized and more frequently attested in Japanese than in Korean. A more detailed comparison with Korean appears to be a promising lead for observing an earlier stage in the pragmaticalization process I have suggested for no_2.

6 Conclusion and outlook

In this chapter, I have distinguished the complementizer no_1 from the evidential particle no_2 and subsumed the various uses of no_2 discussed in 1 as "external anchoring." There is no consensus on such a distinction – in addition to the contentious COMP-exclamatives, which I argue in Section 3.1 should not be considered instances of no_2, the classification of *no* in connective uses varies. Noda (1997), for instance, labels scope-adjusting uses "*no-da* of scope" but includes what I classify as connective no_1 under her label "*no-da* of mood," grouping it with no_2. In Sections 1 through 3, I have defended the view that a sharp distinction is possible, and that gray areas stem from functional overlap (as in exclamatives) or represent bridging contexts. However, my discussion of *no*'s uses has, by no means, been exhaustive and made use of varied terminology for readings of *no*-utterances and bias patterns for compatibility with extant descriptions. This calls for an expansion of the empirical scope within Japanese and more unified description in parallel to the formal analysis.

6.1   *Pragmaticalization of COMP-evidentiality*

As for the pragmaticalization process $no_1 > no_2$, I have identified *daroo*-utterances that narrate evidence-based inference as bridging contexts in Section 5 and argued that the process of externalizing evidence has likely been aided by functional overlap with COMP-exclamatives. While the coincidence of all these factors and the resulting development of no_2 as an evidential particle could be unique to Japanese, more detailed examination of complementizers with evidential properties in other languages could bring parallel processes to light. Broadening the empirical scope to further languages to test the claims against a wider range of data is another area for further research.

6.2   *Formalizing external anchoring*

The formal analysis of no_2 as an utterance modifier in Section 4 attempts to capture external anchoring by taking no_2 to mark the mutually accessible version of what is, in a Gricean sense, "adequate" evidence for assertion, application of which to the quite-productive soliloquous uses of no_2 is not entirely straightforward due to addressee reference. I maintain, however, that a modified version of assertability is preferable to notions of evidentiality that do not directly reflect the status of no_2 as a contributor to non-propositional meaning parallel to utterance modifiers like *daroo*, and *yo*, as well as illocutionary force, with which it conspires to convey the prejacent's status within the participants' epistemic states. Developing an analysis of no_2 within this class of expressions reflecting its relation to assertability without addressee reference remains a third major challenge for future work. This connects to the general issue that approaches within both descriptive and formal work on *no* in particular, pragmatic particles and bias-related phenomena in general, remain highly fragmented. On this background, unified concept of evidentiality on the speech-act level compatible with external anchoring in both soliloquous and addressee-oriented case as well as phenomena like evidential bias has the potential of significantly advancing the understanding of pragmatic meaning.

Abbreviations

ACC	accusative	INT	interrogative
ADN	adnominal	LOC	locative
COMP	complementizer	NEG	negation, negative

COND	conditional	NOM	nominative
CONJ	conjecture	NPST	nonpast
COP	copula	PRT	particle
CTOP	contrastive topic	PN	personal name
DAT	dative	POT	potential
DEC	declarative	PST	past
DEM	demonstrative	RES	resultative
DET	determiner	SBJV	subjunctive
EVID	evidential	SFP	sentence-final particle
EXCL	exclamative	TOP	topic
EXPL	expletive	VOL	volitional

Notes

1 The indices 1 and 2 reflect the assumed diachronic order from complementizer to particle.
2 I take final falling intonation to encode a feature of speaker-, as opposed to addressee-, orientation in non-polite Japanese speech, as reflected in the formalization in Section 4, building on Gunlogson's (2003) similar views.
3 Davis labels FIs "rhetorical questions," a label I prefer to avoid, reserving the term "question" for information-seeking (final rising, addressee-oriented) interrogatives.
4 More precisely, Davis (2011) notes that *ka-yo* FIs are more "assertive" than plain ones in that they intuitively convey that the speaker accepts the prejacent as true.
5 Taniguchi (2016) calls the effect of no_2 "positive bias," which should not be confused with the initial negative epistemic bias that is present with or without no_2, the difference being the likelihood of belief revision.
6 I gloss over cases where FIs are used to convey acceptance of the prejacent without belief revision, which are a productive use of FIs, but one where no_2 is generally dispreferred.
7 *Daroo* can be morphology-analyzed as a copula *d(e)a(r)-* and the no-longer-productive conjecture ending *-oo* but occurs in a more peripheral position than the copula, typical for non-propositional utterance modifiers.
8 I omit interaction of *daroo* with interrogative force or final rising intonation due to space, focusing on assertions.
9 *N.b.* that *da* (COP) is dropped in the plain version of (8), as in all non-polite utterances but falling declaratives, but obligatorily intervenes between the noun *hidarikiki* and morphologically nominal no_2 as *na* (COP.ADN).
10 Ito and Oshima (2014) focus on inner and outer negation and their prosodic distinction, discussing no_2 in passing.
11 See Romero and Han (2004) for similar observations on context and bias in English negative polar questions.
12 Büring and Gunlogson's (2000) observations, which Sudo (2013) extends to Japanese, expand on Ladd's (1981) observations on the bias patterns of negative polar questions in English.
13 Predicates ending on *-i*, which, like adjectives, modify nouns but, like verbs, inflect for tense.
14 Or shortly before this, the assertion crucially being a direct reaction to the observation.
15 *Sasuga* has a positive nuance, that is, is generally used with positively evaluated predicates, which *yappari* lacks.
16 There are many variations of the notion of being an established fact, such as shared or world knowledge, mutual acceptance, or uncontroversiality, which I cannot

discuss here due to space. The basic idea behind the notion is that the speaker asserts a proposition *as if* it were based on externally available evidence, even if that is not necessarily the case.

17 The particle *yo* most frequently occurs in assertions, where it typically indicates that the speaker seeks the addressee to revise epistemic bias, but see Hasegawa (2010) for uses in self-talk, Section 1.1 for *yo* in FIs.

18 I use this label regardless of which surface order complementizer and copula appear in the respective languages.

19 Another strategy is stressed -*wa*, parallel to contrastive focus, indicated by boldface in the English translation.

20 See also an earlier version in Hiraiwa and Ishihara (2002) for a more detailed discussion of the proposed transformative link between *in situ* focus constructions and clefts.

21 I have added an additional instance of COMP-COP to (20), a case they discuss in a footnote without differentiation between complementizer and particle.

22 On their split-CP analysis following Rizzi (1997), no_1 in (19) and (20) heads a finiteness phrase (FINP), whereas the copula *da*, which they label a focus particle, heads a focus phrase (FOCP), another CP layer.

23 While I cannot provide a more precise implementation of due to space, what matters for the distinction between explanation and elaboration is directionality rather than the precise nature of the entailment relation.

24 I use the proffer to cover all utterance types, including soliloquous utterances, that is, all cases in which φ is pronounced by the speaker, regardless of force and sentence-final intonation, etc.

25 Noda (1997) also discusses data from translations, noting similar uses in French and Spanish.

26 While Noda's classification differs from mine (*cf.* Section 6), I use no_2 for "non-connective *no-da* of mood."

27 See Repp (2013) and d'Avis (2016) for more discussion on types of exclamatives in German.

28 See also Hiraiwa and Ishihara (2002) and Noda (1997) for similar observations.

29 For an earlier version of the present analysis with more detailed discussion on and motivation for utterance felicity conditions and implementation of context change, as well as the role of *daroo*, *cf.* Rieser (2017)

30 See Jary (2010) for an overview of different approaches to assertability, some of which might be better suited to capture the contribution of no_2. Discussing fundamentals of this issue is well beyond the scope of this chapter.

31 More broadly, speaker- and addressee-orientation are the categories to be differentiated, which in non-polite Japanese speech corresponds to sentence-final intonation.

32 In declaratives, *yo* is often characterized as a prompt to the addressee to accept the prejacent in spite of previous negative bias. In the case of the potentially soliloquous (49), this arguably amounts to a marking of (potential) revision of a previous belief $\neg\varphi$.

33 I follow Hara (2006) in the required degree of certainty for *daroo*-assertion being (greater than) 50%.

34 In the spirit of "maximize presupposition," *cf.*, for instance, Singh (2011) for detailed discussion.

35 Broadly defined as the emergence of pragmatical (non-propositional) lexical meaning, often via discourse-structuring functions, *cf.* Diewald (2011); Davis and Gutzmann (2015)

36 Not to be confused with -*soo* appearing in (14), Section 1.4.

37 He labels this a nominalizer in line with his views on Japanese *no*.

References

Büring, Daniel & Christine Gunlogson. 2000. *Aren't positive and negative polar questions the same?* Ms. UCSC/UCLA.

Davis, Christopher. 2011. *Constraining Interpretation: Sentence Final Particles in Japanese*: University of Massachusets – Amherst dissertation.

Davis, Christopher & Daniel Gutzmann. 2015. Use-conditional meaning and the semantics of pragmaticalization. In *Proceedings of Sinn und Bedeutung*, vol. 19, 197–213. Konstanz.

d'Avis, Franz. 2016. Different languages – different sentence types? On exclamative sentences. *Language and Linguistics Compass* 10(4). 159–175.

Diewald, Gabriele. 2011. Pragmaticalization (defined) as grammaticalization of discourse functions. *Linguistics* 49(2). 365–390.

Grice, Herbert P. 1975. *Logic and conversation*, 41–58. New York: Academic Press.

Gunlogson, Christine. 2003. *True to Form: Rising and Falling Declaratives as Questions in English*: UCSC dissertation.

Hara, Yurie. 2006. *Grammar of Knowledge Representation: Japanese Discourse Items at Interfaces*: University of Delaware dissertation.

Hara, Yurie & Christopher Davis. 2013. *Darou* as a deictic context shifter. *Proceedings of Formal Approaches to Japanese Linguistics (FAJL)* 6. 41–56.

Hasegawa, Yoko. 2010. The sentence-final particles *ne* and *yo* in soliloquial Japanese. *Pragmatics* 20(1). 71–89.

Hiraiwa, Ken & Shinichiro Ishihara. 2002. Missing links: Cleft, sluicing, and "no da" construction in Japanese. *MIT Working Papers in Linguistics* 43. 35–54.

Hiraiwa, Ken & Shinichiro Ishihara. 2012. Syntactic metamorphosis: Clefts, sluicing, and in-situ focus in Japanese. *Syntax* 15(2). 142–180.

Horie, Kaoru. 2008. The grammaticalization of nominalizers in Japanese and Korean: A contrastive study. In López-Castro María José & Elena Seoane (eds.), *Rethinking grammaticalization: New perspectives*, 169–188. Amsterdam and Philadelphia: John Benjamins.

Ito, Satoshi & David Y. Oshima. 2014. On two varieties of negative polar interrogatives in Japanese. In *Proceedings of Japanese/Korean Linguistics (J/K)*, 23. Stanford: CSLI.

Izvorski, Roumyana. 1997. The present perfect as an epistemic modal. *Proceedings of Semantics and Linguistic Theory (SALT)* 7. 222–239.

Jary, Mark. 2010. *Assertion*. London: Palgrave Macmillan.

Kuno, Susumu. 1986. *Shin nihongobunpoo kenkyuu* [New research on Japanese grammar]. Tokyo: Taishukan Publishing.

Ladd, D. Robert. 1981. A first look at the semantics and pragmatics of negative questions and tag questions. *Proceedings of Chicago Linguistic Society (CLS)* 17. 164–171.

McCready, E. 2014. What is evidence in natural language? In E. McCready, Katsuhiko Yabushita & Kei Yoshimoto (eds.), *Formal approaches to semantics and pragmatics*, 155–180. Berlin: Springer.

McCready, E. & Norry Ogata. 2007. Evidentiality, modality and probability. *Linguistics and Philosophy* 30(2). 147–206.

Mieda, Reiko. 2003. 'daroo' no imi to hataraki: jodooshi kara shuujoshi made [The meaning and functioning of 'daroo': From auxiliary to sentence-final particle]. *Hitotsubashi University Center for Student Exchange journal* 6. 63–76.

Morimoto, Junko. 1994. *Hanashite no shukan o arawasu fukushi ni tsuite* [On adverbs that represent the speaker's subjectivity]. Tokyo: Kuroshio Publishers.

Najima, Yoshinao. 2007. *Noda no imi, kinoo: Kanrenseiriron no kanten kara* [The meaining, functions of *noda*: From the perspective of relevance theory]. Tokyo: Kuroshio Shuppan.

Noda, Harumi. 1997. *"no(da)" no kinoo* [The functions of *no(da)*]. Tokyo: Kuroshio Publishers.

Ono, Hajime. 2006. *An Investigation of Exclamatives in English and Japanese: Syntax and Sentence Processing*. University of Maryland dissertation.

Repp, Sophie. 2013. D-linking vs. degrees: Inflected and uninflected 'welch' in exclamatives and rhetorical questions. In Holden Härtl (ed.), *Interfaces of morphology: A Festschrift for susan olsen.*, 59–89. Berlin: De Gruyter.

Rett, Jessica. 2011. Exclamatives, degrees and speech acts. *Linguistics and Philosophy* 34(5). 411–442.

Rieser, Lukas. 2017. *Belief states and evidence in speech acts: The Japanese sentence final particle no*: Kyoto University dissertation.

Rizzi, Luigi. 1997. The fine structure of the Left Periphery. *Elements of Grammar: Handbooks in Generative Syntax* 1. 281–337.

Romero, Manuel & Chung-Hye Han. 2004. On negative *Yes/No*-questions. *Linguistics and Philosophy* 27. 609–658.

Searle, John R. 1969. *Speech acts*. Cambridge: Cambridge University Press.

Singh, Raj. 2011. Maximize presupposition! and local contexts. *Natural Language Semantics* 19(2). 149–168.

Sudo, Yasutada. 2013. Biased polar questions in English and Japanese. In Daniel Gutzmann & Hans-Martin Gärtner (eds.), *Beyond expressives: Explorations in use-conditional meaning*, 275–296. Leiden: Brill.

Takubo, Yukinori. 2009. Conditional modality: Two types of modal auxiliaries in Japanese. In Barbara Pizziconi & Mika Kizu (eds.), *Japanese modality: Exploring its scope and interpretation*, 150–182. London: Palgrave Macmillan.

Taniguchi, Ai. 2016. Setence-final *ka-yo* in Japanese: A compositional account. In *Proceedings of FAJL 8: Formal approaches to Japanese linguistics*, 165–176. (MITWPL 79). Cambridge: MIT Press.

3 Mandarin Chinese sentence-final *de* as a marker of private evidence

Hooi Ling Soh

1 Introduction[1]

Previous studies on Mandarin sentence-final *de* have mainly focused on constructions where *de* appears with the copula/focus marker *shi*, which are often referred to as the *shi* . . . *de* constructions (Simpson & Wu 2002; Paul & Whitman 2008; Cheng 2008; Hole 2011). The *shi* . . . *de* constructions are cleft-like in that they put a particular constituent in focus.

(1)   Ta   shi   lai   zhao   wo   de.   *Shi* . . . *de* sentence
      3SG   FOC   come   look.for   1SG   DE
      'It is (the case) that she came to look for me.'

The appearance of *de* in bare *de* sentences has not received exclusive focus partly because its contribution in such sentences is elusive (e.g., Cheng (2008) analyzes *de* in a bare *de* sentence as an assertion operator that relates to sentential emphasis/focus).

(2)   Ta   lai   zhao   wo   de.   Bare *de* sentence
      3SG   come   look.for   1SG   DE
      'She came to look for me.'

A significant challenge for determining the contribution of *de* concerns how bare *de* sentences are related to *shi* . . . *de* sentences. Adding to the challenge is the intuition that there is a variant of *shi* . . . *de* sentences with a silent (or omitted) *shi*, as in (3) (Li & Thompson 1981; Hole 2011).

(3)   Ta   ~~shi~~   lai   zhao   wo   de.   ~~Shi~~ . . . *de* sentence
      3SG   FOC   come   look.for   1SG   DE   (with a silent *shi*)
      'It is (the case) that she came to look for me.'

Some previous authors assume without argument that bare *de* sentences are *shi* . . . *de* sentences with a silent *shi* (e.g., Hole (2011)). On the other hand, Cheng (2008) argues that bare *de* sentences are distinct from *shi* . . . *de* sentences.

DOI: 10.4324/9781351057837-4

In this chapter, I present a novel observation about a restriction in the use of *de* in bare *de* sentences. Specifically, *de* is infelicitous in utterance contexts where the evidence for the asserted proposition is shared between the speaker and the addressee or is readily available in the utterance context. I propose that *de* marks the speaker's belief that the status of the evidence for the asserted proposition is *private* at utterance time, with *private* defined using the notion of accessibility:

(4) *Private evidence*: evidence for a proposition that is *accessible* to the speaker and not the addressee.
(5) *Accessibility*: an individual has access to his/her own knowledge base and readily available evidence in the utterance context.

I show how the proposed analysis accounts for the discourse restrictions as well as interpretive effects associated with *de* in a bare *de* sentence. I then consider a prediction of the analysis regarding the distribution of *de* in yes/no questions. I show that the pattern of restrictions observed with *de* in yes/no questions follows from the proposed analysis, coupled with a specific proposal about the syntax of *de*, and certain standard assumptions about the syntax of yes/no questions and modal auxiliaries. Specifically, I claim that *de* heads a projection below TP and above a modal projection for non-epistemic modals. I then discuss apparent counterexamples to the discourse restrictions and suggest that they are not bare *de* sentences but rather *shi . . . de* sentences with a silent *shi*. Finally, I discuss implications of the analysis on the syntax of modal auxiliaries, the relation between bare *de* sentences and *shi . . . de* sentences, and the syntax of discourse particles. The current proposal connects Mandarin sentence-final *de* with German discourse particle *ja* (Kratzer 1999, 2004; Gutzmann 2009) and English parenthetical *I'm telling you* (Reese & Soh 2018). The semantics of these particles/expressions make reference to the speaker's belief about whether the (evidence for the) asserted proposition is shared knowledge between the speaker and the hearer and whether the (evidence for the) proposition is "verifiable on the spot."

2   Discourse restrictions and interpretive effects of sentence-final *de*

The felicity of the use of *de* depends on two factors: (i) whether or not the evidence for the asserted proposition is shared between the speaker and the addressee and (ii) whether the evidence is readily available in the utterance context.

2.1   *Assertion based on evidence known to the speaker and the addressee*

Assertions based on evidence known to both the speaker and the addressee are infelicitous with *de*. Assertions based on sensory experiences in the utterance context that are necessarily shared by the speaker and the addressee provide clear examples of this restriction in the use of *de*. Consider the context in (6).

(6) <u>Context</u>: The speaker and the addressee are visiting a tropical island for the first time, and when they arrive, the weather is hot.
  a. *Zhe-li hen   re.*
     here   very hot
     'It's hot here.'
  b. *#Zhe-li hen   re   de.*
     here   very hot DE
     'I'm telling you, it's hot here.'

The speaker may utter (6a) felicitously to comment on the condition of the weather, but not (6b).

2.2 *Assertions based on evidence known to the speaker but not the addressee*

Assertions based on evidence known to the speaker but not the addressee are, <u>in general,</u> felicitous with *de*. Consider the context in (7).

(7) <u>Context</u>: The speaker knows that the girl standing across the room has a boyfriend, and believes that the addressee does not know that.
  a. *Ta   you nan-peng-you.*
     3SG have boyfriend
     'She has a boyfriend.'
  b. *Ta   you nan-peng-you de.*
     3SG have boyfriend   DE
     'I'm telling you, she has a boyfriend.'

The speaker may utter either (7a) or (7b) felicitously to let the addressee know that the girl has a boyfriend. However, (7a) and (7b) have different discourse effects: (7a) serves as a neutral statement of fact, while (7b) is considered an advice or warning.

2.3 *Assertions based on evidence readily available in the utterance context*

Some assertions based on evidence known to the speaker but not the addressee are nevertheless infelicitous with *de*. These assertions involve evidence that is <u>readily available</u> in the utterance context. They are readily available in the sense that minimal effort is required for the addressee to access the information. Because evidence readily available in the utterance context is sensory in nature or has a sensory component, assertions based on sensory experience provide clear examples to illustrate this restriction. Consider the context in (8).

(8)   Context: The speaker and the addressee are at a party, facing each other. The speaker can see Ling-ling's boyfriend, who is somewhere behind the addressee.

    a. *Ling-ling de   nan-peng-you zai zhe.*
       Ling-ling POSS boyfriend   at here
       'Ling-ling's boyfriend is here.'

    b. *#Ling-ling de   nan-peng-you zai zhe de.*
       Ling-ling POSS boyfriend   at here DE
       'I'm telling you, Ling-ling's boyfriend is here.'

The speaker may utter (8a) felicitously to express the idea that Ling-ling's boyfriend is here, but not (8b). The evidence is considered "readily available" in that the effort required to access the information is minimal: the addressee only needs to turn his/her head to access the relevant evidence.

2.4   Summary

A bare *de* sentence is infelicitous in utterance contexts where the evidence for the asserted proposition is shared between the speaker and the addressee or is readily available in the utterance context. The use of *de* in a bare *de* sentence is sometimes associated with the speaker's intention to "offer advice or warning" or to "encourage the addressee to partake in a certain activity on the basis of the speaker's personal experience."

3   Accounting for discourse restrictions and interpretive effects of sentence-final *de*

To account for the discourse restrictions and interpretive effects of sentence-final *de*, I present an analysis of *de* as a discourse marker, marking private evidence, as elaborated in (9).

(9)   Sentence-final *de* (in a bare *de* sentence) marks the speaker's belief that the status of the evidence for the asserted proposition is <u>*private*</u> at utterance time.

(4)   *Private evidence*: evidence for a proposition that is <u>accessible</u> to the speaker and not the addressee.

(5)   *Accessibility*: an individual has access to his/her own knowledge base and readily available evidence in the utterance context.

The interpretive effects of *de* relating to the speaker's intention to "offer advice or warning" or to "encourage the addressee to partake in a certain activity on the basis of the speaker's personal experience" follow naturally from the proposed analysis. Although it is generally the case that the speaker offers information that s/he believes the addressee does not know when making an assertion, this is not always the case. A speaker may felicitously assert a proposition that s/he has a reasonable belief that the addressee knows as well. For example, the utterance in (10) is felicitous in the specified context, even though the speaker can reasonably assume that both s/he and the addressee experience the weather as being hot.

(10) <u>Context</u>: The speaker and the addressee are visiting a tropical island. The
weather is hot.
Zhe-li hen   re.
here   very hot
'It's hot here.'

This is because what a speaker asserts is taken as proposals to change the common ground, with the goal of having all discourse participants accept the relevant proposition for the purpose of the conversation (Stalnaker 1999:86). There is no requirement for the proposition to be unknown to the addressee.[2] On the other hand, advice/warning and encouragements to partake in a certain activity on the basis of a personal experience are usually offered in contexts in which the speaker believes that s/he knows something that the addressee does not. Because the use of *de* explicitly marks the evidence for the asserted proposition as being not accessible to the addressee, it is natural to associate the discourse function of such utterances to offering advice/warning or encouragements.

4 Sentence-final *de* in yes/no questions

The proposed analysis predicts that *de* has restricted distribution in questions. Specifically, *de* may not have a question operator within its scope. This is because *de* marks the nature of the speaker's evidence for the truth of a certain proposition within its scope. Questions are neither true nor false, and it is unclear what evidence for a question means.

I consider this prediction in yes/no questions. Mandarin Chinese has two main types of yes/no questions: (i) A-not-A questions and (ii) *ma*-questions. A-not-A questions are formed by the reduplication of a verbal element (e.g., verb, preposition, auxiliary) and the insertion of a negative morpheme *bu* (or *mei*) between the reduplicated form. An example is given in the following:

(11) *Ta   lai-bu-lai   zhao   ni?*
3SG come-not-come look.for 2SG
'Is he coming to look for you?'

Ma-questions are formed with the sentence-final question particle *ma*, as in (12).

(12) *Ta   lai   zhao   ni   ma?*
3SG come look.for 2SG Q
'Did he come to look for you?'

I show in the following subsections that sentence-final *de* is compatible with some yes/no questions but not others. In particular, A-not-A questions involving reduplicated verbs, prepositions, and non-epistemic modal auxiliaries are incompatible with *de*, while *ma*-questions and A-not-A questions involving reduplicated dummy auxiliary *shi* 'be' and epistemic modal auxiliaries are compatible with *de*.

4.1   *The pattern of restrictions*

De is not compatible with A-not-A questions involving a reduplicated verb or preposition, as shown in the following:

(13) a. *Ta   lai-bu-lai   zhao   ni?*
        3SG   come-not-come look.for 2SG
        'Is he coming to look for you?'
    b. **Ta   lai-bu-lai   zhao   ni   de?*
        3SG   come-not-come look.for 2SG DE

(14) a. *Ta   zai-bu-zai jia?*
        3SG   at-not-at   home
        'Is she at home?'
    b. **Ta   zai-bu-zai jia   de?*
        3SG   at-not-at   home DE

It is also incompatible with A-not-A questions formed with a reduplicated non-epistemic modal such as *hui* 'will, can (ability),' *keyi* 'can (permission, ability),' and *neng* 'can (ability).'

(15) a. *Ta   hui-bu-hui shuo fayu?*
        3SG   can-not-can speak French
        'Can he speak French?'
    b. **Ta   hui-bu-hui shuo fayu   de?*
        3SG   can-not-can speak French DE

(16) a. *Ta   hui-bu-hui   bang ta?*
        3SG   will-not-will help 3SG
        'Will he help him?'
    b. **Ta   hui-bu-hui bang ta   de?*
        3SG   will-not-will help 3SG DE

(17) a. *Ta   ke-bu-keyi   wan hui   jia?*
        3SG   can-not-can late return home
        'Can he come home late?'
    b. **Ta   ke-bu-keyi wan hui   jia   de?*
        3SG   can-not-can late return home DE

(18) a. *Ta　neng-bu-neng anjing-de　zuo yi-zheng-ge　xiawu?*
　　　 3SG　can-not-can　quietly-MOD sit　one-whole-CL　afternoon
　　　 'Can he sit quietly for the whole afternoon?'
　　b. **Ta　neng-bu-neng anjing-de　zuo yi-zheng-ge　xiawu　de?*
　　　 3SG　can-not-can　quietly-MOD sit　one-whole-CL afternoon DE

On the other hand, *de* can appear in *ma*-questions (Cheng 2008).[3] An example is given in the following:

(19) a. *Ta　lai　zhao　ni ma?*
　　　 3SG　come look.for 2SG Q
　　　 'Did she come to look for you?'
　　b. *Ta　lai　zhao　ni de ma?*
　　　 3SG　come look.for 2SG DE Q
　　　 'Did she come to look for you?'

It may also appear with A-not-A question involving reduplicated *shi* 'be' and reduplicated epistemic modal auxiliary *hui* 'could (possibility).'

(20) a. *Ta　shi-bu-shi　lai　zhao　ni?*
　　　 3SG　be-not-be　come　look.for　2SG
　　　 'Did she come to look for you?'
　　b. *Ta　shi-bu-shi lai　zhao　ni de?*
　　　 3SG　be-not-be come look.for 2SG DE
　　　 'Did she come to look for you?'

(21) a. *Ta　hui-bu-hui　wan-quan bu　zhidao?*
　　　 3SG　could-not-could completely not know
　　　 'Could he be completely unaware (of it)?'
　　b. *Ta　hui-bu-hui　wan-quan bu zhidao de?*
　　　 3SG　could-not-could completely not know DE
　　　 'Could he be completely unaware (of it)?'

In addition to the pre-verbal position, both the A-not-A form of *shi* and epistemic modal *hui* can appear in a sentence-initial position. Note that *de* is compatible with A-not-A questions with sentence-initial *shi* and epistemic modal *hui* as well.

(22) a. *Shi-bu-shi ta　lai　zhao　ni?*
　　　 be-not-be 3SG come look.for 2SG
　　　 'Did she come to look for you?'
　　b. *Shi-bu-shi ta lai　zhao　ni de?*
　　　 be-not-be 3SG come look.for 2SG DE
　　　 'Did she come to look for you?'

(23) a. *Hui-bu-hui　ta wan-quan bu zhidao?*
　　　 could-not-could 3SG completely not know
　　　 'Could he be completely unaware (of it)?'

b. *Hui-bu-hui   ta   wan-quan bu zhidao de?*
could-not-could 3SG completely not know DE
'Could he be completely unaware (of it)?'

4.2   *The syntax of de: an account of the restrictions*

In this section, I show that the pattern of restrictions observed with *de* in yes/no questions follows from the proposed analysis, coupled with a specific proposal about the syntax of *de*, and certain standard assumptions about the syntax of yes/no questions and modal auxiliaries. I follow Cheng (2008) in pursuing an explanation in terms of the relative scope of the question operator in relation to *de*. I assume that epistemic modals appear structurally higher than non-epistemic modals (Cinque 1999; Tsai 2015). In particular, I assume that Mandarin epistemic modals may head a projection above TP, namely, Mod^{E}P (Tsai 2015). In addition, I assume that they may also appear in T. Specifically, while sentence-initial epistemic modals appear in Mod^E, pre-verbal epistemic modals appear in T. On the other hand, I assume that non-epistemic modals appear in a projection lower than TP and above vP, namely, Mod^{NE} (cf. Tsai 2015).

(24)

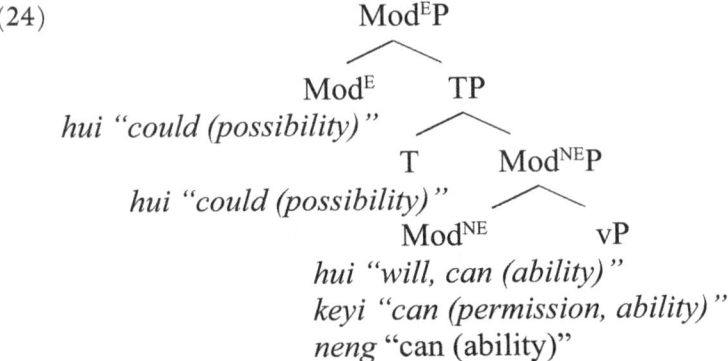

I assume that the auxiliary *shi* occupies a structurally higher position than other auxiliaries, such as *neng* 'can' and *hui* 'will' (Soh 2007), and that pre-verbal *shi* appears in T and sentence-initial *shi* appears in Mod^E, both occupying positions higher than Mod^{NE}.

(25)

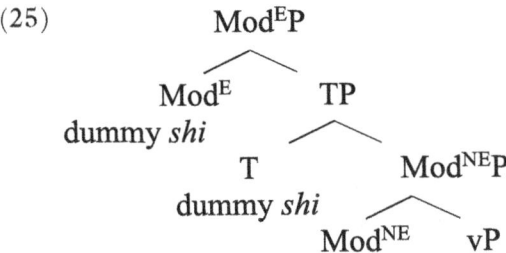

As for *ma*-questions, I assume that the question marker *ma* is in C (Cheng 1991; Paul 2014), and it has scope over Mod^{E}P.

(26)

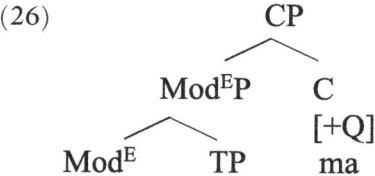

CP
ModᴱP   C
Modᴱ TP [+Q]
           ma

For A-not-A questions, I assume that an A-not-A question contains a [+Q] feature that raises to the CP domain (at LF) (Huang 1982, 1988; Ernst 1994). As shown in (27), the [+Q] feature is generated in the same position where the A-not-A form is found (Ernst 1994; Soh & Gao 2006, cf. Law 2006; Lin 1992), and I assume that the scope of the yes/no question is the node immediately dominating the A-not-A form (Ernst 1994; Soh & Gao 2006), while the raising of the [+Q] feature to the CP domain marks the force of the sentence as a question.

(27)

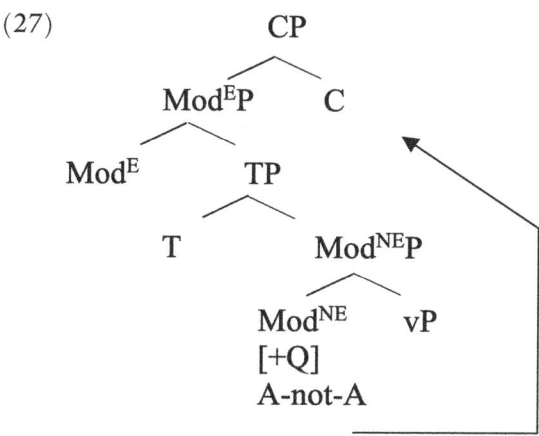

CP
ModᴱP   C
Modᴱ   TP
    T   ModᴺᴱP
       Modᴺᴱ   vP
       [+Q]
       A-not-A

I propose that *de* heads a projection between TP and Mod^{NE}P (cf. Cheng 2008).[4,5]

(28)

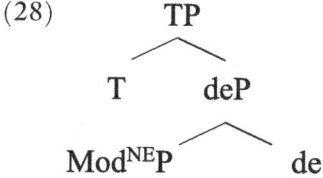

TP
T   deP
ModᴺᴱP   de

The account is straightforward. Sentence-final *de* cannot appear in A-not-A questions involving reduplicated verbs, prepositions, and non-epistemic modal auxiliaries (e.g., *hui* 'will, can (ability),' *keyi* 'can (permission, ability),' *neng* 'can (ability)') because it would scope over the [+Q] feature associated with the A-not-A form of these questions. For example, (29) shows the structure of an A-not-A question with a reduplicated non-epistemic modal. The structure is ruled out because *de* scopes over the [+Q] feature in Mod^{NE}.

(29) *

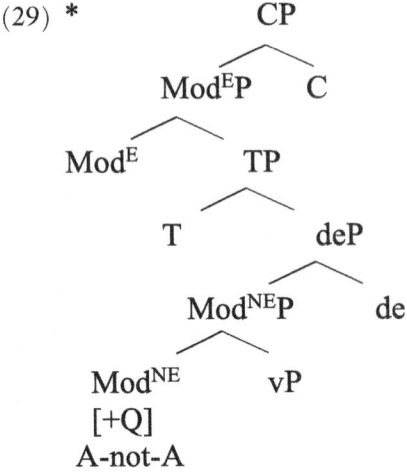

On the other hand, *de* can appear in *ma*-questions and A-not-A questions involving reduplicated dummy auxiliary *shi* 'be' and epistemic modal auxiliary *hui* 'could (possibility)' since the [+Q] feature associated with these questions are above *de*. For example, consider the structure of an A-not-A question formed with an epistemic modal in T, given in (30). The structure is acceptable as the [+Q] feature is outside the scope of *de*.

(30)

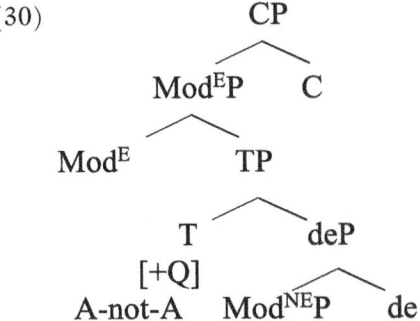

My account for the incompatibility of *de* with certain A-not-A questions is similar to Ernst's (1994) account of the incompatibility of certain adjuncts (e.g., *yiding* 'definitely') with certain A-not-A questions in Mandarin Chinese. Like *de*, the adverb *yiding* cannot appear in A-not-A questions, where the A-not-A forms are within the surface scope of the adverb. The adverb can appear in *ma* questions and A-not-A questions, where the A-not-A forms take surface scope over the adverb.

(31) a. **Ta yiding   qu-bu-qu?*
　　　 3SG definitenly go-not-go
　　　 'Is he definitely going?'

　　 b. *Ta yiding   qu ma?*
　　　 3SG definitenly go Q
　　　 'Is he definitely going?'

　　 c. *Ta shi-bu-shi yiding   qu?*
　　　 3SG be-not-be definitenly go
　　　 'Is he definitely going?'

Ernst (1994) proposes that the relevant adverbs are not able to have a question operator within its scope.[6] The incompatibility of *de* with certain yes/ no questions is in line with Ernst's (2009) observation that some speaker-oriented adverbs are not compatible with questions.

4.3   *The interpretation of questions with* de

Evidential markers in questions differ in terms of whether a "perspective shift" is required, whereby the evidential is interpreted as regarding the answerer's information source rather than the questioner's (Aikenvald 2003; Maslova 2003; Lim 2010; Murray 2010; Soh 2019). Given the proposal that *de* marks the speaker's belief that the evidence for the asserted proposition is private, when the speaker uses *de* in questions, does *de* continue to mark the speaker's belief that the speaker has private evidence for the asserted proposition, or is there a "perspective shift," such that it marks the speaker's belief that the addressee has private evidence for the asserted proposition? The use of *de* in the context given in (32) suggests that *de* continues to mark the speaker's belief that s/he has private evidence for the relevant proposition in questions.

(32) <u>Context</u>: The speaker and the addressee are at a party.
　　 a. *Ling-ling de   nan-peng-you zai zhe ma?*
　　　 Ling-ling POSS boyfriend   at here Q
　　　 'Is Ling-ling's boyfriend here?'
　　 b. *Ling-ling de   nan-peng-you zai zhe   de ma?*
　　　 Ling-ling POSS boyfriend   at here DE Q
　　　 'Is Ling-ling's boyfriend here?'

(32a) is a neutral question, while (32b) is associated with an implication that the speaker has reason to think that Ling-ling's boyfriend is at the party – for example, someone had mentioned to the speaker that Ling-ling's boyfriend would be at the party. In asking the question with *de*, the speaker indicates that s/he has some private evidence (e.g., hearsay evidence) for the relevant proposition while seeking an answer from the addressee regarding the truth of the proposition. The status of the evidence is not questioned. The holder of the private evidence does not appear to shift to the addressee with *de*. Sentence-final *de* in questions thus patterns like the inferential form of questions in Yukaghir, which involves assumption about the speaker and not about the addressee (Maslova 2003).

5   Apparent counterexamples and ~~shi~~ . . . *de* sentences

It is important to note that there are cases where a bare *de* appears to be used in contexts where the evidence for the asserted proposition is accessible to the addressee, contrary to expectation. These cases involve a prior discussion of the relevant proposition, and the use of *de* serves to <u>confirm</u> the relevant proposition in response to a contrary view or doubt held by the addressee. I refer to these cases as "confirmation" cases. An example is given in (33).

(33) <u>Context</u>: A is looking for his watch. B indicated that he believed that the watch was in the room (where they are), but A expressed doubt about that and thought that he might have left it somewhere else.
      b: (Upon finding the watch)
      Kan! shou-biao zai zhe   de.
      look watch   at here DE
      'Look, the watch is here.'

The discourse effect of *de* in confirmation cases is similar to that of *(shi)* . . . *de* constructions, which, according to Li and Thompson (1981:589), serve "to characterize or explain a situation by affirming or denying some supposition, as opposed to simply reporting an event." Due to the distinct contexts in which *de* in confirmation cases are used, I suggest that *de* in these cases involve *shi* . . . *de* sentences with a silent *shi*, as shown in (34).

(34) b: (Upon finding the watch)
      Kan! shou-biao ~~shi~~ zai zhe   de.
      look watch   FOC at here DE
      'Look, the watch is here.'

This analysis is supported by the fact that *shi* may be pronounced in these sentences without any difference in discourse effects.

   The current analysis supports a more nuanced view of the relation between bare *de* sentences and *shi* . . . *de* sentences with a silent *shi*, providing evidence for the existence of both these types of constructions (compare Li & Thompson 1981; Cheng 2008; Hole 2011). These two types of constructions are distinguished by the discourse environments they may appear in. Unlike a bare *de* sentence, the evidence for the proposition expressed by the prejacent in a *shi* . . . *de* sentence (with or without a silent *shi*) does not have to be private at speech time.

6   Summary and implications

To summarize, I have made the following proposals regarding the semantics and syntax of sentence-final *de* in a bare *de* sentence in Mandarin Chinese: (i) *de* marks the speaker's belief that the status of the evidence for the asserted proposition is *private* at utterance time; (ii) *de*P is below TP and above Mod^{NE}P.

The current analysis has implications on the syntax of modal auxiliaries, the relation between bare *de* sentences and *shi . . . de* sentences, and the syntax of discourse particles. With respect to the syntax of modal auxiliaries, the distribution of *de* in A-not-A questions provides a new kind of evidence in support of the claim that Mandarin epistemic modals occupy a structurally higher position than non-epistemic modals (Tsai 2015). The current analysis supports a more nuanced view of the relation between bare *de* sentences and *shi . . . de* sentences with a silent *shi*, providing evidence for the existence of both bare *de* sentences and *shi . . . de* sentences with a silent *shi* and offering a new way to distinguish a true bare *de* sentence from a *shi . . . de* sentence with a silent *shi*. In terms of the syntax of discourse particles, the proposed analysis supports the availability of two syntactic areas where discourse-related particles may appear: one in the CP edge above items associated with sentence force, such as the question particle *ma* (see, for example, Paul (2014)) and one in the clause medial area between TP and above Mod^{NE}P (Soh & Gao 2006, Erlewine, to appear, 2017). It connects *de* with sentence-final *-le* in Mandarin, which has been argued to occupy a position below TP and above Mod^{NE}P (for non-epistemic modals). Like *de*, sentence-final *-le* has been associated with discourse properties and has been noted to be a marker of "currently relevant state" (Li & Thompson 1981) and analyzed as involving speaker presupposition (Soh & Gao 2008; Soh 2008, 2009).

Finally, the current proposal connects *de* with discourse particles that mark the speaker's belief about whether the (evidence for the) asserted proposition is shared knowledge between the speaker and the hearer and whether it is "verifiable on the spot," such as German *ja* (Kratzer 1999, 2004; Gutzmann 2009) and English parenthetical *I'm telling you* (Reese & Soh 2018). German discourse particle *ja* (in its unstressed uses) requires that the asserted proposition be shared knowledge between the speaker and the addressee or verifiable on the spot (Kratzer 1999, 2004; Gutzmann 2009).[7] Mandarin *de* and German *ja* thus appear to make reference to the same discourse features, but with opposite values.[8] In Reese and Soh (2018), we show that English parenthetical *I'm telling you* is also sensitive to the same discourse features, sharing the same values with Mandarin *de* (see Reese & Soh (2018) for further discussion about the connection with German *ja*). Further comparisons between Mandarin *de*, German *ja*, and English *I'm telling you* will likely contribute to clarifications about similarities and differences among these closely related discourse particles and the semantic parameters they operate on.

Abbreviations

1	first person	POSS	possessive marker
2	second person	Q	question
3	third person	MOD	modification marker
SG	singular	CL	classifier
FOC	focus marker		

Notes

1 **Acknowledgements:** I would like to thank Brian Reese and Hanlin Zhu for extensive discussions. Many thanks to my native speaker consultants for their patience and care with the data. The current project received support from the Chiang Ching-Kuo Foundation for International Scholarly Exchange (Scholar Grant for Professors, 2016–2017) and an Imagine Fund Annual Award from the University of Minnesota, which I gratefully acknowledge. All errors are mine.

2 *Common ground*: It is common ground that ϕ in a group if all members accept (for the purpose of the conversation) that ϕ, and all believe that all accept that ϕ, and all believe that all believe that all accept that ϕ, etc. (Stalnaker 2002:716).

3 Cheng (2008) observes that sentence-final *de* may not appear in A-not-A questions and wh-questions but may appear in yes/no questions formed by the question particle *ma*. It is noted that the contrast in their behaviors is related to the relative scope of the question operator in relation to *de*. I leave aside the distribution of *de* in wh-questions, as judgments are variable for reasons unclear to me at this point.

4 Cheng (2008) proposes that *de* in a bare *de* sentence is associated with the presence of an assertion operator that takes a proposition as its argument. It is noted that *de* may be the head of the AssertionP, which hosts the assertion operator. My analysis thus differs from Cheng's (2008) in placing *de* lower in the structure. Most other studies on the syntax of *de* focus exclusively on *shi . . . de* sentences, which I assume to be distinct from bare *de* sentences. See, for example, Simpson & Wu (2002), Paul & Whitman (2008), Hole (2011), Paul (2014) and Song (2015).

5 Note that the structure in (28) with a head-final deP immediately dominating a head-initial Mod^{NE}P along with the one in (26) with a head-final CP immediately dominating a head-initial Mod^{F}P are exceptions to the final-over-final constraint (FOFC) (Biberauer *et al.* 2014). See Erlewine (2017) for a discussion of how the Mandarin data motivate a view of FOFC holding only within individual spell-out domains (Richards 2016), within the theory of cyclic spell-out.

6 Ernst's (1994) account involves movement of the [+Q] feature to C, followed by the movement of the relevant adjuncts to a position c-commanding C at LF, due to the isomorphic principle, which preserves surface scope (cf. Law 2006).

7 An earlier analysis by Lindner (1991) proposes that in using *ja*, the speaker indicates that in his/her eyes, the proposition *p* is not controversial.

8 There is a difference between Mandarin *de* and German *ja* in their current descriptions. The restriction is stated in terms of whether the <u>evidence for the asserted proposition</u> is private (not common knowledge and not verifiable on the spot) in case of *de*, while it is stated in terms of whether <u>the asserted proposition</u> is common knowledge or verifiable on the spot (not private) in case of *ja*.

References

Aikenvald, Alexandra Y. 2003. Evidentiality in typological perspective. In Alexandra Y. Aikenvald and R.M.W. Dixon (eds.), *Studies in evidentiality*, 1–31. Amsterdam/Philadelphia: John Benjamins Publishing Company.

Biberauer, Theresa, Anders Holmberg & Ian Roberts. 2014. A syntactic universal and its consequences. *Linguistic Inquiry* 45. 169–225.

Cheng, Lisa Lai-Shen. 1991. *On the Typology of Wh-Questions*. MIT dissertation.

Cheng, Lisa Lai-Shen. 2008. Deconstructing the *shi . . . de* construction. *Linguistic Review* 25. 235–266.

Cinque, Guglielmo. 1999. *Adverbs and functional heads*. Oxford: Oxford University Press.

Erlewine, Michael Yoshitaka. To appear: Sentence-final particles at the vP phase edge. In *Proceedings of the 25th North American Conference on Chinese Linguistics (NACCL 25)*. The Ohio State University.

Erlewine, Michael Yoshitaka. 2017. Low sentence final particles in Mandarin Chinese and the Final-over-Final Constraint. *Journal of East Asian Linguistics* 26. 37–75.

Ernst, Thomas. 1994. Conditions on Chinese A-not-A questions. *Journal of East Asian Linguistics* 3. 241–264.

Ernst, Thomas. 2009. Speaker-oriented adverbs. *Natural Language and Linguistic Theory* 27. 497–544.

Gutzmann, Daniel. 2009. Hybrid semantics for modal particles. *Sprache und Datenverarbeitung* 33. 45–59.

Hole, Daniel. 2011. The deconstruction of Chinese *shi . . . de* clefts revisited. *Lingua* 121. 1707–1733.

Huang, C.-T. James. 1982. *Logical Relations in Chinese and the Theory of Grammar*. MIT dissertation.

Huang, C.-T. James. 1988. *Wo pao de kuai* and Chinese phrase structure. *Language* 64. 274–311.

Kratzer, Angelika. 1999. Beyond 'Ouch' and 'Oops'. How descriptive and expressive meaning interact. Comment on Kaplan's paper at the Cornell Conference on Context Dependency. March 26. http://semanticsarchive.net/Archive/WEwNGUyO/

Kratzer, Angelika. 2004. Interpreting focus: Presupposed or expressive meanings? A comment on Geurts and Van der Sandt. *Theoretical Linguistics* 30. 123–136.

Law, Paul. 2006. Adverbs in A-not-A questions in Mandarin Chinese. *Journal of East Asian Linguistics* 15. 97–136.

Li, Charles N. & Sandra A. Thompson. 1981. *Mandarin Chinese: A functional reference grammar*. Berkeley, CA: University of California Press.

Lim, Dong Sik. 2010. *Evidentials and interrogatives: A case study from Korean*: University of Southern California Dissertation.

Lin, Jo-Wang. 1992. The syntax of *zenmeyang* 'how' and *weishenme* 'why' in Mandarin. *Journal of East Asian Linguistics* 1. 293–331.

Lindner, Katrin. 1991. 'Wir sind ja doch alte Bekannte' The use of German *ja* and *doch* as modal particles. In Werner Abraham (ed.), *Discourse particles: Descriptive and theoretical investigations on the logical, syntactic, and pragmatic properties of discourse particles in German*, 163–201. Amsterdam/Philadelphia, PA: John Benjamins.

Maslova, Elena. 2003. Evidentiality in Yukaghir. In Alexandra Y. Aikenvald & R.M.W. Dixon (eds.), *Studies in evidentiality*, 219–236. Amsterdam/Philadelphia: John Benjamins Publishing Company.

Murray, Sarah E. 2010. Evidentials and questions in Cheyenne. In Suzi Lima (ed.), *Proceedings of SULA 5: Semantics of under-represented languages in the Americas*, 139–155. Amherst: GLSA Publications.

Paul, Waltraud. 2014. Why particles are not particular: Sentence final particles in Chinese as heads of a split CP. *Studia Linguistica* 68. 77–115.

Paul, Waltraud & John Whitman. 2008. Shi. . . de focus clefts in Mandarin Chinese. *The Linguistic Review* 25(3–4). 413–451.

Reese, Brian & Hooi Ling Soh. 2018. Parenthetical *I'm telling you* as a marker of private evidence. *Proceedings of the Linguistic Society of America* 3(62). 1–13. doi:10.3765/plsa.v3i1.4360.

Richards, Norvin. 2016. *Contiguity theory*. Cambrige, MA: MIT.

Simpson, Andrew & Zoe Wu. 2002. From D to T–Determiner incorporation and the creation of tense. *Journal of East Asian Linguistics* 11(2). 169–209.

Soh, Hooi Ling. 2007. Ellipsis, Last Resort, and the dummy auxiliary *shi* 'be' in Mandarin Chinese. *Linguistic Inquiry* 38. 178–188.

Soh, Hooi Ling. 2008. The syntax and semantics of change/transition: Evidence from Mandarin Chinese. In Susan Rothstein (ed.), *Theoretical and cross-linguistic approaches to the semantics of aspect*, 387–419. Philadelphia, PA: John Benjamins.

Soh, Hooi Ling. 2009. Speaker presupposition and Mandarin Chinese sentence final -*le*: A unified analysis of the "change of state" and the "contrary to expectation" reading. *Natural Language and Linguistic Theory* 27. 623–657.

Soh, Hooi Ling. 2019. Colloquial Malay discourse particle *punya* as a modal evidential. *Oceanic Linguistics* 58. 386–413.

Soh, Hooi Ling & Meijia Gao. 2006. Perfective aspect and transition in Mandarin Chinese: An analysis of double -*le* sentences. In Pascal Denis, E. McCready, Alexis Palmer & Brian Reese (eds.), *Proceedings of 2004 Texas linguistics society conference: Issues at the semantics-pragmatics interface*, 107–122. Somerville, MA: Cascadilla Press.

Soh, Hooi Ling & Meijia Gao. 2008. Mandarin sentential -*le*, perfect and English *already*. In: Johannes Dölling, Tatjana Heyde-Zybatow & Martin Schäfer (eds.), *Event structures in linguistic form and interpretation*, 447–473. Berlin: Mouton de Gruyter.

Song, Wei. 2015. *The sentence final de and the post-verbal de in the shi . . . de construction in Mandarin Chinese*. MA Plan B paper. University of Minnesota.

Stalnaker, Robert. 1999. *Context and content: Essays on intentionality in speech and thought*. Oxford: Oxford University Press.

Stalnaker, Robert. 2002. Common ground. *Linguistics and Philosophy* 25. 701–721.

Tsai, Wei-Tien Dylan. 2015. On the topography of Chinese modals. In Ur Shlonsky (ed.), *Beyond functional sequence: The cartography of syntactic structures*, vol. 10, 257–294. Oxford: Oxford University Press.

4 How are contrasts marked? – the case of *ne* in Mandarin Chinese

Satomi Ito

1 Introduction[1]

Semantics of interrogatives has had a history of more than 40 years that began with Hamblin's (1973) seminal work. Although the exact definition of *interrogatives* differs by the scholar, the agreed-on definition of an interrogative is a set of answers to itself. Because answers are represented as propositions and a proposition is represented as a set of possible worlds that support it, the semantics of an *interrogative* is defined as a set of sets of worlds that supports the possible answers to the interrogative. In this chapter, I call the set of worlds that represents the answer a "cell." I argue that the particle *ne* in Mandarin Chinese marks the contrast between cells of the partition.

On the one hand, partition semantics is one of the strongest devices to analyze natural languages; on the other hand, it cannot analyze the flow of discourse. This problem was solved by Isaacs and Rawlins (2008). They combine the dynamic semantics for conditionals with the partition semantics and analyze the conditional questions. In this chapter, I show that the multiple occurrences of the particle *ne* in alternative questions is accounted for in the framework of the dynamic semantics.

This chapter comprises sections. Section 1 presents the introduction, Section 2 defines the notion of contrast, Section 3 summarizes various functions of the particle *ne* observed in the literature, Section 4 argues that the particle *ne* that appears at the end of a clause marks contrast among propositions and that the particle *ne* attached to a nominal constituent marks topic, and Section 5 presents the conclusion.

2 Notion of contrast

The notion of contrast has been used in topic and focus: a contrastive topic (CT) is a constituent that the sentence discusses and is chosen from among the salient alternatives; a contrastive focus (CF) is a prominent constituent in a sentence chosen from among the salient alternatives. CT and CF are defined relative to alternatives. In this section, I show that the notion of contrast intersects topic and focus and define it separately from a CT or CF.

DOI: 10.4324/9781351057837-5

Lee (2003) shows examples from Korean, (1) and (2), and compares the noun with the particle *-un* in (1) and the noun with the particle *-ul* in (2) to show that both a CT and CF are interpreted relative to a contextually salient set of alternatives; thus, the notion of contrast intersects topic and focus. In Korean, the particle *-un* signals that NP is supposed to be known both to the speaker and the listener (Kim *et al.* 2017:138). Thus, an NP with *-un* that appears at the beginning of a sentence is naturally considered a topic of the sentence. Additionally, Lee (2003) argues that the NP with *-un* in example (1B) contrasts with an implicit NP; thus, it is a CT. He demonstrates that the question (1A) "Do you have money"? is interpreted by speaker B as a conjunction of questions such as "Do you have coins?" and "Do you have bills?" Accordingly, "coins (*tongceon*)" is in contrast with "bills" even though "bills" does not appear in the question. Thus, the particle *-un* can mark the NP as CT if the question is interpreted as a conjunction of questions through the conventional implicature.

(1) a: *Ne   ton   iss   ni?*
         you   money have   Q
         'Do you have money?'

    b: *Na   tongceon-un   iss-e.*
         I   coins-CT   have-DEC
         'I have coins, (but not bills).'

By contrast, an answer to an alternative question cannot be marked as CT. In the following dialogue, NP *ton* (money) in (2B) is followed by the accusative marker *-ul*, not by the topic marker *-un*.

(2) a: *aki-ka   ton-ul   mence cip-ess-ni   animyen phen-ul*
         Baby-NOM   money-ACC   first pick-PAST-Q if-not   pen-ACC
         mence cip-ess-ni?
         first   pick-PAST-Q
         'Did the baby pick the money first, or did she pick the pen first?'

    b: *(aki-ka)   ton-ul   /   ?*ton-un   mence cip-ess-e.*
         (Baby-NOM)   money-ACC   /   money-CT   first pick-PAST-DEC
         'The baby picks the money first.'

Obviously, *ton* (money) in (2B) is in contrast with *phen* (pen), because they both are presented as alternatives in the preceding question. *Ton* (money) is also focus because it is supported by the impossible *-un* marking and focus accent (reported in Lee 2003). Thus, with contrastiveness and focus, *ton* (money) is the CF of the sentence.

In examples (1) and (2), despite the notion of contrast being common to CT and CF, the markings of topic and focus override the contrastiveness, leading to different markings (different particles and accents). In this chapter,

I show that the particle *ne* in Mandarin Chinese marks contrastiveness regardless of topic or focus.

3   Analyses of the particle *ne*

According to Li and Thompson (1981), six sentence-final particles are in Mandarin Chinese: *ma* turns the proposition into a question, *le* indicates that the proposition is relevant to the current state, *ba* indicates that the speaker solicits agreement from the listener, *ne* indicates that the speaker utters the proposition as a response to expectation, *ou* indicates that the speaker utters the proposition as a friendly warning, and *a* reduces forcefulness of the utterance. Of these particles, *ne* is peculiar in that it performs different functions in different contexts. Some papers on the particle *ne* even argue that several homonyms are pronounced as *ne*: each homonym is licensed by different presuppositions (see references in Ito 2018a, 2018b). In this section, I show the various effects caused by the particle *ne* to appear.

3.1   *The particle ne in various contexts*

The particle *ne* in Mandarin Chinese is attached to declaratives, interrogatives, *if*-clauses, and nouns and causes various effects, depending on what it is attached to. In this section, I summarize four usages of the particle *ne*.

First, the particle *ne* appears at the end of a declarative and indicates that the speaker contrasts his utterance with the listener's state of knowledge. Li and Thompson (1981) claim that the utterance accompanying the particle *ne* is a response to the listener's expectation. For instance, example (3) is uttered as a response to the assumption that the restaurant is already open.[2] If the sentence is uttered without *ne*, it shows that the speaker states the proposition without considering the listener's assumption.

(3) *Yingye   shijian   mei   dao   ne.*
    open   hour   NEG   arrive   NE
    'We aren't open yet.'

By contrast, Zhou (2008, 2009) investigates the function of *ne* in declaratives and argues that the particle *ne* indicates that the speaker requires the listener to acknowledge the truth of the proposition and to speculate the intention of the speaker on the basis of the information found in the context. Although the conclusion of Li and Thompson (1981) seems to differ from that of Zhou (2008, 2009), their claims have at least one point in common: the use of the particle *ne* is involved with the speaker's speculation of the listener's state of knowledge, possibly intending to contrast his/her utterance with the speaker's belief.

Second, the particle *ne* appears at the end of an interrogative and causes various effects on the illocutionary act. Unlike the particle at the end of declaratives, there are various suggestions regarding the function of the particle at the end of interrogatives: Shao (1989) states that *ne* indicates the speaker's urgent request for an answer, Liu *et al.* (2002) state that *ne* makes the question polite, and Kimura and Moriyama (1992) argue that *ne* indicates that the speaker is confused at the content of the interrogative. These various proposals indicate that proposing a unified analysis on the particle *ne* is difficult when the particle follows an interrogative. I show example (4) to explain the various effects of the particle. Example (4) is uttered in a situation in which the listener (a child) lost a toy car and his mother attempts to find its whereabouts. This interrogative can either describe an urgent request by the speaker, a polite question, or the speaker's confusion because the toy car is lost. All these interpretations depend on the prosody in which the interrogative is uttered and the relationship between the speaker and the listener. Hence, the effect on an illocutionary act is due to the prosody and the relationship between the speaker and the listener in the conversation, not the particle *ne*.

(4) *Che   shi   hui   kai-lai   kai-qu   de,   xiang-xiang, jintian*
    car   be   may   drive-in drive-away NMLZ   think-RED   today
    dao   nar   qu   le   ne?
    to   where go   PFV   NE
    'A car may drive in and away. Think back, where did the car go today?'[3]

In addition to the effect on the illocutionary level, scholars suggest that the particle *ne* is licensed by the presupposition of the sentence. Jin (1996) and Kang (2007) argue that the particle *ne* is licensed by the shared knowledge between the speaker and the listener. Their suggestion is similar to that proposed for the particle in declaratives: the particle *ne* presupposes that the speaker acknowledges the current context, including the listener's state of knowledge. However, what type of presupposition the particle *ne* requires is unclear. In this sense, interrogatives are the most difficult sentence type to analyze of all the contexts in which the particle *ne* appears.

Third, the particle *ne* marks the topic of the sentence, as shown in (5). Fang (1994) argues that the particle *ne* is attached to the first nominal in the sentence to indicate that the nominal is a topic.

(5) (In contrast to the former housekeepers)
    Zhe   Xiao   Ye   ne,   gan-huo   hai   bucuo,   wo   jiu   pa   ta
    this   Miss   Ye   NE   do-work   even   good   1SG   only   afraid 3SG
    he   Yiwen   he-bu-qilai.
    with Yiwen   suit-NEG-become
    'Miss Ye is doing even better work (than other housekeepers), but I'm only afraid that she can't be on good terms with Yiwen.'

Fang (1994) also mentions that the particle *ne* often appears at the end of an *if*-clause, as shown in (6). Given that an *if*-clause sets the scope of the main clause, an *if*-clause is regarded to be a topic of the whole conditional; thus, it is compatible with the particle *ne*.

(6) *Ni   yao   juede   heshi   ne,   jiu   ba   ta   liu-xia-lai.*
2SG   if   think   appropriate   NE   then   OBJ   3SG   keep-down-come
'If you think that she is appropriate (for the job), then keep her (as a housekeeper).'

Last, the particle *ne* functions as an interrogative marker. As I mentioned in the beginning of this section, the particle can appear at the end of interrogatives. In these cases, the particle is not a question marker but some other constituent, such as a *wh*-word or *yes/no*-question marker, that turns the clause into an interrogative. By contrast, the particle *ne* as an interrogative marker is only compatible with a nominal constituent, and even a predicate is not allowed to follow. The interrogative formed by a nominal constituent and the particle *ne* is called a "truncated question" because it is a question with a predicate truncated. The truncated predicate is recovered in accordance with the context. For instance, example (7) is interpreted as "Would you like some drink?" "Did you buy a drink?" or "Where is the drink?" depending on the context in which it is uttered.

(7) *Yinliao   ne?*
drink   NE
'Would you like some drink?'

Lu (1982) regards this usage of the particle *ne* as the original meaning of the particle and argues that the particle *ne* is a question marker. Since then, most reference books on Chinese grammar follow his idea and regard the particle *ne* as an interrogative particle. Accordingly, the authors of these reference books regard that there are at least two homonyms for *ne*: an interrogative particle and a noninterrogative one.

Thus far, I have introduced various proposals on the function of the particle *ne* in various contexts. Numerous researchers have attempted to propose a unified analysis covering all usages of the particle but have not demonstrated the common feature of all usages or the proper derivation of meanings. In addition to these descriptive works, a few theoretical works propose unified analyses. Chu (2006) and Xu (2008) analyze the particle *ne* in the framework of relevance theory and argue that it indicates relevance to the context, explaining all the usages of the particle. Although their arguments are convincing, they do not define context or specify how the particle interacts with the given context. By contrast, Constant (2014) argues that the particle *ne* marks CT on the basis of the clear definition of a context, namely, QUD. In the next section, I introduce the brief sketch of Constant's (2014) analysis.

3.2   *The particle ne as a CT marker*

As Fang (1994) mentioned, the particle *ne* and topic have a strong relationship. However, Cao (1977) argues that the first nominal of a clause is a topic in Mandarin Chinese. Thus, the particle *ne* marks as a topic the first nominal that is already a topic by virtue of its position. Hence, the particle probably serves a function other than marking the topic. Constant (2014) proposes that the particle *ne* marks CT. He argues that the particle *ne* is a counterpart of the B-accent in English. The B-accent is a fall-rise intonation at the end of a clause, shown in (8c), typically observed in an answer to a subquestion, such as (8b). (8b) is called a subquestion because it is an instance of the big question shown in (8a), which also is the question that triggers the B-accent in its answer:

(8)   a.   *Who ate what?* (= a big question)
      b.   *What did Fred and Mary eat?* (= a subquestion)
      c.   *Fred ate the beans. Mary ate the eggplant.*

Since first demonstrated by Bolinger (1965), the function of this accent has been widely discussed (e.g., Jackendoff 1972; Büring 2003). The shared view on this accent is that it indicates that the topic of the clause is contrastive to other individuals in the context. Since the particle *ne* in Mandarin Chinese often marks a topic, as shown in (5), identifying the function of the particle *ne* with that of the B-accent seems to be promising at first glance.

Constant (2014) argues that the particle *ne* marks CT by providing four pieces of evidence to support it. First, the particle *ne* does not mark an exhaustive focus, as shown in (9). Because topic and focus are mutually exclusive, it suggests that the particle *ne* marks a topic. Second, the particle *ne* does not always mark a topic, as shown in (10). The first nominal in example (10) is a topic of the sentence, but it is not in contrast with any individual. This finding indicates that the particle *ne* is not an ordinary topic marker. Third, the particle *ne* does not mark a universally quantified expression, as shown in (11). A universally quantified expression is not in contrast with any nonempty set and thus cannot be contrastive. Fourth, the particle *ne* marks an *if*-clause but not a reason-clause, as shown in (12). The particle *ne* cannot follow a reason-clause, because of the absence of alternative situations in contrast with it, whereas an *if*-clause implies a contrast between the content of an *if*-clause and the real world, allowing the particle *ne*. Based on this evidence, Constant's (2014) conclusion is that the particle *ne* must follow a constituent that is in a topic position and is in contrast with something in the context; thus, the particle *ne* is a CT marker.

(9)   a: *Shei   zui   gao?   B:Zhangsan   (#ne)   zui   gao.*
           who   most   tall   Zhangsan   NE   most   tall
      a: 'Who is the tallest?' B: 'Zhang is the tallest.'

(10) (As the first utterance in the course of thermodynamics)
    Relixue   (*#ne*), *dabufen de   ren   keneng mei*
    Thermodynamics NE   most   GEN people possibly NEG
    tingshuo guo.
    hear-say EXP
    'As for thermodynamics, most people possibly haven't heard about it.'

(11) *Suoyou   de   shiqing (#ne) dou hen nan ban.*
    everything GEN matters NE   all   very hard handle
    'Everything is hard to handle.'

(12) *Women benlai   yiwei ta   gou   zige,*
    1PL   originally think 3SG enough qualification
    a. *keshi, yaoshi ta   shijishang bu   hege   ne,*
       but   if   3SG in-fact   NEG qualified NE
       women bu   neng gu   ta.
       1PL   NEG can   hire 3SG
       'We used to think he was qualified, but if he is not qualified in fact,
       we cannot hire him.'

    b. *keshi, yinwei ta   shijishang bu   hege   (*ne),*
       but   because 3SG in-fact   neg qualified NE
       women bu   neng gu   ta.
       1PL   NEG can   hire 3SG
       'We used to think he was qualified, but as he is not qualified in fact,
       we cannot hire him.'

Constant (2014) extends his analysis to the particle *ne* that appears at the end of interrogatives. He argues that both nominal CT and clausal CT move to the spec of CP, causing two positions of the particle *ne*, shown in examples (13) and (14). In example (13), the particle *ne* is attached to the topic of the clause, namely, *baba* (father), whereas in (14), the particle *ne* appears at the end of the clause.

(13) *Mama hen   wan cai   hui-lai.   [Baba] ne gancui*
    mother very late finally come-back father NE simply
    bu   hui-lai.
    NEG come-back
    'Mother came back very late. Father simply didn't come back.'

(14) *Ni   dong   le.   [Ta dong-bu-dong   ]ne?*
    2SG understand CRS 3SG understand-NEG-understand NE
    'You understood. Did he understand at all?'

Constant (2014) explains the different positions of the particle *ne* in examples (13) and (14) by proposing a distinction between direct marking and indirect marking of CT. Figure 4.1 is a tree of example (13) and shows an instance of direct CT-marking; Figure 4.2 is a tree of example (14) and shows an instance of indirect CT-marking. The particle *ne* is defined as a CT-abstraction operator (CT-λ) and is located in CP. It checks the CT-feature of nominals and clauses (shown as subscripted CT in Figures 4.1 and 4.2) by spec-head agreement.

In example (13), the subject noun *baba* (father) with a CT-feature moves up into the CP of the clause to check the feature, as shown in Figure 4.1, resulting in the word order as it is. In example (14), the CT-feature of the subject pronoun *ta* (he) percolates to the whole clause, causing the movement of the clause into the CP, as shown in Figure 4.2. As a result of the movement, the particle *ne* appears at the end of the clause.

3.3   *The problem with Constant's analysis*

Although Constant's (2014) unified analysis appears successful, there are problems with his proposal. First, if the percolation is optional, as he argues, (13) and (14) can be rephrased as (15) and (16), respectively, without any change in meaning, which is not attested.

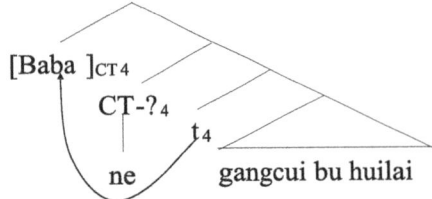

Figure 4.1 Topical *ne*.

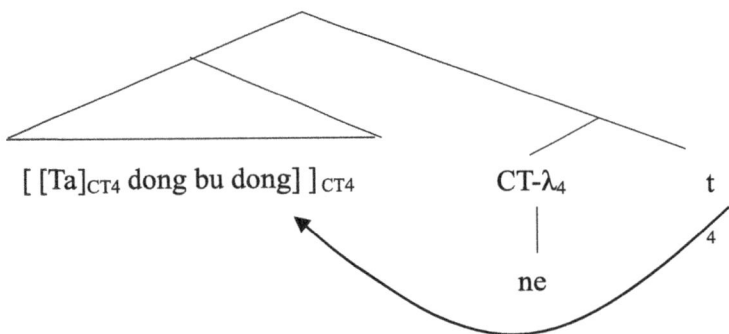

Figure 4.2 Sentence-final *ne*.

(15) *Mama   hen   wan   cai   hui-lai.   Baba   gancui   bu*
mother very   late   finally come-back father   simply   NEG
hui-lai   (?ne).
come-back   NE
'Mother came back very late. Father simply didn't come back.'

(16) *Ni   dong   le.   Ta   ne   (dong-bu-dong)?*
you   understand   CRS   he   NE   understand-NEG-understand
'You understood. Did he understand at all?'

The rephrased versions are not as good as expected: the particle *ne* at the end of clause (15) is slightly strange, and the particle *ne* attached to the subject noun in (16) makes the predicate redundant if it is not ill-formed.

Second, the particle *ne* can appear at the end of a topic-less sentence, as shown in example (17). In a topic-less sentence, no nominal has a CT-feature. Hence, Constant's (2014) analysis cannot account for the use of the particle *ne* in this example.

(17) *Xia-bu-xia   yu   ne?*
fall-NEG-fall   rain   NE
'Is it raining?'

Third, Constant's (2014) evidence in (9)–(12) only indicates that the particle *ne* is licensed in the context where there are alternatives that can be contrasted with the constituent followed by the particle. (9) is the superlative, that is, the subject *Zhangsan* is the only person who has the property of being the tallest, and thus there is no alternative for it. (10) is the first utterance of a discourse, and thus, no alternative is expected to be contrasted with; the first nominal in (11) is a universally quantified expression, and thus, there is no individual to be compared with. The contrast between (12a) and (12b) is brought about by the presence or absence of alternatives and does not support that the constituent with the particle *ne* should be a topic.

Fourth, on some occasions, CT cannot be found in the sentence. In example (18), a reprint of (4), no CT can be found. The car is a topic throughout these two clauses and thus is not a CT. Also difficult is regarding the whole clause as a CT. Theoretically, the notion of CT must be defined with respect to nominals; empirically, finding a proposition that contrasts with the clause is difficult.

(18) *Che   shi   hui   kai-lai   kai-qu   de,   xiang-xiang,   jintian*
car   be   may   drive-in   drive-away   NMLZ   think-RED   today
dao   nar   qu   le   ne?
to   where   go   PFV   NE
'The car may drive in and away. Think back, where did the car go today?'

In summary, although the particle *ne* can follow a CT constituent of the clause, especially when attached to the first nominal constituent in a clause, not all usages of the particle *ne* can be explained under Constant's theory. The topic accompanying the particle *ne* can be contrastive, but the contrastiveness is brought about by the context, not the particle *ne*. Hence, I dismiss the unified theory that the particle *ne* marks a CT. Instead, I categorize the particle *ne* into two groups: attached to a clause and attached to nominal constituents. The former marks contrast among possible alternatives found in the information state, and the latter marks a topic, as Fang (1994) argues.

4   The particle *ne* as a contrast marker

In this section, I propose that a proposition with the particle *ne* is contrasted with its alternative proposition. As a framework of analysis, I use Hamblin semantics, proposed by Hamblin (1973) and Karttunen (1977). In Hamblin semantics, an *interrogative* is defined in terms of sets of possible worlds, and a *proposition* is defined as a set of possible worlds. The difference is that the former is a partition of possible worlds, and each partition supports the possible answer, whereas the latter is a set of possible worlds that supports the proposition. In Isaacs and Rawlins (2008), the model is combined with file-change semantics to analyze both the temporary state and the changes in state along the time axis. Assuming a model in which the original information state includes every possible world, upon uttering a proposition, the speaker excludes the possible worlds that do not support the proposition, narrowing the information state to the possible worlds compatible with the propositions. By contrast, uttering an interrogative, the speaker partitions the information state into the possible answers by dividing it into the group of possible worlds that support the answers. Based on this framework, I argue that the particle *ne* marks the contrast between the cells, the sets of possible worlds partitioned by the interrogative or the context.

In Section 4.1, I examine the occurrence of the particle *ne* in interrogatives and argue that there are two types of *ne*: one type marks the contrast between the cells partitioned by the interrogative, and the other marks the contrast between the content of the interrogative and the proposition in the context. In Section 4.2, I examine how the particle *ne* marks the contrast between the disjuncts in alternative questions. In Section 4.3, I argue that the particle *ne* in declaratives marks the contrast between the utterance and a proposition found in the context, leading to the implication that the utterance is a speaker's response to the listener's expectation. In Section 4.4, I briefly show that the particle *ne* marks the topic and derives truncated questions.

4.1   *Association with the particle* ne *in interrogatives*

Before discussing the function of the particle *ne*, I clarify what constituent the particle *ne* associates with. Constant (2014) associates the particle *ne* in an interrogative sentence with the topic of the sentence, which I have rejected in 3.3. Although no evidence identifies what constituent is associated with the particle *ne* in interrogatives, several traditional Chinese grammarians have regarded that it scopes over the whole sentence (e.g., Li 1924; Wang 1943; Zhu 1981). I tentatively describe this intuition by representing the constituent associated with *ne* as [ ]$_C$, distinguishing it from a CT. The representation of the association with *ne* in (19) is as follows:

(19) *Ni   dong   le.   [Ta]*$_{CT}$ *dong-bu-dong]*$_C$ *ne?*
      2SG understand CRS 3SG   understand-NEG-understand   NE
      'You understood. Did he understand at all?'

In (19), *ta* (he) is a CT and contrasted with the subject noun in the preceding clause. Nevertheless, the particle *ne* is not associated with the subject in the preceding clause but is associated with the whole clause. Unlike in Constant's (2014) analysis, the particle does not mark the CT but marks the whole clause as contrastive. I propose that the particle *ne* looks for groups of possible worlds in the current information state. For instance, an A-not-A question such as (20) contains two propositions, one positive and one negative, represented in (20b); thus, the A-not-A question supplies two sets of possible worlds that can be contrasted.

(20) a. *Ta   dong-bu-dong*   *ne?* (= the latter half of (19))
          he   understand-NEG-understand   NE
          'Did he understand at all?'
      b. {{w: he understood(w)=1}, {w: he understood(w)=0}}

Likewise, the particle *ne* in a *wh*-question is associated with the whole clause and marks the utterance as contrastive. Example (21), the latter half of (4), is a *wh*-question; by uttering it, the information state is partitioned into sets of worlds, each of which supports a possible answer to it. The partition is represented as (21b), namely, a set of sets of worlds that satisfy each proposition with the *wh*-word replaced by any entity. Thus, the particle *ne* can mark the contrast between the sets of possible worlds.

(21) a. (*Che*) *dao   nar   qu   le   ne?* (= the latter half of (4))
              car   to   where go   PFV   NE
          'Where did the car go?'
      b. {{w: the car went to x(w)| x∈D$_{<c>}$}}

In summary, the contrast that the particle *ne* marks is found in the interrogative meaning. As shown in the representation of (20b) and (21b), there are several propositions in the current information state. The particle *ne* marks the contrast between these propositions.

Figures 4.3 and 4.4 visualize the denotations shown in (20b) and (21b). Figure 4.3 describes how the information state is partitioned based on (20a).

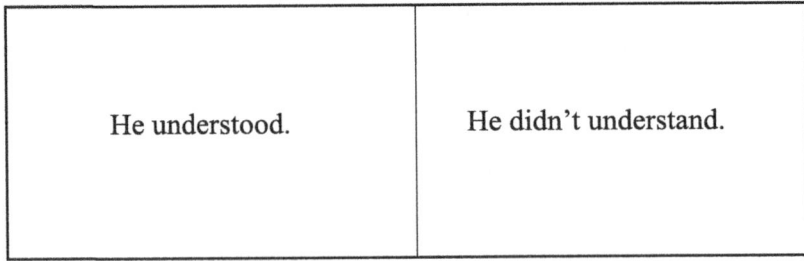

He understood.	He didn't understand.

Figure 4.3 The denotation of (20).

Under the table	Behind the sofa
Under the bed	In the housekeeper's bag

Figure 4.4 The denotation of (21).

The information state is partitioned into the two cells, with one cell representing "he understood" and the other cell representing "he didn't understand." Figure 4.4 is an instance of the information state partitioned by (21b). For convenience of explanation, four answers are assumed: *under the table, behind the sofa, under the bed*, and *in the housekeeper's bag*. In this hypothetical world, the set of possible worlds is partitioned into four cells.

The particle *ne* marks the contrast between these cells in the information state. It works under the condition that there is more than one cell in the information state and that cells are mutually exclusive.

Based on the discussion thus far, my proposal is that the particle *ne* is a function that takes a variable of type <s, <s,t>>, namely, an interrogative. It checks whether the information state created by the interrogative has more than one cell. If the information state contains more than one cell, it passes the requirement of the particle *ne*. The requirement is formalized, as shown in (22).

(22) Semantics of *ne* – interrogatives
$\llbracket ne \rrbracket = \lambda X.\exists q \in X\,[f(X) = p \wedge \{w:p(w) = 1\} \cap \{w:q(w) = 1\} = \emptyset]$
$(X \in D_{<s,<s,t>>},\ p,q \in D_{<s,t>},\ w \in W,\ f = $ a function that chooses a proposition)

The particle *ne* ensures that there is a proposition that is not compatible with the proposition chosen from the interrogative by the function *f*. Because the function *f* can freely choose one proposition from the interrogative, every proposition has a proposition that is not compatible with it. The proposition not compatible with it is found in the same information state: one of the other possible answers. In other words, an interrogative followed by the particle *ne* is always adequate, because we can find two sets of worlds exclusive from each other. Moreover, the presence of the particle *ne* emphasizes the partition of the information state. Speakers can add the particle *ne* whenever they want to emphasize the partition, and conversely, the existence of the partition is the condition for the particle *ne* to appear.

There is a type of interrogative that cannot be compatible with the particle *ne*. Mandarin Chinese has two types of *yes/no*-questions: A-not-A questions and *ma*-questions. *Ma*-questions are formed with the sentence-final particle *ma*. These differ from A-not-A questions in that the positive answer to the interrogative is expected by the speaker (Liu *et al.* 2002), and *ma*-questions can be answered by expressions that show agreement with the questioner, such as *dui* (right) or *shi* (it is; Yuan 1993; Guo 2000). Ito (2018b) shows that ma-questions ask for the admittance of the proposition to the information state, whereas A-not-A questions partition the information state. In this sense, a *ma*-question does not have a proper proposition to be contrasted with itself. Hence, *ma*-questions are not followed by the particle *ne*.

Next, I re-consider the illocutionary effect of the particle *ne* under definition (22). As I mentioned in 3.1, interrogatives accompanying the particle *ne* convey various nuances: an urgent request (Shao 1989), a polite question (Liu *et al.* 2002), and the speaker's confusion (Kimura & Moriyama 1992). These nuances are the result of emphasizing the partition in the information state. By emphasizing the partition in the information state, the question may sound demanding because it forces the listener to choose one of the answers immediately. On other occasions, the question may sound polite because it implies that there are other options. In monologues, highlighting the contrast among the possible answers indicates that the speaker is at a loss as to what the answer is. The nuances reported thus far are by-products of the function of the particle *ne*.

Thus far, I have described interrogatives uttered out of the blue. In these instances, the contrasted propositions are collected from the meaning of the interrogative. However, not all interrogatives with the particle *ne* retrieve the contrasted proposition among the meaning of interrogatives. There are other cases in which the contrasted proposition is retrieved from the context. These are the cases of rhetorical questions, as shown in (23); in this example, the speaker insists that the father should not eat with the former housekeeper instead of asking what type of meal the father eats with her. Hence, the utterance contrasts with a proposition in the speaker's mind, a proposition such as "You should not eat with the former housekeeper."

(23) *Ba,   ta   bu   zou   le   ma,   jie-wan   le   zhang   jiu*
        Dad   3SG   NEG   leave PFV   Q   pay-finish PFV bill   then

de   le   bei,
enough PFV   PRTCL

chi shenme fan   ne!
eat   what   meal   NE
'Dad, she (the housekeeper) left, didn't she? You paid the bill, so it's enough for her, what meal did you eat with her = you shouldn't eat with her.'

Rhetorical questions can be presented in various forms, but one of the means to describe rhetorical questions is interrogatives with the particle *ne* at their ends. Native speakers tend to use the particle *ne* to describe rhetorical questions more often than to describe ordinary questions. To confirm this tendency, I asked seven native Chinese speakers whether they accept the particle *ne* after the underlined part of dialogue (24). This dialogue is excerpted from a TV drama, and the particle *ne* appears only at the end of lines 7 and 11. The questionnaire is created by replacing the particles in lines 7 and 11 with parentheses and adding parentheses at the end of line 5, where no particle originally appears. The results are shown in the parentheses in (24). The numerator is the number of native Chinese speakers who accept the particle; the denominator is the number of consulted subjects.

(24) (In a restaurant, a waiter and a waitress are loading a box onto the carrier of a bicycle.)[4]
1 Waiter: *Zhe   xiang   shi   putaojiu.*
             this   box   be   wine
             'This is a box of wine.'
2 Waitress: *Putaojiu, jiu   zhege wo   xihuan.*
              wine   only   this   1SG like
              'Wine, I love it.'
(Ms. Liu enters the restaurant.)
3 Waiter: *Yingye shijian mei   dao   ne.*
            open   hour   NEG   arrive NE
            'We aren't open yet.'
(Mrs. Liu ignores him and approaches them.)
4 Waitress: *Bu   shi gen ni   shuo le   ma,*
              NEG be   to   you   say   PFV   question
              hai mei   dao   yingye shijian, zou-zou-zou!
              yet   NEG arrive open   hour   go-go-go
              'Hasn't he told you that we aren't open yet? Go away!'
5 Mrs. Liu: *Nimen   zhe shi gan shenme?* (6/7)
              2PL   this be   do   what
              'What are you doing?'
6 Waiter: *Guan   ni   shenme shi?   Momingqimiao.*
            Involve 2SG what   matter baffling
            'That's none of your business! It's baffling.'

7 Mrs. Liu: <u>*Nimen   dasuan   ba   zhexie   dongxi   ban-dao   shenme*</u>
        2PL   plan   OBJ   these   thing   move-to what
        <u>*difang   qu* ?</u> (0/7)
        location go
        'Where are you going to bring these boxes?'

8 Waitress: *Ni   zhege   ren   dao   shi   man   guai*
        2SG this   person unexpectedly be   very   strange
        de   o.
        de   PRTCL
        'What a weirdo you are.'
        Pao   dao   zheli   guan   xianshi   lai   le.
        run   to   here   involve other people's business come   PFV
        Ni   kuai   zou   a!
        2SG quickly go   PRTCL
        'You're meddling in other people's affairs. Go away immediately!'

9 Mrs. Liu: *Shi-bu-shi   yao   wang   jia-li   ban   na?*
        be-NEG-be plan to   home-LOC move PRTCL
        'Is it that you bring them to home?'

10 Waitress: *Ni   zhege   ren   hen   guai   de   o.*
        2SG this   person very strange NMLZ PRTCL
        'You're weird.'

11 Mrs. Liu: <u>*Wo   shi   xin   lai   de   jingli,*</u>
        1SG be   newly come REL manager
        <u>*neng-bu-neng   guan* ?</u> (5/7)
        can-NEG-can be-in-charge-of
        'I am the new manager of this restaurant. Can't I be in charge
        of these things?'

(The waiter and waitress look embarrassed.)

12 Mrs. Liu: *Zhexie   dongxi   dou   shi   dian-li   de,   nimen*
        these thing   all   be   restaurang-LOC GEN you
        yaoshi   shuo-bu-chu   shenme   yao   na-hui-qu,   jiu
        if   say-NEG-out what   plan take-back-go then
        zhi   neng   suan   nimen   shi   touqie   la.
        only can   count   you   be steal   PRTCL
        'All of these boxes belong to the restaurant. If you can't give any
        reason to take them out, you are thieves.'

The result shows that six of seven native Chinese speakers add the particle *ne* in line 5, none of the speakers accept the use of the particle *ne* in line 7, and five of seven speakers accept the use of the particle *ne* on line 11. The distribution of the particle *ne* in lines 5 and 7 differs from that of the original script of the TV drama: line 5 is uttered without the particle *ne*, and line 7 is followed by the particle *ne* in the original text. Furthermore, an anonymous reviewer points out that s/he can either use the particle *ne* or not in lines 5 and 7. By contrast, the occurrence of the particle *ne* in line 11 is admitted in the original script and supported by most native Chinese speakers and the reviewer. The difference between line 11 and the other lines might be attributed to the richness of the context. Line 11 is judged as a rhetorical question based on the flow of discourse: Mrs. Liu is attempting to declare that she oversees matters in the restaurant. The high rate of acceptance of the particle *ne* in line 11 indicates the close relationship between rhetorical questions and the use of the particle *ne*. The disagreement of the result as to lines 5 and 7 indicates that the speaker can optionally use the particle *ne* to mark the contrast among the proposition supplied by the interrogative if the context does not supply the preposition that should be contrasted with the interrogative.

To integrate the rhetorical use of the particle *ne*, I modify the semantics of the particle *ne* as follows. In rhetorical questions, the contrasted proposition is retrieved from the former information state. The current information state can be discarded to recover the former information state. Assuming that the former state of the information state can be accessed, the semantics of the particle *ne* in rhetorical questions is defined as shown in (25): the particle *ne* marks the contrast between the proposition chosen from the interrogative meaning and the proposition in the recovered information state.

(25) Semantics of *ne* for rhetorical questions

$[\![ne]\!] = \lambda X.\exists q \in s\ [f(X) = p \wedge \{w: p(w) = 1\} \cap \{w: q(w) = 1\} = \emptyset]$

$(X \in D_{<s,<s,t>>}, p,q \in D_{<s,t>}, w \in W, f = $ a function that chooses a proposition, s = the recovered information state)

In conclusion, the particle *ne* checks whether the sentence is qualified to accompany it. There are two means to obtain the contrasted proposition: among the possible answers or in the recovered information state. As a result, the use of the particle *ne* indicates that the speaker wants to either contrast the possible answers or the proposition that s/he has in mind to one of the answers to the declarative; in the former case, the particle *ne* is optional, and in the latter case, it is obligatory.

4.2 *Association with the particle ne in alternative questions*

The association with the particle *ne* in alternative questions differs between A-not-A questions and *wh*-questions and other interrogatives. In nonrhetorical use, the particle *ne* appears at the end of interrogatives and marks the contrast between cells created by the interrogative meaning.[5] By contrast, the particle *ne* is not limited to the sentence-final position and can appear at each end of the disjuncts. Accordingly, I need to explain the multiple occurrences of the particle. In this section, I discuss the structure of alternative questions and then account for the multiple occurrences of the particle *ne*.

4.2.1 Structure of alternative questions

Shao (1994) argues that alternative questions are similar to A-not-A questions in that both consist of positive and negative clauses and form polar questions, as shown in (26a–b). According to his analysis, A-not-A questions are derived from alternative questions by deleting the connective *haishi*.

(26) a. *Daodi   kao   ta   haishi   bu   kao   ta   ?*
       at-all   test   3SG   or   NEG   test   3SG
       'Do we test him or not at all?'
    b. *Daodi   kao   bu   kao   ta   ?*
       at-all   test   NEG   test   3SG
       'Do we test him or not at all?'

In contrast with Shao (1994), Huang (1991) and Huang *et al.* (2009:250–260) argue that A-not-A questions are not derived from alternative questions. They argue that an alternative question is a conjunction of two clauses, and an A-not-A question is formed via the reduplication of the verb. Moreover, the two constructions have different question operators: in alternative questions, the interrogative conjunction *haishi* (or) is a question operator and coordinates clauses, and in A-not-A questions, an overt A-not-A operator is assumed, and it reduplicates the verb to form an A-not-A form.

    Huang (1991) presents four pieces of evidence to support the claim. The first piece of evidence is from the behavior of prepositions: a preposition cannot form an alternative question, whereas it can form an A-not-A question, as shown in the contrast between (27a) and (27b). Prepositions in Mandarin Chinese originate from verbs and are not fully grammaticalized as prepositions. On the one hand, they preserve verbal characteristics, such as reduplication; on the other hand, they have lost the ability to form a clause. The dual status of the preposition is reflected in the different acceptability between prepositional alternative questions and prepositional A-not-A questions. The evidence that supports alternative questions consists of a coordination of two clauses, and A-not-A questions are formed by an A-not-A operator.

(27) a. **Ni   gen   haishi   bu   gen   ta   shuo-hua?*
       you   with   or   neg   with   him   speak-story
       'Do you talk with him?'
    b. *Ni   gen   bu   gen   ta   shuo-hua?*
       you   with   NEG   with   him   speak-story
       'Do you talk with him?'

    The second piece of evidence is from the form of verbs. When a verb consists of more than one syllable, either the first syllable or the full form of the verb is reduplicated in A-not-A questions, whereas only the full form is reduplicated in alternative questions. Huang (1991) and Huang *et al.* (2009)

argue that the reduplication by A-not-A operator is a morphological process, and coordinating two clauses is a syntactic process, leading to the different acceptability between (28a) and (28b).

(28) a. *Ni   xi   haishi   bu   xihuan   zheben   shu?
        you like or   NEG like   this   book
        'Do you like this book?'
    b. Ni   xi   bu   xihuan   zheben   shu?
        you like NEG like   this   book
        'Do you like this book?'

The third piece of evidence is on the extraction of the interrogative feature from inside the subject NP. Although both alternative questions and A-not-A questions can be embedded into the subject positions, the alternative question can extend its scope over the whole clause, and the A-not-A question cannot, as shown in the contrast between (29a) and (29b). If the connective *haishi* is assumed to have an interrogative feature, it can move out of the subject clause and include the whole sentence as its scope. By contrast, an A-not-A operator cannot move out of the subject clause and fail to extend its scope to the whole sentence. The difference is caused by the difference in interrogative operators: the interrogative connective *haishi* can undergo covert movement across the boundary, whereas A-not-A operator cannot, because it would result in a covert movement of a covert operator.

(29) a. *[Wo   qu   Meiguo   haishi   bu   qu   Meiguo]   hao?*
        I   go   USA   or   NEG   go   USA   good
        'Which is better, going to USA or not?'
    b. *[Wo   qu   bu   qu   Meiguo]   hao?*
        I   go   NEG   go   USA   good
        'Which is better, going to USA or not?'

Huang (1991) and Huang *et al.* (2009) conclude that alternative questions are derived from two clauses combined by the interrogative connective *haishi*, whereas A-not-A questions are derived by the reduplication of the verbs, caused by the A-not-A operator.

Based on their analysis, I assume that an alternative question has two clauses, and an A-not-A question has one clause. The position of the particle *ne* also supports that the structure of the two constructions differs. The particle *ne* can appear at each end of disjuncts in alternative questions, but its appearance is limited to the end of the clause in the case of A-not-A questions, as shown in (30a–b).

(30) a. *Daodi   kao   ta   ne   haishi   bu   kao   ta   ne?*
        at-all   test 3sg ne   or   neg test 3sg ne
        'Do we test him or not at all?'

b.	*Daodi*	*kao*	(**ne*)	*bu*	*kao*	*ta*	*ne?*
	at-all	test	ne	neg	test	3sg	ne

'Do we test him or not at all?'

4.2.2 *Semantics of alternative questions*

Structurally, the multiple occurrences of the particle do not cause problems. Semantically, they cause a problem when applying definition (22). First, the multiple occurrences of the particle *ne* indicate that there is more than one contrast. In the case of (30a), the first alternative is a positive proposition, and the second alternative is a negative proposition; thus, the two alternatives are exclusive from each other. Hence, the particle *ne* marks the contrast twice even though there is only one partition in the information state: a set of worlds in which the positive proposition is true, and a set of worlds in which the negative proposition is true. Furthermore, if the particle *ne* is allowed to mark one and the same partition as contrastive multiple time, as many particles as the speaker desires can be added to a sentence. Nonetheless, one particle *ne* is attached to one clause, forbidding the duplication of the particle, such as *ne-ne*.

Second, what is contrasted in an alternative question cannot be predicted by the semantics proposed in 4.1. Disjuncts in an alternative question are not always exclusive of each other; thus, determining which partition the particle *ne* marks is difficult. Example (31) accompanies one occurrence of the particle *ne*. Determining which partition the particle marks is difficult because the two disjuncts have independent truth values:

(31) *Daodi kao ni haishi kao ta ne?*
　　 at-all test 2SG or test 3SG NE
　　 'Do we test you or test him at all?'

Example (31) divides the information state into four parts (Figure 4.5): we test you and test him, we test you and don't test him, we don't test you and test him, and we do not test you and do not test him.

We test you. We test him.	We test you. We don't test him.
We don't test you. We test him.	We don't test you. We don't test him.

Figure 4.5 The denotation of (31).

We test you. We test him.	We test you. We don't test him.
We don't test you. We test him.	We don't test you. We don't test him.

Figure 4.6 The denotation of the first clause of (31).

We test you. We test him.	We test you. We don't test him.
We don't test you. We test him.	We don't test you. We don't test him.

Figure 4.7 The denotation of the second clause of (31).

Although this partition looks like the one describing a *wh*-question, there is a crucial difference: although a *wh*-question divides the information state without any overlap, an alternative question divides the information state with an overlap. The overlapped parts are shown in Figures 4.6 and 4.7.

The first alternative, *we test you*, divides the set of possible worlds into a set of worlds in which we test you and a set of worlds in which we do not test you, ignoring the distinction between we test him and we do not test him. The second alternative, *we test him*, divides the set of possible worlds into a set of worlds in which we test him and a set of worlds in which we do not test him, ignoring the distinction between we test you and we do not test you. Thus, the partition imposed by the first disjunct differs from that imposed by the second disjunct. Hence, determining which partition the particle *ne* marks is impossible.

If the particle *ne* occurs multiple times, as shown in (32), it is more difficult to determine which partition the particle is associated. One method to solve the problem might be limiting the particle's scope to the clause to which it is attached. In this case, the particle marks the contrast between the proposition described by the clause and its negative counterpart, contradicting the native speakers' intuition that the two disjuncts are contrasted with each other.

(32) *Daodi   kao   ni   ne   haishi   kao   ta   ne?*
     at-all   test   2SG   NE   or   test   3SG   NE
     'Do we test you or test him at all?'

To solve these problems, I propose that the particle *ne* marks alternatives in order, from the first clause to the second clause. The marking is conducted dynamically in that the two clauses are interpreted successively, as in the file-change semantics proposed by Heim (1983). Each disjunct of an alternative question creates one information state, piled up on the stack of information states. Such a combination of dynamic semantics and partition semantics was proposed by Isaacs and Rawlins (2008). I briefly explain their analysis as follows.

Isaacs and Rawlins (2008) analyze conditional questions such as, "If Alfonso comes to the party, will Joanna leave?" by combining the dynamic semantics for conditionals with the partition semantics for questions. Conditional questions are problematic in that the answers to them are not limited to *yes* and *no*. For example, the addressee of the question can utter "Alfonso isn't coming" as an answer to the conditional question. Denying the content of the antecedent also counts as an answer to the conditional question. The third type of answer dispels the issue raised by the antecedent. To account for the third type of answer, they propose a three-step analysis to analyze conditional questions. First, a temporary copy of the current context is created. Second, the temporary copy is updated with the propositional content of the antecedent. Finally, the question in the consequent is imposed on the temporary context. This three-step analysis is based on the stack-based model of contexts that Kaufmann (2000) proposes.

In the stack-based model of contexts, an utterance is interpreted relative to a macro-context, an ordered pair of contexts. Two operations are applied to a given macro-context: assertion and inquisition. An *assertion* updates the macro-context to create a new context that supports the content of the assertion. The updated macro-context is placed on the top of the stack, supplying a new macro-context for the coming assertion. An *inquisition* divides the top member of the macro-context into answers. These two operations are applied to interpret conditional questions: the antecedent operates an assertion, and the consequent operates an inquisition. They argue that the denial of the antecedent removes the temporary context created by the antecedent, recovering the context before the conditional question is uttered. Hence, this type of answer counts as an answer to conditional questions.

I apply the three-step analysis of conditional questions to alternative questions in Mandarin Chinese. As I mentioned at the beginning of this section, an alternative question in Mandarin Chinese is a coordination of two clauses. Each clause updates the macro-context in order. In the following, s, s', s"∈macro-context: the context *s* is the original context, the context *s'* is the context updated by the propositional content of the antecedent, and *s"* is the context updated by the propositional content of the consequent. The push operator adds the context *s'* on the top of the stack of contexts at stage 1; next, the disjunctive connection *haishi* plays the role of pop operator and removes it at stage 2. At stage 3, the push operator adds the context *s"* on the top of the stack. From stage 4 on, the process of pop-and-push is repeated until the answer is given by the addressee of the question.

(32) Stage 1:
    Daodi   kao   ni
    at-all   test   2SG
    'we test you'
    $s + [\text{ASSERT (we test you)}] = s'$
    $\text{push}(<s, <>>, s'>) = <s', <s, <>>>$
Stage 2:
    haishi
    or
    $\text{pop}(<s', <s, <>>>) = <s, <>>>$
Stage 3:
    kao   ta ?
    test   3SG
    'test him'
    $s + [\text{ASSERT (we test him)}] = s''$
    $\text{push}(<s, <>>, s''>) = <s'', <s, <>>>$
Stage 4:
    (haishi)
    or
    $\text{pop}(<s'', <s, <>>>) = <s, <>>>$
Stage 5:
    kao   ni
    test   2SG
    'we test you'
    $s + [\text{ASSERT (we test you)}] = s'$
    $\text{push}(<s, <>>, s'>) = <s', <s, <>>>$
    . . .
Stage *n*:
    . . .

Assuming that the state of information changes, as shown in (32), the particle *ne* marks the contrast at states 1 and 3. When the particle *ne* marks the antecedent at state 1, there is a proposition in contrast with it in the information state, as shown in (33b); when it marks the consequent at state 3, there is a proposition in contrast with it in the information state, as shown in (33d).

(33) a. *Daodi kao ni   ne*
      at-all   test 2SG   NE
      'Do we test you?'
  b. $\exists q \in s \, [\text{we-test-you} \wedge f(\text{we-test-you}) = p \wedge \{w: \text{we-test-you}(w)=1\} \cap \{w: q(w)=1\}=\emptyset]$
  c. *haishi kao ta   ne?*
      or   test 3SG NE
      'or do we test him?'
  d. $\exists q \in s \, [\text{we-test-him} \wedge f(\text{we-test-him}) = p \wedge \{w: \text{we-test-him}(w)=1\} \cap \{w: q(w)=1\}=\emptyset]$

The contrast between the two disjuncts is induced because the contrasted proposition is included in the recovered state of the information state. In (32), state 1 is the recovered state at state 3, state 3 is the recovered state at state 5, and the change in states continues until the state is defined to one by the answer.

4.3   Function of the particle ne in declaratives

Now, I examine the function of the particle *ne* in declaratives. A declarative denotes a proposition; thus, there is no partition in the information state that the particle *ne* can mark. In this section, I show that the definition of the particle *ne* in rhetorical questions can be applied to the particle *ne* in declaratives.

Declaratives do not partition the information state. Instead, they restrict the current information state to the state that supports the proposition described by the declarative. Uttering a declarative (assertion) reduces the context set, provided that there are no objections from the other participants in the conversation (Stalnaker 1978). The particle *ne* at the end of a declarative thus cannot find cells to contrast.

As I mentioned in Section 3.1, the particle *ne* at the end of a declarative is reported to indicate that the speaker acknowledges the current context, including the listener's state of knowledge. For example, Li and Thompson (1981) argue that the particle *ne* indicates the declarative is a response to the listener's expectation, and Zhou (2008, 2009) argues that the particle *ne* requires the listener to exploit the information found in the context. In these explanations, the particle *ne* always triggers a proposition found in the common ground. For instance, example (34), from dialogue (24), asserts the proposition "we aren't open yet," contrasted with the listener's expectation, such as "the restaurant is open." Although the listener's expectation is merely resumed by the speaker, the speaker contrasts his/her utterance with what s/he assumes the listener would expect. What the particle *ne* at the end of declaratives marks is the contrast between the two propositions.

(34) a. *Yingye   shijian   mei   dao   ne.*
       open   hour   NEG   arrive   NE
       'We aren't open yet.'
   b. {w: we-aren't-open(w)=1} vs. {w: we-are-open(w)=1}

The third line of dialogue (35) also shows that the man's assertion is contrasted with the proposition triggered by the preceding utterance. The man's utterance *wo mangzhe gan lunwen ne* (I'm writing a paper) both asserts that he is writing a paper and denies the proposition that he is in love with someone. The latter proposition is introduced by the woman's question *shi-bu-shi tan lian'ai le* (Are you in love with someone?). Because the question imposes a partition on the information state, both the proposition *you are in love with someone* and the proposition *you aren't in love with someone* are available in the current information state. The speaker of line 3 resorts to the propositions to show the contrast with his utterance.

(35) man: *Wo   yijing   lianxu   wutian   meiyou   shui   guo   yige*
           1SG   already   serial   five-days   NEG   sleep   EXP   one
           zhengjiao   le
           good-sleep   CRS
           'I haven't slept five days.'

woman: *Guaibude   ni   lianse   dou   hei   le.   Mang   shenme*
        no-wonder   you   face   all   black   CRS   busy   what
        ne?
        NE
        'No wonder you look pale. Why are you busy? Are you in love with someone?'

man: *Bie   kai   wanxiao   le,   wo   mang   zhe   gan*
      don't   open   joke   CRS   1SG   busy   DUR   rush
      lunwen   ne.
      paper   NE
      'No joking. I'm busy writing a paper.'

I suggest applying the semantics of the particle *ne* for rhetorical questions to the particle *ne* at the end of declaratives. As I proposed in 4.1, the semantics of the particle *ne* in rhetorical questions differs from that in other interrogatives. In nonrhetorical questions, the particle *ne* marks the contrast among the propositions found in the current information state; in other words, it emphasizes the partition imposed by the interrogative meaning. By contrast, the particle *ne* in rhetorical questions marks the contrast between the proposition from the current information state and that from the recovered information state. The semantics of the particle *ne* at the end of a declarative is defined similarly to that at the end of rhetorical questions. I modify definition (25) such that the particle *ne* operates on rhetorical questions and declaratives, as shown in (36).

(36) Semantics of *ne* for rhetorical questions and declaratives
$[\![ne]\!] = \lambda X.\exists q \in s \; [f(X) = p \wedge \{w:p(w) = 1\} \cap \{w:q(w) = 1\} = \emptyset]$
($X \in D_{<s,<s,t>>}$ or $D_{<s,t>}$, $p,q \in D_{<s,t>}$, $w \in W$, f = a function that chooses a proposition, s = the recovered information state)

Now, the variable *X* can be either of type <s,<s,t>> or of type <s,t>. Function *f* is vacuous if *X* is of type <s,t>, because *X* has only one proposition.

In this section, I have proposed a unified analysis of the particle *ne* for rhetorical questions and declaratives. Rhetorical questions and declaratives differ in the current information state: the former is partitioned, and the latter is not. However, the particle *ne* functions similarly: it marks the contrast between the proposition in the current information state and the proposition in the recovered information state.

4.4   *Function of* ne *attached to noun phrases*

I have proposed definitions of the particle *ne* for interrogatives, rhetorical questions, and declaratives. In all these cases, the particle *ne* appears at the end of a clause. However, as I mentioned in 3.1, the particle *ne* is also attached to noun phrases. As I have shown thus far, the particle operates on type <s, <s, t>> and type <s, t>, not on type e or <e,t>. In this chapter, I distinguish the particle attached to the nominal constituents from the particle following clauses. The particle *ne* following nominals marks topic, not contrast.

On two occasions, the particle *ne* is attached to nominals: the particle is attached to the first nominal constituent of the sentence, as shown in (37), and the particle is attached to a nominal constituent with no predicate followed, as shown in (38). The former indicates that the nominal constituent is the topic of the sentence. By contrast, the latter forms an interrogative, asking whereabouts or the condition of the object denoted by the nominal. In this chapter, I call the former a topical use and the latter an interrogative use.

(37) *Baba   ne,   bu   hui   zuo   fan.*
      father   ne   neg   can   do   meal
      'As for dad, he can't cook.'

(38) *Baba   ne?*
      father   ne
      'Where's dad?'/'What about dad?'

The topical use of the particle *ne* is reported by Fang (1994). Unlike Constant's (2014) proposal, the topic marked with the particle *ne* is not contrastive. I show the contrast between the true CT marker *ke* and the particle *ne* in examples (39) and (40).

(39) a.   *Wo   keyi   daying   ni,   Baba   ke   bu   ken.*
          I   can   agree   you   father   KE   NEG   agree
          'I can agree with you, but dad won't agree.'
     b.   *Wo   keyi   daying   ni,   Baba   ne   bu   ken.*
          I   can   agree   you   father   NE   NEG   agree
          'I can agree with you. As for dad, he won't agree.'

(40) a.   *Lisi   yuchun,   Zhangsan   ke   bu   yuchun.*
          Lisi   fool   Zhangsan   ke   neg   fool
          'Lisi is a fool, but Zhangsan isn't a fool.'
     b.   *Lisi   yuchun,   Zhangsan   ne   bu   yuchun.*
          Lisi   fool   Zhangsan   ne   neg   fool
          'Lisi is a fool. As for Zhangsan, he isn't a fool.'

In example (39a), the CT marker *ke* appears in the postcedent, and the clause is in contrast with the antecedent. When we replace the CT marker with the particle *ne*, as shown in (39b), the effect of contrast is reduced, if not completely lost. Similarly, the effect of contrast brought about by the CT marker in example (40a) is reduced if the CT marker is replaced with the particle *ne*. The contrastiveness observed in (13), which I reproduce in (41), is caused by the coordination of two clauses that have the same structure but not caused by the particle *ne*.

(41) *Mama   hen   wan   cai   hui-lai.   Baba   ne   gancui   bu*
     mother   very   late   finally   come-back   father   ne   simply   neg
     hui-lai.
     come-back
     'Mother came back very late. Father simply didn't come back.'

The interrogative use of the particle *ne*, which is also called a truncated question, is derived from the topical use of the particle. Li (2016) proposes that the interrogative force of truncated questions is due to the deleted *wh*-phrase in the predicate. According to his analysis, the CT moves to the spec of TopP, leaving the *wh*-phrase inside TP. Then, the TP is deleted.

(42) A-i: *Libai   he   le   shenme?   B: Hongjiu.*
            Libai   drink   asp   what   red-wine
     A-ii: *Dufu ne?*
     Dufu   ne
     'What did Libai drink? – Red wine. What about Dufu?'

(43) $[_{CP2}$ Q $[_{CP1}$ ~ $[_{TopP}$ [Dufu]$_{F1}$ $[_{Top'}$ ne $[_{TP}$ t_1 ~~drank what~~ $]]]]]$

His analysis does not require the particle *ne* to be a CT marker but only requires it to be a topic marker. Hence, the topical and interrogative usage are accounted for based on the assumption that the particle *ne* attached to a nominal constituent marks topic.

5   Conclusion

In this chapter, I have defined the notion of contrast and discussed the research on the Chinese particle *ne*. I have shown that various explanations are proposed for this particle: some studies are detailed descriptions of the particle, and others propose a unified theory. I have argued that the unified theory cannot cover all the usages of the particle *ne*, and I have proposed two groups for the particle *ne*: one appears at the end of a clause, and the other is attached to the nominals. Third, I have proposed that the particle *ne* marks a contrast among propositions in the information state and have argued that the contrasted propositions are found in either the interrogative meaning or the contexts. Finally, I have shown that the particle *ne* attached to nominals marks topic of the sentence, and the topical use evolves the interrogative use of the particle.

Abbreviations

1	first person	NEG	negator
2	second person	NMLZ	nominalizer
3	third person	NOM	nominative
ACC	accusative	OBJ	object marker
CRS	currently relevant state	PAST	past
CT	contrastive topic	PFV	perfective aspect
DEC	declarative	PL	plural
DUR	durative	PRTCL	particle
EXP	experiential	Q	question
GEN	genitive	RED	reduplication
LOC	locative	REL	relativizer
NE	contrast	SG	singular

Notes

1 **Acknowledgements:** This work was supported by JSPS KAKENHI Grant Number 16K02620 and Tokyo University of Foreign Studies, ILCAA Joint Research Project *Semantics of Discourse Particles in East and Southeast Asian Language*, PI: E. Mc-Cready (April 2015 – March 2018). Special thanks to the members of ILCAA Joint Research and Chungmin Lee for the useful discussion and advice.
2 Examples (3)–(7) are excerpted from the TV drama *Tian jiaoshou jia de ershibage baomu (Twenty-eight housekeepers at Professor Tian's home)*.
3 This example might sound strange because the car in this sentence is animated. The animation occurs because the sentence is uttered by a mother to her child to ask where his toy car is.
4 This dialogue is excerpted from *Tian jiaoshou jia de ershibage baomu (Twenty-eight housekeepers at Professor Tian's home)*. All stage directions are added by the author.
5 In the case of polar questions formed by the particle *ma* (*ma*-interrogatives), the particle *ne* cannot appear at the end of the clause. Ito (2018b) discusses the incompatibility of these particles from the view of illocutionary force.

References

Bolinger, Dwight L.M. 1965. *Forms of English: Accent, morpheme, order.* Harvard University Press.

Büring, Daniel. 2003. On D-trees, beans, and B-accents. *Linguistics and Philosophy* 26(5). 511–545.

Cao, Feng-fu. 1977. *A functional study of topic in Chinese: The first step toward discourse analysis.* University of Southern California.

Chu, Chauncey C. 2006. A contrastive approach to discourse particles: A case study of the Mandarin UFP Ne. *Journal of Foreign Languages* 3. 7–29.

Constant, Noah. 2014. *Contrastive Topic: Meanings and Realizations.* Ph.D. thesis, University of Massachusetts.

Dekker, Paul, Maria Aloni & Alastair Butler. 2007. The semantics and pragmatics of questions. In Maria Aloni, Alastair Butler & Paul Dekker (eds.), *Questions in Dynamic Semantics*, 1–40. Leiden: BRILL.

Fang, Mei. 1994. Beijinghua ju zhong yuqici de gongneng yanjiu [A study on the function of clause-internal particle in Mandarin Chinese conversation]. *Zhongguo Yuwen* 1994(2).

Guo, Rui. 2000. Ma-wenjude quexindu he huida fangshi [On certainty and answers of ma-questions]. *Shijie Hanyu Jiaoxue* 2. 13–24.

Hamblin, Charles L. 1973. Questions in Montague English. *Foundations of Language* 10(1). 41–53.

Heim, Irene. 1983. File change semantics and the familiarity theory of definiteness. In *Meaning, use and the interpretation of language*, 164–190. Berlin: Walter de Gruyter.

Huang, C.T. James. 1991. Modularity and Chinese A-not-A questions. In C. Georgopoulos & Roberta Ishihara (eds.), *Interdisciplinary approaches to language*, 305–332. Amsterdam: Kluwer Academic Publishers.

Huang, C.T. James, Yen-hui A. Li & Yafei Li. 2009. *The syntax of Chinese*. Cambridge: Cambridge University Press.

Isaacs, James & Kyle Rawlins. 2008. Conditional questions. *Journal of Semantics* 25(3). 269–319.

Ito, Satomi. 2018a. Gimonbun chuuno gokijosi "ne" no kinoo: gimon ennzannshi ka taihi wadai maakaa ka o megutte [On the function of the sentence-final particle "ne": is it a question marker or a contrastive topic marker?]. *Journal of Chinese Language and Culture* 7. 20–46.

Ito, Satomi. 2018b. Danwakinoo-kara miru Chuugoku-ni okeru bunmatsujoshi "ma" to "ne" no hikaku [Comparing the sentence-final particle "ma" and "ne" from the viewpoint of discourse function]. *Bulletin of the Sinological Society Ochanmizu University* 37. 17–33.

Jackendoff, Ray S. 1972. *Semantic interpretation in generative grammar*. Cambridge, MA: MIT Press.

Jin, Li-Xin. 1996. Guanyu yiwenju zhong de "ne" [On the particle *ne* in interrogatives]. *Yuyan Jiaoxue yu Yanjiu* 1994(4). 43–49.

Kang, Liang-Fang. 2007. Yiwenju jumo yuqizhuci ne tanxi [An analysis on the sentence-final particle ne at the end of interrogatives]. *Chongqing Wenlixueyuan Xuebao (Shehui kexue ban)* 2007(6). 24–29.

Karttunen, Lauri. 1977. Syntax and semantics of questions. *Linguistics and Philosophy* 1(1). 3–44.

Kaufmann, Stefan. 2000. Dynamic context management. In M. Faller, S. Kaufmann, & M. Pauly (eds.) *Formalizing the dynamics of information*, 171–187. Stanford, CA: CSLI Publishing.

Kim, Soohee, Emily Curtis & Cho Haewon. 2017. *Korean grammar: The complete guide to speaking Korean naturally*. North Clarendon, VT: Tuttle Publishing.

Kimura, Hideki & Takuro Moriyama. 1992. Kikite joho hairyo to bunmatu keishiki [The hearer's consideration on the information and the sentence-final forms]. In Yasunori Okochi (ed.), *Nihongo to Chugokugo no taisho kenkyu [Essays on the contrastive analysis of Japanese and Chinese]*. Tokyo: Kurosiho Shuppan.

Lee, Chungmin. 2003. Contrastive topic and/or contrastive focus. *Japanese/Korean Linguistics* 12. 352–364.

Lee, Chungmin. 2017. Contrastive topic, contrastive focus, alternatives, and scalar implicatures. In Chungmin Lee et al. (eds.), *Contrastiveness in information structure, alternatives and scalar implicatures*, 3–21. Amsterdam: Springer.

Li, Charles N. & Sandra A. Thompson. 1981. *Mandarin Chinese: A functional reference grammar*. Berkeley, CA: University of California Press.

Li, Haoze. 2016. Fragment questions: Deleting question items. *NELS* 46. 279–292.

Li, Jin-Xi. 1924. *Xinzhu guoyu wenfa [Newly-published Chinese grammar]*. Beijing: Shangwu Yinshuguan.

Liu, Yue-Hua, Wen-wu Pan & Hua Gu. 2002. *Shiyong Xiandai Hanyu Yufa (Chongding ben) [Practical contemporary Chinese grammar (The second edition)]*. Beijing: Shangwu Yinshuguan.

Lu, Jian-Ming. 1982. You "fei yiwen xingshi + ne" zaocheng de yiwenju [Interrogatives which are derived from "non-interrogative form + ne"]. *Zhongguo Yuwen* 1982(6). 435–438.

Shao, Jing-Min. 1989. Yuqici "ne" zai yiwenju zhong de zuoyong [The function of the sentence-final particle *ne* in interrogatives]. *Zhongguo Yuwen* 1989(3). 170–175.

Shao, Jing-Min. 1994. Xaindai hanyu xuanzewen yanjiu [A study on alternative questions in contemporary Chinese]. *Yuyan jiaoxue yu yanjiu* 1994(2). 49–67.

Stalnaker, Robert C. 1978. Assertion. In Peter Cole (ed.), *Pragmatics*, 315–332. New York: Academic Press.

Wang, Li. 1943. *Zhongguo xiandai yufa [Chinese contemporary grammar]*. Beijing: Shangwu Yinshuguan.

Xu, Jing-Ning. 2008. *Xiandai hanyu huayu qingtai yanjiu [A study on the conversational mood in contemporary Chinese]*. Beijing: Kunlun Chubanshe.

Yabushita, Katsuhiko. 2017. Partition semantics and pragmatics of contrastive topic. In Chungmin Lee et al. (eds.), *Contrastiveness in information structure, alternatives and scalar implicatures*, 23–45. Amsterdam: Springer.

Yuan, Yu-Lin. 1993. Zhengfanwenju ji xiangguande leixingxue canxiang [A-not-A questions and their related typological parameters]. *Zhongguo yuwen* 2. 103–112.

Zhou, Yan-Hong. 2008. Chugokugo no gokijosi "ne" no honshitsutekina imi [On the basic meaning of the sentence-final particle ne in Mandarin Chinese]. *Chugokugo Kyoiku* 6. 130–153.

Zhou, Yan-Hong. 2009. *Chugokugo no gokijosi "ne" [The Sentence-Final Particle ne in Mandarin Chinese]*. Ph.D thesis, Osaka University.

Zhu, De-Xi. 1981. *Yufa jiangyi [A note on grammar]*. Beijing: Shangwu Yinshuguan.

5 Cantonese question particles

Yurie Hara

1 Introduction[1]

Cantonese has a number of constructions that express a polar question, as in (1) and (2).[2] Examples in (1) are taken from Lam (2014b, 2014a). All of them encode a polar question meaning, but they differ in terms of the context's bias/neutrality. (1a), a so-called A-NOT-A question, can only be asked in a neutral context. (1b), with a sentence-final particle HO2, is used when the speaker is biased toward the positive answer, while (1c), with ME1, is asked when the speaker has a bias toward the negative answer.[3]

(1) a. *zi3ming4 jau5 mou5 fu6ceot1 gwo3 si4gaan3 aa3?*
   Jimmy have not.have devote ASP time PRT
   'Has Jimmy spent time (on the project), or not?' (A-NOT-A Q)

   b. *zi3ming4 jau5 fu6ceot1 gwo3 si4gaan3 gaa3 ho2?*
   Jimmy have devote ASP time PRT HO2
   'Jimmy has spent time (on the project), hasn't he?' (HO2 Q)

   c. *zi3ming4 jau5 fu6ceot1 gwo3 si4gaan3 me1?*
   Jimmy have devote ASP time ME
   'Jimmy hasn't spent time (on the project), has he?' (ME1 Q)

In contrast, an AA4 question like (2), which is simply marked with a final question particle AA4, is not as restricted. It can be used in both neutral and biased contexts.[4]

(2) *zi3ming4 jau5 fu6ceot1 gwo3 si4gaan3 aa4?*
   Jimmy have devote ASP time AA4
   'Has Jimmy spent time (on the project)?' (AA4 Q)

The goal of this chapter is to provide a semantic analysis that derives each interpretation. Lam (2014a) argues that HO2 and ME1 questions are complex speech acts of questioning and asserting, while A-NOT-A questions are simple acts of questioning. Lam's (2014a) account of A-NOT-A questions fails to explain why they are more restricted than AA4 questions, which can be used

DOI: 10.4324/9781351057837-6

in both biased and neutral contexts. Incidentally, Yuan and Hara (2013); Yuan (2015) claim that Mandarin A-NOT-A questions are also complex speech acts of questioning and asserting, where the content of the assertion is a tautology, '*p* or not *p*.' Yuan and Hara (2013) argue that the assertion of '*p* or not *p*,' in effect, indicates the ignorance of the speaker, hence the neutrality requirement. However, Yuan and Hara's analysis also poses a conceptual problem because in truth-conditional semantics, an assertion of '*p* or not *p*' is equivalent to that of '*q* or not *q*.' This chapter thus offers a solution to this problem in the framework of inquisitive semantics (Groenendijk & Roelofsen 2009). Contra Lam (2014a), the semantics of an A-NOT-A question is also multi-dimensional in that it has a question meaning as well as a secondary assertion meaning, which indicates lack of 'anticipation of prior expectation-rejection shift.' The chapter also reports one force-choice experiment and one naturalness rating experiment which jointly support the proposal.

2 Lam (2014a) on (non-)biased questions

Lam (2014a) analyzes the three interrogative constructions in (1) and proposes that an A-NOT-A question denotes a simple speech act of questioning, while ME1 and HO2 questions are complex speech acts of questioning and asserting.

Lam (2014a) provides convincing pieces of evidence supporting that A-NOT-A questions are neutral, HO2 questions have positive bias, and ME1 questions have negative bias.

First, only A-NOT-A questions can be used in neutral contexts, as in (3). Examples (3)–(6) are adapted from Lam (2014a).

(3) Scenario: Jimmy is asked to take a seat in an interrogation room of a police station. A police officer asked for Jimmy's name and then says this.

    a. *nei5 hai6 m4 hai6 mei5gwok3 jan4?*
       'Are you American?'   (A-not-A)
    b. #*nei5 hai6 mei5gwok3 jan4 ho2?*
       'You are American, right?'   (HO2)
    c. #*nei5 hai6 mei5gwok3 jan4 me1?*
       'You aren't American, are you?'   (ME1)

Second, A-NOT-A questions cannot be responded by 'You are right' (Asher & Reese 2005).

(4) a: *gam1 go3 ji6jyut6 jau5 mou5 jaa6gau2 hou6?*
       'Is there a 29th this February?'   (A-NOT-A)
    b: #*nei5 aam1, nei5 aam1. jau5/mou5*
       2SG   right, 2SG right not.have/have
       'You are right, you are right. There is(n't).'

In contrast to an HO2 question, the responder B can say, 'You are right,' to agree with the positive answer.

(5) a: *gam1 go3 ji6jyut jau5 jaa6gau2 hou6 ho2?*
        'There is a 29th this February, isn't there?'   (HO2)
     b: *nei5 aam1, nei5 aam1.* ✓ *jau5/*mou5*
        'You are right, you are right. There ✓is/*isn't.'

Similarly to an ME1 question, the responder B can say, 'You are right,' to agree with the negative answer.

(6)   a: *gam1 go3 ji6jyut jau5 jaa6gau2 hou6 me1?*
        'There isn't a 29th this February, is there?'   (ME1)
      b: *nei5 aam1, nei5 aam1.* *jau5/✓ mou5*
        'You are right, you are right. There *is/✓isn't.'

Based on these data,[5] Lam (2014a) concludes that A-NOT-A questions are pure questions in that they are simple speech acts of questioning, thus can be used only when the context is neutral. On the other hand, HO2 questions are complex speech acts of questioning and assertion of p, while ME1 questions are also complex speech acts of questioning and assertion of $\neg p$.[6] Lam's analysis is summarized in Table 5.1.

Table 5.1 Lam's analysis of Cantonese polar questions

Syntax	Observation	Analysis
A-NOT-A	neutral	QUEST(p)
HO2	p bias	QUEST(p)&ASSERT(p)
ME1	$\neg p$ bias	QUEST(p)&ASSERT($\neg p$)

I agree with Lam (2014a) in that A-NOT-A questions are only used in neutral contexts, but contra Lam (2014a), I claim that A-NOT-A questions also have multi-dimensional semantics. To see this, let us compare A-NOT-A questions with another polar question, namely, AA4 questions. First, AA4 questions are similar to A-not-A questions in that they are used in neutral contexts, as in (7).

(7) a. Scenario: Jimmy is asked to take a seat in an interrogation room of a police station.
         A police officer asked for Jimmy's name and then says this.
     b. *nei5 hai6 mei5gwok3 jan4 aa4?*
         'Are you American?'   (AA4)

Also, just like A-NOT-A questions, AA4 questions cannot be responded by 'You're right,' suggesting that AA4 questions are true questions without assertive contents.

(8) a: *gam1 go3 ji6jyut6 jau5 jaa6gau2 hou6 aa4?*
     'Is there a 29th this February?'   (AA4)
   b: *#nei5 aam1, nei5 aam1. jau5/mou5*
     'You are right, you are right. There is(n't).'

However, the parallel breaks down with respect to the following situation. In (9), A first asserted, 'There is a 29th this February!' (*p*). Thus, when B responds, the context is biased toward *p* (see Gunlogson 2003). In this biased context, an A-NOT-A question is odd, while an AA4 question is good:

(9) a: *gam1 go3 ji6jyut6 jau5 jaa6gau2 hou6 aa3!*
     'There is a 29th this February!'
  b1: *#zan1 hai2? gam1 go3 ji6jyut6 jau5 mou5 jaa6gau2 hou2?*
     'Really? Is there a 29th this February or not?'   (A-NOT-A)
  b2: *zan1 hai2? gam1 go3 ji6jyut jau5 jaa6gau2 hou6 aa4?*
     'Really? Is there a 29th this February?'   (AA4)

As summarized in Table 5.2, A-NOT-A questions can be used only in neutral contexts, while AA4 questions can be used in both neutral and biased contexts. In other words, an A-NOT-A question explicitly encodes its neutrality requirement in the semantics, while an AA4 question simply performs a question act. Lam's (2014a) analysis fails to account for this contrast. Thus, this chapter claims that A-NOT-A questions perform complex speech acts and AA4 questions perform simple question acts. The next section briefly reviews Yuan and Hara (2013), who make a similar claim for Mandarin polar questions.

Table 5.2 Difference among "neutral" questions

Syntax	Neutral	Biased
A-NOT-A	OK	#
AA4	OK	OK ($\neg p$ bias)

3 Yuan and Hara (2013) and Yuan (2015) on Mandarin A-not-A questions

Yuan and Hara (2013) and Yuan (2015) analyze Mandarin polar questions and argue that MA questions like (10) are simple questions, while A-NOT-A questions like (11) perform questioning and asserting of ignorance at the same time. Mandarin data in this section are taken from Yuan and Hara (2013).

(10) *Lin xihuan Wu ma?*
      Lin like Wu Q
      'Does Lin like Wu?'   (Mandarin MA Q)
(11) *Lin xihuan bu xihuan Wu (ne)?*
      Lin like not like Wu NE
      'Does Lin like or not like Wu?'   (Mandarin A-not-A Q)

Yuan and Hara's analysis is motivated by the following contrast. Just like Cantonese AA4 and A-NOT-A questions, MA questions can be used in both neutral and biased contexts, while A-NOT-A questions cannot be used in biased contexts:

(12) a: *Lin xihuan Wu.*
          Lin like Wu
          'Lin likes Wu.'
      b: ✓Lin xihuan Wu ma?   (MA Q)
          #Lin xihuan bu xihuan Wu (ne)?   (A-NOT-A Q)

According to Yuan and Hara (2014) and Yuan (2015), the Mandarin morpheme MA is a question operator. It takes a proposition p denoted by its sister TP and yields a context change potential (CCP; Heim (1982)), which adds a Hamblin (1958) set $\{p, \neg p\}$ created out of the proposition p onto the question under discussion (QUD) stack (Roberts 1996).[7]

(13) $\llbracket MA \rrbracket = \lambda p \cdot \lambda C \cdot [QUD(C) + \{p, \neg p\}]$

Turning to Mandarin A-NOT-A questions Yuan and Hara (2013) follow Huang (1991) and propose that the surface structure of (11) is derived from a deep structure depicted in (14).

(14)

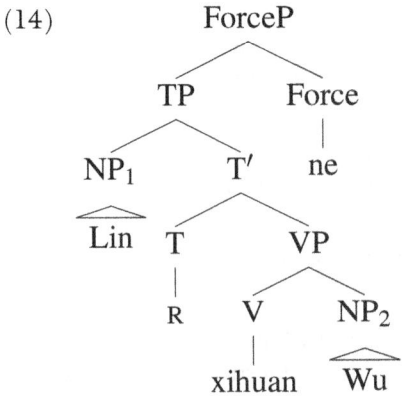

The reduplication feature R defined in (15) creates a Hamblin set; thus, the TP denotes a set of propositions as in (16).

(15) $[\![R]\!] = \lambda P.\lambda x.\{P(x), \neg P(x)\}$

(16) $[\![TP]\!] = [\![R(\text{like.Wu})(\text{Lin})]\!] = \{p, \neg p\}$ p = 'Lin likes Wu'

The particle NE is another question operator which yields a multi-dimensional meaning, as indicated by '×' in (17). On the one hand, it produces a question CCP, which adds the set of propositions S to the QUD stack. On the other hand, it outputs a single proposition by connecting each proposition in S with the disjunction '∨':

(17) $[\![NE]\!] = \lambda S.\lambda C.[\text{QUD}(C) + S] \times \lambda S.\left(r_1 \vee r_2 \vee \ldots \vee r_{|S|} \right) r_i \in S \text{ for all } 1 < i \leqslant |S|$

Furthermore, Yuan and Hara (2013) show that A-NOT-A questions obligatorily end with the low-boundary tone 'L%.' Adopting Bartels's (1997) analysis of English intonation, Yuan and Hara (2013) propose that the L% tone in a Mandarin A-NOT-A question is an intonational morpheme which is paratactically associated with the syntactic structure like (14). Semantically, it denotes an assertion, that is, a CCP which adds a proposition to the Stalnaker (1978) common ground (CG):[8]

(18) $[\![L\%]\!] = \lambda p \cdot \text{ASSERT}(p) = \lambda p \cdot \lambda C.[\text{CG}(C) + p]$

This morpheme is looking for a proposition as its argument. Now, among the two meanings generated by the structure in (14), the primary meaning is already a CCP of questioning; thus, the morpheme $L\%$ can only attach to the secondary meaning, that is, the disjunction $p \vee \neg p$. As a result, the whole A-NOT-A construction with the L% tone expresses a complex speech act, questioning and asserting. Yuan and Hara (2013) claim that this assertion of $p \vee \neg p$ is the source of the neutrality requirement of A-NOT-A questions. $p \vee \neg p$ is a tautology; thus, asserting $p \vee \neg p$ is an uninformative act. Following Gricean principles, the questioner is indicating his or her ignorance toward the issue $p \vee \neg p$. When the context is biased, the speaker cannot be ignorant about the issue $p \vee \neg p$; thus, an A-NOT-A question cannot be use in a biased context.

In short, an MA question is a simple act of questioning, while an A-NOT-A question is a complex act of questioning and asserting, as summarized in Table 5.3. The neutrality meaning is reinforced by the assertion component of the A-NOT-A question. The same explanation could be given to the contrast of Cantonese AA4 and A-NOT-A questions in (9). However, Yuan and Hara's implementation of the neutrality requirement faces a conceptual problem for both Mandarin and Cantonese. That is, in truth-conditional semantics, $p \vee \neg p$ is equivalent to $q \vee \neg q$ since they are both tautologies, thus always true. Similarly, ASSERT$(p \vee \neg p)$ is

Table 5.3 Yuan and Hara's analysis of Mandarin polar questions

Syntax	Observation	Analysis
A-NOT-A	anti-bias	$\text{QUEST}(p)\&\text{ASSERT}(p\vee\neg p)$
MA	neutral	$\text{QUEST}(p)$

equivalent to $\text{ASSERT}(q \vee\neg q)$; hence, it cannot indicate the ignorance toward a particular issue $p \vee\neg p$. In order to solve this problem, this chapter adopts another semantic framework, that is, radical inquisitive semantics.[9]

4   Proposal: inquisitive semantics

In classical truth-conditional semantics, the meaning of a sentence is determined by its truth-condition.

(19) **Truth-condition**: One knows the meaning of a sentence ⇔ one knows under which circumstances the sentence is *true* and under which it is *false*.

(Groenendijk & Roelofsen 2013:2)

In recent work by Groenendijk and his colleagues (Groenendijk & Roelofsen 2009; Ciardelli *et al.* 2013; Ciardelli 2009; Ciardelli & Roelofsen 2011:among others),[10] it is argued that the truth-conditional semantics is not capable of analyzing interrogative sentences. In order to analyze both declarative and interrogative sentences, the new framework, inquisitive semantics, centers on support-conditions:

(20) **Support-condition**: One knows the meaning of a sentence ⇔ one knows which information states *support* the given sentence, and which don't.

(Groenendijk & Roelofsen 2013:2)

Let us see the difference between the two frameworks with figures. Each figure represents an information state σ which contains only four possible worlds. In world 11, for instance, both p and q are true; in world 01, p is false but q is true; and so on. In truth-conditional semantics, both $p\vee\neg p$ and $q\vee\neg q$ are true in all four worlds. Thus, $p\vee\neg p$ and $q\vee\neg q$ cannot be distinguished from one another, as noted earlier. In inquisitive – that is, support-conditional – semantics, on the other hand, the two sentences are distinguished as follows: the information state depicted in Figure 5.1(a) supports $p\vee\neg p$, while the information state depicted in Figure 5.1(b) supports $q\vee\neg q$.

Another important feature of inquisitive semantics is that a polar question $?\varphi$ is defined in terms of disjunction.

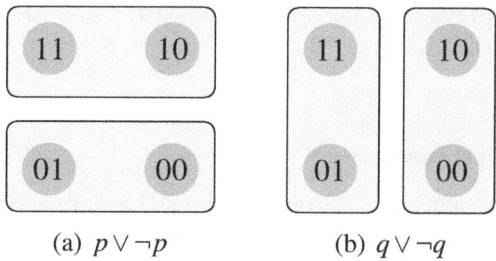

(a) $p \vee \neg p$ (b) $q \vee \neg q$

Figure 5.1 Support for disjunctive sentences.

(21) Questions and support:
A question $?\varphi = \varphi \vee \neg \varphi$ is supported in $\sigma \Leftrightarrow \sigma$ either supports φ or supports $\neg \varphi$.

4.1 Groenendijk (2013) on Dutch biased questions

Groenendijk (2013) analyzes biased questions marked by a stressed particle *toch* in Dutch, which seems to have the same effect as Cantonese HO2 questions. Dutch examples in this section are taken from Groenendijk (2013).

Let us start with a declarative sentence with stressed TOCH, as in (22). The sentence *p*-TOCH conveys a secondary meaning which indicates the speaker's *prior expectation* of $\neg p$:[11]

(22) *Ad is* TOCH *in Amsterdam.*
'Ad is in Amsterdam after all.'
Secondary meaning:
The speaker expected that Ad would not be in Amsterdam.

When TOCH is used in a question, *p*-TOCH?, as in (23), it gives rise to a *current* expectation of *p* 'Ad is in Amsterdam.'

(23) *Ad is in Amsterdam,* TOCH?
'Ad is in Amsterdam, right?'

The interpretation might be clearer with possible answers to (23). If the answer is 'yes,' the prior expectation of *p* is confirmed. 'No' answers can be given either with or without TOCH. In (24c), TOCH indicates that the *prior* expectation *p* is rejected.

(24) a. *Ja, Ad is in Amsterdam.*
    b. *Nee, Ad is niet in Amsterdam.*
    c. *Nee, Ad is* TOCH *niet in Amsterdam.*

As mentioned previously, the interpretation of p-TOCH? is similar to that of a Cantonese HO2 question. The questioner is biased toward the positive answer p.

4.2   *Radical inquisitive semantics*

In analyzing TOCH sentences, Groenendijk (2013) employs a radical version of inquisitive semantics (Groenendijk & Roelofsen 2010; Aher 2012; Sano 2015). In radical inquisitive semantics, the semantics of sentences are characterized by positive and negative semantic relations between sentences and information states, *support* and *reject*.[12]

(25)   The atomic clause: ($|p|$ is the set of worlds where p is true)
   support $\sigma \vDash^+ p$ iff $\sigma \neq \emptyset$ and $\sigma \subseteq |p|$
   reject $\sigma \vDash^- p$ iff $\sigma \neq \emptyset$ and $\sigma \cap |p| = \emptyset$

An information state σ is a set of possible worlds. A state σ supports an atomic sentence p just in case σ is consistent and p is true in all worlds in σ. In contrast, σ rejects p just in case σ is consistent and p is false in all worlds in σ.

As for negation, a state σ supports $\neg\varphi$ just in case it rejects φ, and it rejects $\neg\varphi$ just in case it supports φ.

(26)   The clauses for negation:
   a. $\sigma \vDash^+ \neg \varphi$ iff $\sigma \vDash^- \varphi$
   b. $\sigma \vDash^- \neg \varphi \sigma$ iff $\sigma \vDash^+ \varphi$

Turning to conjunction, a state σ supports $\varphi \wedge \psi$ just in case it supports both φ and ψ, and it rejects $\varphi \wedge \psi$ just in case it rejects either φ or ψ.

(27)   The clauses for conjunction:
   a. $\sigma \vDash^+ \varphi \wedge \psi$ iff $\sigma \vDash^- \varphi$ and $\sigma \vDash^- \psi$
   b. $\sigma \vDash^- \varphi \wedge \psi$ iff $\sigma \vDash^- \varphi$ or $\sigma \vDash^- \psi$

Similarly, a state σ supports $\varphi \vee \psi$ just in case it supports either φ or ψ, and it rejects $\varphi \vee \psi$ just in case it rejects both φ and ψ.

(28)   The clauses for disjunction:
   a. $\sigma \vDash^+ \varphi \vee \psi$ iff $\sigma \vDash^+ \varphi$ or $\sigma \vDash^+ \psi$
   b. $\sigma \vDash^- \varphi \vee \psi$ iff $\sigma \vDash^- \varphi$ and $\sigma \vDash^- \psi$

In order to analyze TOCH, Groenendijk (2013) introduces a basic sentential operator, ($\neg$). Thus, the TOCH-declarative (22) translates as ($\neg$)p.

Now, recall that an interrogative sentence is defined as $?\varphi =_{\mathrm{def}} \varphi \vee \neg\varphi$. Now, an interrogative operator for TOCH? is defined as:

(29) $?(\neg)\varphi =_{\mathrm{def}} \varphi \vee (\neg)\neg\varphi$

Consequently, the TOCH-question (23) translates as $?(\neg)p = p \vee (\neg)\neg p$.

As discussed in Section 4.1, sentences with TOCH give rise to prior/current expectations. Thus, in defining semantics for TOCH sentences, Groenendijk (2013) introduces two notions: (1) the expectations in an information state σ, and (2) the history of σ.

First, a model includes a function ε which takes any information state σ and yields an expectation state $\varepsilon(\sigma) \subseteq \sigma$.

Second, in order to talk about different stages in the history of an information state, σ is now changed into a sequence of states. If σ is such a sequence, length(σ) returns the number of stages in σ. For $n <$ length(σ), σn refers to the nth stage in σ from the current stage σ_0. Thus, when σn is more recent than σm, $m > n$.

To define the semantics of $(\neg)\varphi$, Groenendijk (2013) introduces another semantic relation, *prior expectation–rejection shift*. It characterizes the changes of expectations through the stages. Initially, some proposition was expected, but it became no longer expected at some later stage. At the most recent stage, the proposition is rejected.

(30) Prior expectation–rejection shift
    Let $t <$ length(σ).
    $\sigma_t \vDash^{\bullet}_{\mathcal{M}} \varphi$ iff $\exists t'$: length $(\sigma) > t' > t$ such that:

    1. $\varepsilon_{\mathcal{M}}(\sigma_{t'}) \vDash^{+}_{\mathcal{M}} \varphi$ and
    2. $\forall t''$: if $t' > t'' >$, then $\varepsilon_{\mathcal{M}}(\sigma_{t''}) \nvDash^{+}_{\mathcal{M}} \varphi$ and
    3. $\sigma_{t+1} \vDash^{-}_{\mathcal{M}} \varphi$

Based on (30), semantics for TOCH sentences, that is, $(\neg)\varphi$, is defined as follows.

(31) Semantics for TOCH

    a. $\sigma_t \vDash^{+}_{\mathcal{M}} (\neg)\varphi$ iff $\sigma_t \vDash^{+}_{\mathcal{M}} \varphi$ and $\sigma_t \vDash^{\bullet}_{\mathcal{M}} \neg\varphi$
    b. $\sigma_t \vDash^{-}_{\mathcal{M}} (\neg)\varphi$ iff $\sigma_t \vDash^{-}_{\mathcal{M}} \varphi$ and $\sigma_t \vDash^{\bullet}_{\mathcal{M}} \neg\varphi$

Let us see how the interpretation of (22), repeated here as (32), is derived. As its primary speech act, it asserts $p\left(\sigma_0 \vDash^{+}_{\mathcal{M}} p\right)$. At the same time, as its secondary act, it indicates that $\neg p$ is a prior expectation, which is now rejected $\left(\sigma_0 \vDash^{\bullet}_{\mathcal{M}} \neg p\right)$.

(32) *Ad is* TOCH *in Amsterdam.* $((\neg)p)$

That is, 'Ad would not be in Amsterdam' used to be expected, $\varepsilon_{\mathcal{M}}(\sigma_2)\vDash^+_{\mathcal{M}}\neg p$ but at some point, it stopped being expected, $\forall t''$: if $2 > t'' > 0, \varepsilon_{\mathcal{M}}(\sigma_{t''})\nvDash^+_{\mathcal{M}}\neg p$. Finally, it is rejected, $\sigma_1\vDash^-_{\mathcal{M}}\neg p$.

Let us turn to an interrogative TOCH?, namely, $?(\neg)\varphi$. Given that $?(\neg)\varphi =_{\text{def}} \varphi\vee(\neg)\neg\varphi$, the semantics is derived as follows.

(33)   Derived semantics for TOCH?

    a. $\sigma_t\vDash^+_{\mathcal{M}} ?_{(\neg)}\varphi$ iff $\sigma_t\vDash^+_{\mathcal{M}}\varphi$, or $\left(\sigma_t\vDash^+_{\mathcal{M}}\neg\varphi\text{ and }\sigma_t\vDash^\bullet_{\mathcal{M}}\varphi\right)$

    b. $\sigma_t\vDash^-_{\mathcal{M}} ?_{(\neg)}\varphi$ never

Thus, the TOCH-question (23), repeated here as (34), asks $p\vee\neg p$, that is, $\sigma_0\vDash^+_{\mathcal{M}} p$ or $\sigma_0\vDash^+_{\mathcal{M}}$, and at the same time, in case that the answer was negative, it anticipates a current expectation–rejection, $\sigma_0\vDash^\bullet_{\mathcal{M}} p$.

(34)   *Ad is in Amsterdam*, TOCH?　　　　　　　　　$(?(\neg)p = p\vee(\neg)\neg p)$

Thus, 'Ad is in Amsterdam' is currently expected, $\varepsilon_{\mathcal{M}}(\sigma_2)\vDash^+_{\mathcal{M}} p$. But there was some move in the conversation that made 'Ad is in Amsterdam' no longer expected, $\forall t''$:if $2 > t'' > 0$, then $\varepsilon_{\mathcal{M}}(\sigma_{t''})\nvDash^+_{\mathcal{M}} p$.

If the answer to (34) is 'yes,' there is no prior expectation–rejection shift. If the answer is 'no,' 'Ad is in Amsterdam' is rejected, $\sigma_1\vDash^-_{\mathcal{M}} p$:

(35)   a. *Ja, Ad is in Amsterdam.*
     b. *Nee, Ad is niet in Amsterdam.*
     c. *Nee, Ad is* TOCH *niet in Amsterdam.*

In summary, a TOCH declarative, $(\neg)p$, conventionally encodes a rejection of prior expectation $\neg p$ as a secondary assertion. A TOCH?-interrogative, namely, $?_{(\neg)}p$, secondarily asserts the anticipation of a rejection of the current expectation p.

Recall that a Cantonese HO2 question indicates a bias toward the positive answer. Thus, it can be analyzed analogously to the Dutch TOCH?

4.3   *Back to the Cantonese questions*

Based on the data reported by Lam (2014a) and the novel data in (7)–(9) in Section 2, I propose that among the four kinds of the Cantonese questions, only an AA4 question denotes a simplex speech act of questioning, while A-NOT-A, HO2, and ME1 questions are multi-dimensional in that they perform question acts as well as secondary assertion acts.

I define the semantics of each questions which derives the correct interpretations in the framework of radical inquisitive semantics. First, let us take an HO2 question, as it is identical to the Dutch TOCH? question, as in (36).

(36) Semantics of an HO2 question

a. $\sigma \vDash_{\mathscr{M}}^{+} \text{HO2}(\varphi)$ iff $\sigma_t \vDash_{\mathscr{M}}^{+} \varphi$, or $(\sigma_t \vDash_{\mathscr{M}}^{+} \neg\varphi$ and $\sigma_t \vDash_{\mathscr{M}}^{\bullet} \varphi$

b. $\sigma \vDash_{\mathscr{M}}^{-} \text{HO2}(\varphi)$ never

Recall that HO2 questions cannot be used in neutral contexts (3b) and the addressee can respond to a HO2 question by saying, "You're right," to agree with the positive answer (5). Both facts are correctly predicted since HO2(p) semantically indicates that the questioner has an expectation toward p.

Similarly, an ME1 question indicates that the questioner has an expectation toward $\neg p$. Thus, it cannot be used in neutral contexts (3c) and can be responded with, "You're right," to agree with the negative answer (6).

(37) Semantics of an ME1 question

a. $\sigma_t \vDash_{\mathscr{M}}^{+} \text{ME1}(\varphi)$ iff $\sigma_t \vDash_{\mathscr{M}}^{+} \neg\varphi$, or $\left(\sigma_t \vDash_{\mathscr{M}}^{+} \varphi \text{ and } \sigma_t \vDash_{\mathscr{M}}^{\bullet} \neg\varphi\right)$

b. $\sigma_t \vDash_{\mathscr{M}}^{-} \text{ME1}(\varphi)$ never

Now, let us turn to the two questions which appear to be "neutral." First, an AA4 question is defined as a simplex question, as in (38).

(38) Semantics of an AA4 question

a. $\sigma_t \vDash_{\mathscr{M}}^{+} \text{AA}^{4}(\varphi)$ iff $\sigma_t \vDash^{+} \varphi$ or $\sigma_t \vDash_{\mathscr{M}}^{+} \neg q$

b. $\sigma_t \vDash_{\mathscr{M}}^{-} \text{AA}^{4}(\varphi)$ never

Put another way, it does not encode any expectation within its semantics. Thus, it can be used in neutral contexts (7). At the same time, it can also be used in biased contexts (9), repeated here as (39).

(39) a: *gam1 go3 ji6jyut6 jau5 jaa6gau2 hou6 aa3!*
        'There is a 29th this February!'

   c: *zan1 hai2? gam1 go3 ji6jyut jau5 jaa6gau2 hou6 aa4?*
        'Really? Is there a 29th this February?'   (AA4)

In this case, the bias or expectation meaning arises as a *pragmatic* effect. A asserted, 'There is a 29th this February' (= p). If B did not have any prior expectation, B should just accept p. Still, B asks a question $p \vee \neg p$. Hence, B is anticipating a rejection of his/her prior expectation $\neg p$. Furthermore, since it is a simple question, it cannot be responded by, "You are right," as we have seen in (8).[13]

Finally, I agree with Lam (2014a) in that A-NOT-A questions are neutral questions, though contra Lam (2014a), I propose that A-NOT-A questions are complex speech acts. In other words, A-NOT-A questions are anti-bias questions. They semantically negate any anticipation of prior expectation–rejection shift toward p or $\neg p$.

(40) Semantics of an A-not-A question

    a. $\sigma_t \vDash^+_{\mathcal{M}}$ A-NOT-A(φ) iff $\left(\sigma_t \vDash^+_{\mathcal{M}} \varphi \text{ or } \sigma_t \vDash^+_{\mathcal{M}} \neg\varphi\right)$ and $\sigma_t \nvDash^\bullet_{\mathcal{M}} \varphi \vee \neg\varphi$

    b. $\sigma_t \vDash^-$ A - NOT - A(φ) never

Therefore, A-NOT-A questions can be, of course, used in neutral contexts (3a). However, they cannot be used when the speaker expresses his or her bias. Consider (41), which is a repetition of (9) followed by A's answer. As before, A asserted, 'There is a 29th this February' p, but B still attempts to ask a question $p \vee \neg p$. This means that: (i) B had a prior expectation, $\varepsilon_{\mathcal{M}}(\sigma_3) \vDash^+_{\mathcal{M}} p$; (ii) A's first assertion indicates that p is no longer supported by the expectation state, $\varepsilon_{\mathcal{M}}(\sigma_2) \nvDash^+_{\mathcal{M}} p$; (iii) A's answer indicates that p is rejected, $\sigma_1 \nvDash^+_{\mathcal{M}} p$. Thus, $\sigma_1 \vDash^+_{\mathcal{M}} p$. This contradicts the secondary component of the semantics of A-NOT-A question, $\sigma_1 \nvDash^\bullet_{\mathcal{M}} p \vee \neg p$.

(41)   a: *gam1 go3 ji6jyut6 jau5 jaa6gau2 hou6 aa3!*
         'There is a 29th this February!'

       b: #*zan1 hai2? gam1 go3 ji6jyut6 jau5 mou5 jaa6gau2 hou2?*
          'Really? Is there a 29th this February or not?'   (A-NOT-A)

       a: *jau5.*
         'Yes.'

Note also that the conceptual problem that Yuan and Hara (2013) face does not arise here, since in inquisitive semantics, $p \vee \neg p$ is not a tautology. $\sigma_t \nvDash^\bullet_{\mathcal{M}} p \vee \neg p$ is not equivalent to $\sigma_t \nvDash^\bullet_{\mathcal{M}} q \vee \neg q$.

As summarized in Table 5.4, among the four Cantonese polar questions considered in this chapter, only AA4 questions are simplex questions, while HO2, ME1, and A-NOT-A questions have multi-dimensional semantics. The bias meaning that arises from an AA4 question is due to the pragmatic pressure. HO2 and ME1 questions semantically encode prior expectations toward p and $\neg p$, respectively, as their secondary speech acts. Lastly, A-NOT-A questions encode the neutrality requirement in their semantics as lack of anticipation of prior expectation–rejection shift.

Table 5.4 Inquisitive semantics–based analysis of Cantonese polar questions

Syntax	Semantics
HO2	$\sigma_t \vDash^+_{\mathcal{M}} \varphi$, or ($\sigma_t \vDash^+_{\mathcal{M}} \neg\varphi$ and $\sigma_t \vDash^\bullet_{\mathcal{M}} \varphi$)
ME1	$\sigma_t \vDash^+_{\mathcal{M}} \neg\varphi$, or ($\sigma_t \vDash^+_{\mathcal{M}} \varphi$ and $\sigma_t \vDash^\bullet_{\mathcal{M}} \neg\varphi$)
AA4	$\sigma_t \vDash^+_{\mathcal{M}} \varphi$ or $\sigma_t \vDash^+_{\mathcal{M}} \neg\varphi$
A-not-A	($\sigma_t \vDash^+_{\mathcal{M}} \varphi$ or $\sigma_t \vDash^+_{\mathcal{M}} \neg\varphi$) and $\sigma_t \nvDash^\bullet_{\mathcal{M}} \varphi \vee \neg\varphi$

4.4 *Summary*

Cantonese has a variety of (non-)biased polar questions. HO2 and ME1 questions express a bias toward the positive and negative answers, respectively. In contrast, A-NOT-A and AA4 questions seem to be neutral questions. Thus, Lam (2014a) analyzes HO2 and ME1 questions as complex speech acts of questioning and asserting, while A-NOT-A questions are simple acts of questioning. Lam's (2014a) account cannot explain the contrast between A-NOT-A and AA4 questions; A-NOT-A questions can only be used in neutral contexts, while AA4 questions can be used in both neutral and biased contexts. Incidentally, Yuan and Hara (2013) claim that Mandarin A-not-A questions are also complex speech acts of questioning and asserting, where the content of the assertion is a tautology, 'p or not p.' Yuan and Hara (2013) argue that the assertion of 'p or not p,' in effect, indicates the ignorance of the speaker, hence the neutrality requirement. However, Yuan and Hara's analysis is also conceptually problematic. In truth-conditional semantics, an assertion of 'p or not p' is equivalent to that of 'q or not q.' This chapter thus offers a solution to this problem in the framework of inquisitive semantics (Groenendijk & Roelofsen 2009), where meanings of sentences are given based on support-conditions. Contra Lam (2014a), the semantics of an A-NOT-A question is also multi-dimensional in that it has a primary question meaning as well as a secondary assertion meaning which indicates lack of 'anticipation of prior expectation–rejection shift.' Therefore, A-NOT-A questions are anti-bias questions, thus cannot be used when the questioner wants to express his or her bias toward one of the answers, while AA4 questions are simple questions which can be pragmatically rendered into biased questions in biased contexts.

The rest of the chapter is devoted to reinforcing the empirical basis of the proposal. I conducted one force-choice survey and one naturalness rating survey to elicit linguistic judgments from native speakers who are naive to the linguistic phenomenon and theory at issue.

5   Experiments

5.1   *Experiment I: force-choice*

The predictions for the distribution of question forms and context are as follows:

(42)   a.   In NEUTRAL contexts, A-NOT-A questions are most preferred.
     b.   In POSITIVE contexts, HO2 questions are most preferred.
     c.   In NEGATIVE contexts, ME1 questions are most preferred.
     d.   AA4 questions occur in all contexts.

The aim of Experiment I is to verify these predictions.

5.1.1   *Method*

Stimuli. The stimuli had two fully crossed factors – contexts (NEUTRAL/ POSITIVE/NEGATIVE) and question forms (A-NOT-A/HO2/ ME1/AA4).[14]

(43) Contexts:

    a. *Neutral: A mou5 gin3gwo3 Ben, soeng2zi1 keoi5 zung1ji3 mat1je5*
        'A has never met Ben before and is wondering what he likes.'

    b. Positive bias: *A ji5wai4 Ben zung1ji3 daa2gei1, daan6hai6 B waa6*
        keoi5 hai6 syu1cung4. so2ji5 A soeng2 hoeng3 B kok3jing6 haa5.
        'A thought Ben likes video games, but B says he is a bookworm. So A
        asks B to check.'

    c. Negative bias: *A ji5wai4 Ben hai6 syu1cung4, daan6hai6 B waa6 keoi5*
        zung1ji3 daa2gei1. so2ji5 A soeng2 hoeng3 B kok3jing6 haa5.
        'A thought Ben is a bookworm, but B says he likes video games. So A
        asks B to check.'

(44) Target sentences:

    a. *Ben zung1-m4-zung1ji3 daa2gei1?*
        Ben like-not-like play-videogames
        'Does Ben like video games or not?'

    b. *Ben zung1ji3 daa2gei1 aa4?*
        Ben like videogames PRT
        'Does Ben like video games?'

    c. *Ben zung1ji3 daa2gei1 aa3 ho2?*
        Ben like play-videogame PRT PRT
        'Ben likes video games, right?'

    d. *Ben zung1ji3 daa2gei1 me1?*
        Ben likes play-videogames PRT
        'Ben doesn't like video games, does he?'

There were 12 items, and each item had 3 contexts, resulting in 36 questions (12 items × 3 contexts). 108 questions from another experiment were also included.

Procedure. The experiment was conducted in a quiet meeting room at City University of Hong Kong. The stimuli were presented in Chinese characters by Qualtrics.[15] The first page of the test showed the instructions.

In the main section, the participants were asked to read each context and then select the most natural utterance among the four choices, A-NOT-A, HO2, ME1, and AA4 questions.

To avoid minimal pair sentences from appearing next to each other, the main experiment was organized into 12 blocks, and each block contained 3 questions. None of the stimuli were repeated. In order to counter-balance practice and fatigue effects, the order of the blocks and the stimuli within each block were randomized by the Qualtrics software.

Participants. Ten native speakers of Cantonese participated in the rating experiment. They were undergraduate students recruited from City University of Hong Kong and received 80 Hong Kong dollars as compensation.

Statistics. To analyze the results, a generalized linear mixed model (Nelder & Wedderburn 1972) was run using the lme4 package (Bates *et al.* 2015) implemented in R (R Core Team 2017). Context types and question forms were the fixed factors. Speakers and items were the random factors. The *p*-values were calculated by the summary function.

If the frequency of the question forms depends on the type of context, then the dependency is expected to result in a significant interaction between forms and contexts.

5.1.2   *Result and discussion*

Figure 5.2 shows the frequency of each question form in the three context types.

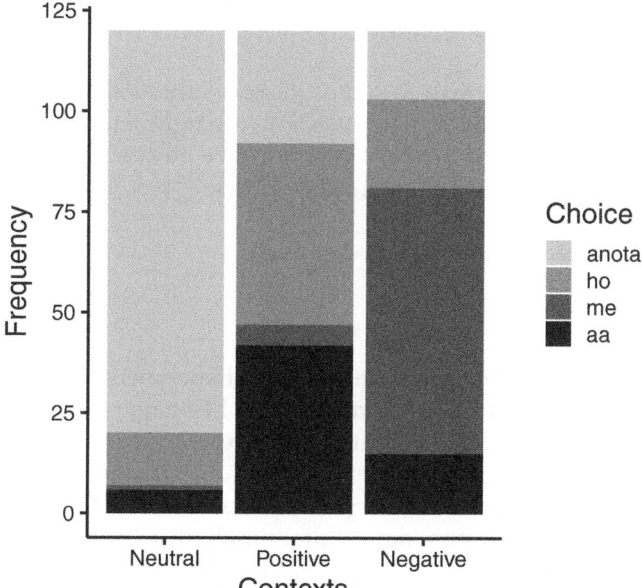

Figure 5.2 Force-choice frequencies.

The first three predictions in (42) were confirmed: A-NOT-A questions were most frequent in NEUTRAL contexts (compared with POSITIVE: $z = -8.291$; $p < 0.001$; with NEGATIVE: $z = -9.139$; $p < 0.001$). Ho2 questions were most frequent in POSITIVE contexts (compared with NEUTRAL: $z = -5.065$; $p < 0.001$; with NEGATIVE: $z = -3.674$; $p < 0.001$). ME1 questions were most frequent in NEGATIVE contexts (compared with NEUTRAL: $z = -5.272$; $p < 0.001$; with POSITIVE: $z = -6.901$; $p < 0.001$).

In contrast, the prediction regarding the AA4 questions (42d) was not confirmed: AA4 questions were significantly most frequent in POSITIVE contexts (compared with NEUTRAL: $z = -5.131$; $p < 0.001$; with NEGATIVE: $z = -4.014$; $p < 0.001$). This may seem puzzling, given the introspection-based data discussed earlier. I speculate that this result comes from the format of Experiment I and the fact that HO2 questions are generally marked forms. Since in Experiment I the participants were forced to choose the best form given a context, the AA4 question, the default form of question, was rarely chosen in NEUTRAL and NEGATIVE contexts. In POSITIVE contexts, on the other hand, although the semantics of HO2 fits the context, the HO2 form itself is marked; thus, a default AA4 becomes more frequent. The next section reports a naturalness rating experiment which tests these speculations.

5.2   Experiment II: naturalness rating

In Experiment II, predictions parallel to Experiment I (45) as well as (46) are tested as a naturalness rating study.

(45)   a. In NEUTRAL contexts, A-NOT-A questions are most natural.
      b. In POSITIVE contexts, HO2 questions are most natural.
      c. In NEGATIVE contexts, ME1 questions are most natural.
      d. AA4 questions are natural in all contexts.

(46)   In general, HO2 questions are degraded.

5.2.1   Method

Stimuli. The same contexts and sentences as Experiment I were used. Each of the 12 conditions had 12 items, resulting in 144 target sentences (12 items × 12 conditions). 36 questions from another experiment were also included.

Procedure. In the main section, the participants were asked to read each stimulus and then judge the naturalness of the stimuli on a 7-point scale (provided in Chinese characters): from "7: very natural" to "1: very unnatural." The experiment was organized into 12 blocks. Each block contained 12 questions. The other aspect of the procedure was the same as Experiment I.

Participants. Ten native speakers of Cantonese who did not participate in Experiment I participated in the naturalness rating experiment. The other aspect of the procedure was the same as Experiment I.

Statistics. The responses were recorded as numerical values: from very natural = 7 to very unnatural = 1. To analyze the results, a general linear mixed model (Baayen 2008; Baayen *et al.* 2008; Bates 2005) was run using the lmerTest package (Kuznetsova *et al.* 2016) implemented in R (R Core Team 2017). Question forms and context types were the fixed factors. Speakers and items were the random factors. The *p*-values were calculated by the Markov chain Monte Carlo method using the LanguageR package (Baayen 2013). If the naturalness of the question forms depends on the type of context, then the dependency is expected to result in a significant interaction between forms and contexts.

5.2.2 *Result and discussion*

Figure 5.3 shows the result of Experiment II. Just like Experiment I, the first three predictions in (45) were confirmed: A-NOT-A questions were most natural in NEUTRAL contexts (compared with POSITIVE: $t = -5.578$; $p < 0.001$; with NEGATIVE: $t = -9.911$; $p < 0.001$). HO2 questions were most natural in POSITIVE contexts (compared with NEUTRAL: $t = -2.091$; $p < 0.05$; with NEGATIVE: $t = -4.369$; $p < 0.001$). ME1 questions were most natural in NEGATIVE contexts (compared with NEUTRAL: $t = -18.65$; $p < 0.001$; with POSITIVE: $t = -21.67$; $p < 0.001$).

In contrast, the prediction regarding the AA4 questions (45d) was not straightforwardly confirmed, since AA4 questions were significantly most natural in NEGATIVE contexts (compared with NEUTRAL: $t = -3.955$;

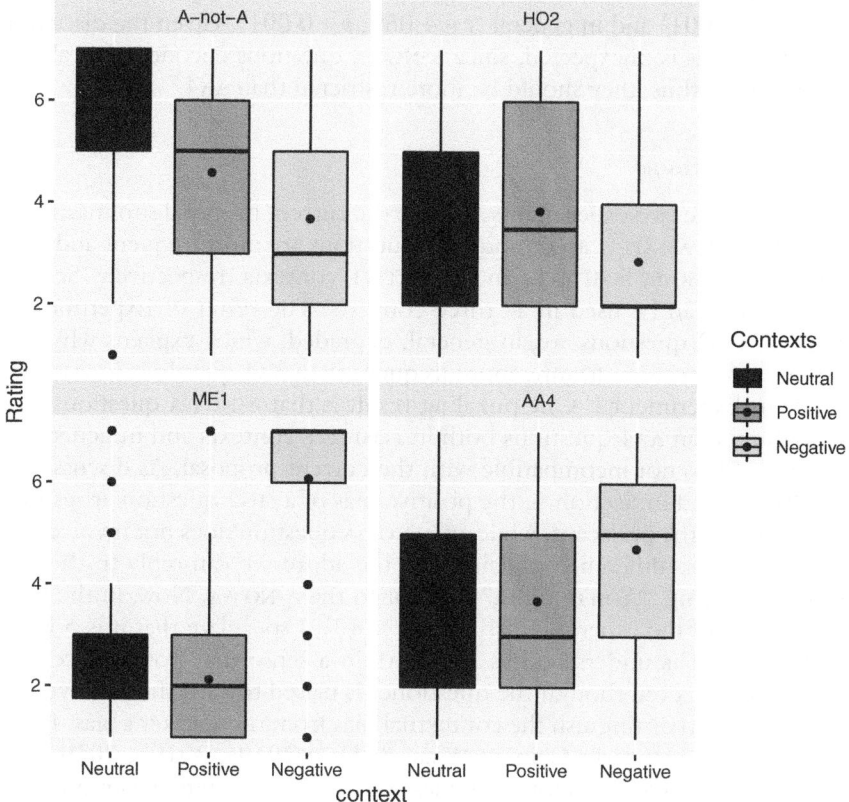

Figure 5.3 Naturalness ratings (sorted by forms).

$p < 0.001$; with POSITIVE: $t = -4.423$; $p < 0.001$). However, if we compare the ratings of AA4 questions with other forms in the same context, they have significantly higher ratings than other non-top-rated forms, as can be seen in Figure 5.4. In NEUTRAL contexts, AA4 questions were more natural than HO2 questions ($t = -2.180$; $p < 0.05$) and ME1 questions ($t = -5.843$; $p < 0.001$). In POSITIVE contexts, AA4 questions were more natural than ME1 questions ($t = -7.100$; $p < 0.001$). In NEGATIVE contexts, AA4 questions were more natural than A-NOT-A questions ($t = -4.874$; $p < 0.001$) and HO2 questions ($t = -8.686$; $p < 0.001$).

Finally, question-form types show a significant main effect. In particular, HO2 questions were least preferred (mean: 3.369444) among the four question types (compared with A-NOT-A (mean: 4.669444): $t = 8.794$ $p < 0.001$; compared with ME1 (mean: 3.630556): $t = 1.766$; $p < 0.1$; compared with AA4 (mean: 4.069444): $t = 4.735$; $p < 0.001$), supporting prediction (46).

In addition, AA4 questions are preferred over HO2 ($t = -4.735$; $p < 0.001$) and ME1 ($t = -2.969$; $p < 0.01$) questions, which is compatible with prediction (45d).

Finally, one of the unexpected results is that, as can be seen in Figures 5.4 and 5.5, A-NOT-A is significantly more preferred than AA4 both in positive contexts ($t = 4.062$; $p < 0.001$) and in general ($t = 4.059$; $p < 0.001$). Given the discussion in Section 4, this is unexpected, since A-NOT-A questions encodes neutrality in their semantics; thus, they should be more restricted than AA4.

5.3   *General discussion*

The results of the two experiments support the current proposal summarized in Table 5.4. First, A-NOT-A, HO2, and ME1 questions are most frequent and most natural in NEUTRAL, POSITIVE, and NEGATIVE contexts, respectively. Second, AA4 questions can be used in all three contexts. The result of Experiment II shows that HO2 questions are, in general, degraded, which explains why HO2 questions were not significantly more frequent than AA4 questions in POSITIVE contexts in Experiment I. One puzzling result is that A-NOT-A questions were more natural than AA4 questions both in POSITIVE contexts and in general. In fact, this result is not incompatible with the current proposal. As discussed by Lam (2014a) and in Section 4, the positive bias of a HO2 question arises from the assertion of the prejacent, while an A-NOT-A question does not involve such an assertion. This difference explains why the addressee can reply to the HO2 question by saying, "You're right," but not to the A-NOT-A. Now, in the POSITIVE contexts of the experiment stimuli like (43), I speculate that it is possible that the context is understood as NEUTRAL in a sense that both answers are equally plausible even though the questioner is biased toward the positive one. Thus, we need to distinguish the contextual bias from the speaker's bias. In our recent work on Mandarin Chinese (Yuan & Hara 2019a, 2019b, 2019c), we claim that an A-NOT-A question expresses contextual neutrality which might be

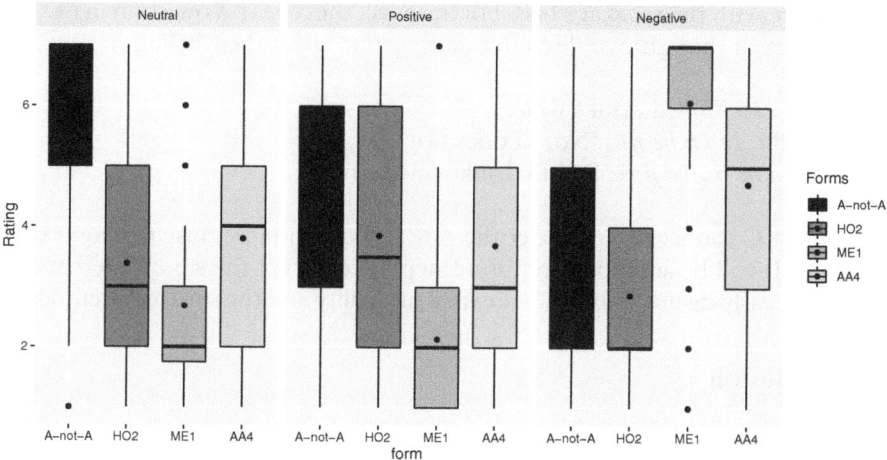

Figure 5.4 Naturalness ratings (sorted by contexts).

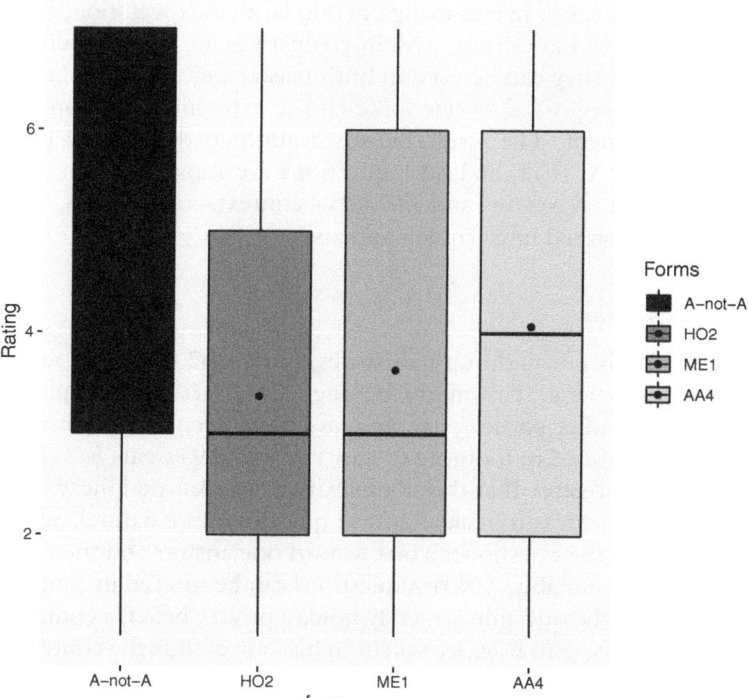

Figure 5.5 Naturalness ratings (main effect of forms).

compatible with the speaker's bias. For instance, the A-NOT-A question in (47) is felicitous even though two discourse participants assert their beliefs in p or $\neg p$.

(47)   a: *Li he jiu.* 'Li drinks wine.'
        b: *Bu, Li bu he jiu.* 'No, Li does not.'
        c: *Li he-bu-he jiu?* 'Did Li drink wine or not?'

Participant C can felicitously utter the A-NOT-A question because the context is neutral.[16] It will be an important future step to construct the stimuli so that the contexts clearly distinguish the contextual neutrality and the speaker's neutrality.

6   Conclusion

6.1   Summary

This chapter investigated four kinds of Cantonese polar questions, HO2, ME1, AA4, and A-NOT-A questions, in the framework of radical inquisitive semantics (Groenendijk & Roelofsen 2010; Aher 2012; Sano 2015). Ho2, ME1, and A-NOT-A questions have multi-dimensional semantics. In addition to their primary speech act of questioning, HO2 and ME1 interrogatives encode secondary assertive acts of positive and negative expectations, respectively, while A-NOT-A interrogatives conventionally encode lack of expectation, hence the neutral requirement. In contrast, AA4 interrogatives are semantically simplex question acts; thus, they can be used in both biased and neutral contexts. The analysis is further supported by one force-choice experiment and one naturalness rating experiment. The results mostly confirmed the current proposal's predictions: A-NOT-A, HO2, and ME1 questions are most frequent and most natural in NEUTRAL, POSITIVE, and NEGATIVE contexts, respectively. Also, AA4 questions can be uttered in all three contexts.

6.2   Future directions

The experiments also brought up new issues. First, HO2 questions seem to be less preferred in general. This might be due to the fact that the particle *ho2* usually embeds another particle, like *aa3*, as can be seen in the stimuli in the appendix. As mentioned in footnote 6, Law *et al.* (2019) treats *ho2* as a speech act modifier. It is possible that this complexity in the left periphery requires a pragmatically rich context to make the HO2 question more natural. Second, we need to tease apart the questioner's bias toward one answer and the contextual bias/neutrality. Presumably, A-NOT-A questions can be uttered in contexts such as a context where the questioner merely holds a private belief, a context where both answers, that is, p and $\neg p$, are salient in discourse, thus the context is neutral, etc. (see Yuan & Hara 2019a, 2019b, 2019c). In contrast, HO2 and ME1 questions explicitly assert his or her bias toward one of the answers.

Another important outstanding issue is the compositionality of the interpretations of these questions. In the current chapter, semantics of each interrogative is stipulated at the level of the entire construction. As discussed in Section 3, Yuan and Hara (2013) and Yuan (2015) propose that an intonational morpheme can be paratactically associated with the main text and yield a secondary meaning. Hara and Yuan (2019, to appear) further develop this notion and provide its syntactic and semantic composition rules that can be applied to discourse particles and prosodic morphemes. It appears to be fruitful to test whether a similar morphological analysis can be given to the Cantonese question particles and the A-not-A construction.

Finally, as mentioned in footnote 12, radical inquisitive semantics has evolved into suppositional inquisitive semantics, which can handle conditional sentences. It would be interesting to see whether the new framework has any implication for the Cantonese conditional questions.

A. Stimuli

(1) a. Neutral: *A seng4jat6 tung4 Jenny sik6 tim4ban2, gin3keoi5 ci3ci3-dou1 m4 sik4 san1dei2, soeng2 zi1 keoi5 hai6 mai6 deoi3 faa1sang1 man5gam2.*
    'A always has dessert with Jenny and found her never eats sundae. A is wondering if she is allergic to peanuts.'

   b. Positive bias: *A ji5wai4 Jenny deoi3 faa1sang1 man5gam2, daan-6hai6 B waa6 keoi5 hai6 deoi3 laai5 man5gam2. so2ji5 A soeng2 ho-eng3 B kok3jing6 haa5.*
    'A thought Jenny is allergic to milk, but B says she is allergic to peanuts. So A asks B to check.'

   c. Negative bias: *A ji5wai4 Jenny deoi3 laai5 man5gam2, daan6hai6 B waa6 keoi5 hai6 deoi3 faa1sang1 man5gam2. so2ji5 A soeng2 hoeng3 B kok3jing6 haa5.*
    'A thought Jenny is allergic to peanuts, but B says she is allergic to milk. So A asks B to check.'

(2) a. *Jenny hai6-m4-hai6 deoi3 faa1sang1 man5gam2?*
    Jenny   is-not-is to peanuts allergy
    'Is Jenny allergic to peanuts or not?'

   b. *Jenny hai6 deoi3 faa1sang1 man5gam2 aa4?*
    Jenny is to peanuts allergy PRT
    'Is Jenny allergic to peanuts?'

   c. *Jenny hai6 deoi3 faa1sang1 man5gam2 aa3 ho2?*
    Jenny is to peanuts allergy PRT PRT
    'Jenny is allergic to peanuts, right?'

   d. *Jenny hai6 deoi3 faa1sang1 man5gam2 me1?*
    Jenny is to peanuts allergy PRT
    'Jenny isn't allergic to peanuts, does she?'

(3)   a.   Neutral: *A m4-sik1 hon4gwok3 di1 je5, soeng2zi1 hon5gwok3jan4 sai1-*
      m4-sai1 dong1bing1.
      'A knows nothing about Korea, he wonders whether they have man-
      datory military service.'

   b.   Positive bias: *A waa6 hon4gwok3 jan4 jiu3 dong1bing1, daan6hai6 B*
      waa6 m4 sai2. so2ji5 A soeng2 hoeng3 B kok3jing6 haa5.
      'A thought Koreans have to serve military service, but B says they
      don't have to. So A asks B to check.'

   c.   Negative bias: *A waa6 hon4gwok3 jan4 m4-sai dong1bing1, daan-*
      6hai6 B waa6 jiu3. so2ji5 A soeng2 hoeng3 B kok3jing6 haa5.
      'A thought Koreans do not have to serve military service, but B says
      they have to. So A asks B to check.'

(4)   a.   *hon4gwok3 jan4 jiu3-m4-jiu3 dong1bing1?*
      Korea people need-not-need serve-military-service
      'Do Koreans need to serve military service or not?'

   b.   *hon4gwok3 jan4 jiu3 dong1bing1 aa4?*
      Korea people need serve-military-service PRT
      'Do Koreans need to serve military service?'

   c.   *hon4gwok3 jan4 jiu3 dong1bing1 aa3 ho2?*
      Korea people need serve-military-service PRT PRT
      'Koreans need to serve military service, right?'

   d.   *hon4gwok3 jan4 jiu3 dong1bing1 me1?*
      Korea people need serve-military-service PRT
      'Koreans do not need to serve military service, do they?'

(5)   a.   Neutral: *A mou5 gin3gwo3 CityU ge3 haau6fai1, soeng2zi1 dou3 hai6*
      mat1je5 sik1.
      'A has never seen the logo of CityU before and is wondering what
      color it is.'

   b.   Positive bias: *A ji5wai4 CityU ge3 haau6fai1 hai6 laam4-sik1 tung4*
      luk6-sik1, daan6hai6 B waa6 keoi5 hai6 hung4 sik1 ge3. so2ji5 A so-
      eng2 hoeng3 B kok3jing6 haa5.
      'A thought the logo of CityU is blue and green, but B says it's red. So
      A asks B to check.'

   c.   Negative bias: *A ji5wai4 CityU ge3 haau6fai1 hai6 hung4 sik1, daan-*
      6hai6 B waa6 keoi5 hai6 laam4-sik1 tung4 luk6-sik1 ge3. so2ji5 A so-
      eng2 hoeng3 B kok3jing6 haa5.
      'A thought the logo of CityU is red, but B says it's blue and green. So
      A asks B to check.'

(6)   a.   *Si1ti2(CITY) ge3 haau6fai1 hai6-m4-hai6 laam4-sik1 tung4luk6-sik1?*
      City(U) GEN logo is-not-is blue and green
      'Is the logo of CityU blue and green or not?'

   b.   *Si1ti2(CITY) ge3 haau6fai1 hai6 laam4-sik1 tung4 luk6-sik1 aa4?*
      City(U) GEN logo is blue and green PRT
      'Is the logo of CityU blue and green?'

   c.   *Si1ti2(CITY) ge3 haau6fai1 hai6 laam4-sik1 tung4 luk6-sik1 aa3 ho2?*
      City(U) GEN logo is blue and green PRT PRT
      'The logo of CityU is blue and green, right?'

      d. *Si1ti2(CITY) ge3 haau6fai1 hai6 laam4-sik1 tung4 luk6-sik1 me1?*
         City(U) GEN logo is blue and green PRT
         'The logo of CityU isn't blue and green, is it?'

(7)   a. Neutral: *A jiu3 heoi3 EMAX tai2 jin2coeng3wui2, daan6hai6 m4 zi1 EMAX hai2 bin1.*
       'A is going to a concert in EMAX, but she doesn't know where is EMAX.'

      b. Positive bias: *A ji5wai4 EMAX hai6 hai2 gau2lung4waan1, daan-6hai6 bi(B) waa6 hai6 hai2 gau2lung4tong4. so2ji5 A soeng2 hoeng3 B kok3jing6 haa5.*
       'A thought EMAX is at Kowloon Bay, but B says it is at Kowloon Tong. So A asks B to check.'

      c. Negative bias: *A ji5wai4 EMAX hai6 hai2 gau2lung4tong4, daan-6hai6 bi(B) waa6 hai6 hai2 gau2lung4waan1. so2ji5 A soeng2 hoeng3 B kok3jing6 haa5.*
       'A thought EMAX is at Kowloon Tong, but B says it is at Kowloon Bay. So A asks B to check.'

(8)   a. *EMAX hai6-m4-hai6 hai2 gau2lung4waan1?*
       EMAX is-not-is at Kowloon-Bay
       'Is EMAX at Kowloon Bay or not?'

      b. *EMAX hai6 hai2 gau2lung4waan1 aa4?*
       EMAX is at Kowloon-Bay PRT?
       'Is EMAX at Kowloon Bay?'

      c. *EMAX hai6 hai2 gau2lung4waan1 aa3 ho2?*
       EMAX is at Kowloon-Bay PRT PRT
       'EMAX is at Kowloon Bay, right?'

      d. *EMAX hai6 hai2 gau2lung4waan1 me1?*
       EMAX is at Kowloon-Bay PRT
       'EMAX is not at Kowloon Bay, is it?'

(9)   a. Neutral: *A mou5 heoi3gwo3 jat6bun2, soeng2zi1 jat6bun2 ho2-m4-ho2 ji5 zoek3 haai4 jap6 uk1.*
       'A has never been to Japan before and is wondering if they can wear shoes when visiting one's home or not.'

      b. Positive bias: *A ji5wai4 ho2ji5 zoek3 haai4 jap6 uk1, daan6hai6 B waa6 m4 ho2ji5. so2ji5 A soeng2 hoeng3 B kok3jing6 haa5.*
       'A thought they can wear shoes when visiting one's home, but B says they cannot. So A asks B to check.'

      c. Negative bias: *A ji5wai4 m4 ho2ji5 zeok3 haai4 jap6 uk1, daan6hai6 B waa6 ho2ji5. so2ji5 A soeng2 hoeng3 B kok3jing6 haa5.*
       'A thought they cannot wear shoes when visiting one's home, but B says they can. So A asks B to check.'

(10) a. *hai2 jat6bun2 ho2-m4-ho2ji5 zoek3 haai4 jap6 uk1?*
       In Japan can-not-can wear shoes go-in house
       'Can we wear shoes when visiting one's home in Japan or not?'

      b. *hai2 jat6bun2 ho2ji5 zoek3 haai4 jap6 uk1 aa4?*
       In Japan can wear shoes go-in house PRT
       'Can we wear shoes when visiting one's home in Japan?'

    c. *hai2 jat6bun2 ho2ji5 zoek3 haai4 jap6 uk1 aa3 ho2?*
       In Japan can wear shoes go-in house PRT PRT
       'We can wear shoes when visiting one's home, right?'

    d. *hai2 jat6bun2 ho2ji5 zoek3 haai4 jap6 uk1 me1?*
       In Japan can wear shoes go-in house PRT
       'We cannot wear shoes when visiting one's home in Japan, can we?'

(11) a. Neutral: *A cung4loi4 mei6 gin3gwo3 Jimmy, hou2 soeng2 zi1 keoi5 bin1 dou6 lai4.*
      'A has never met Jimmy before and is wondering where he is from.'

    b. Positive bias: *A ji5wai4 Jimmy hai6 mei5gwok3jan4 daan6hai6 B waa6 keoi5 hai6 gaa1naa4daai6jan4 so2ji5 A soeng2 hoeng3 B kok3jing6 haa5.*
      'A thought Jimmy is American, but B says he is Canadian. So A asks B to check.'

    c. Negative bias: *A ji5wai4 Jimmy hai6 gaa1naa4daai6jan4 daan6hai6 B waa6 keoi5 hai6 mei5gwok3jan4 so2ji5 A soeng2 hoeng3 B kok3jing6 haa5.*
      'A thought Jimmy is Canadian, but B says he is American. So A asks B to check.'

(12) a. *Jimmy hai6 m4 hai6 mei5gwok3 jan4?*
      Jimmy is not is America person
      'Is Jimmy American or not?'

    b. *Jimmy hai6 mei5gwok3 jan4 aa4?*
      Jimmy is America person PRT
      'Is Jimmy American?'

    c. *Jimmy hai6 mei5gwok3 jan4 aa3 ho2?*
      Jimmy is America person PRT PRT
      'Jimmy is American, right?'

    d. *Jimmy haai6 mei5gwok3 jan4 me1?*
      Jimmy is America person PRT
      'Jimmy isn't American, is he?'

(13) a. Neutral: *A mou5 lau4sam1 soeng5tong4 keoi5 m4 zi1 keoi5 jiu3m4jiu3 zou6 dai6 luk6sap6jip6.*
      'A was not paying attention in class, and he did not know whether he needed to do p. 60 or not.'

    b. Positive bias: *A ji5wai4 keoi5 jiu3 zou6 dai6 luk6sap6jip6 daan6hai6 B teng1dou2 hai6 dai6 sap6luk6jip6 so2ji5 A soeng2 hoeng3 B kok3jing6 haa5.*
      'A thought that he needed to do p. 60, but B heard that it was p. 16. So A asked B to check about it.'

    c. Negative bias: *A ji5wai4 keoi5 jiu3 zou6 dai6 sap6luk6jip6 daan6hai6 B teng1dou2 hai6 dai6 luk6sap6jip6 so2ji5 A soeng2 hoeng3 B kok3jing6 haa5.*
      'A thought that he needed to do p. 16, but B heard that it was p. 60. So A asked B to check about it.'

(14) a. *ngo5dei6 jiu3 m4 jiu3 zou6 dai6 luk6 sap6 jip6?*
      we should not should do number six ten page
      'Do we need to do p. 60 or not?'

b. *ngo5dei6 jiu3 zou6 dai6 luk6 sap6 jip6 aa4?*
we should do number six ten page PRT
'Do we need to do p. 60?'

c. *ngo5dei6 jiu3 zou6 dai6 luk6 sap6 jip6 aa3 ho2?*
we should do number six ten page PRT PRT
'We need to do p. 60, right?'

d. *ngo5dei6 jiu3 zou6 dai6 luk6 sap6 jip6 me1?*
we should do number six ten page PRT
'We don't need to do p. 60, do we?'

(15) a. Neutral: *A tung4 B gong2gan2 keoi5dei6 ge3 pang4jau5 Michael A hou2 soeng2 zi1 keoi5 zung1m4zung1ji3 daa2 laam4kau4.*
'A and B are talking about their friend Michael. A is wondering whether he likes to play basketball or not.'

b. Positive bias: *A ji5wai4 Michael zung1ji3 daa2 laam4kau4 daan-6hai6 B waa6 keoi5 zung1ji3 tek3 zuk1kau4 so2ji5 A soeng2 hoeng3 B kok3jing6 haa5.*
'A thinks Michael likes to play basketball, but B says he likes to play football. So
A asks B to check.'

c. Negative bias: *A ji5wai4 Michael zung1ji3 tek3 zuk1kau4 daan-6hai6 B waa6 keoi5 gin3gwo3 Michael lo2zyu6 go3 laam4kau4 A hou2 ging1ngaa5 zau6 man6.*
'A thinks Michael likes to play football, but B says he saw Michael carrying a basketball. A is surprised and asked:'

(16) a. *Michael zung1 m4 zung1ji3 daa2 laam4kau4?*
Michael like not like hit basketball?
'Does Michael like to play basketball or not?'

b. *Michael zung1ji3 daa2 laam4kau4 aa4?*
Michael like hit basketball PRT
'Does Michael like to play basketball?'

c. *Michael zung1ji3 daa2 laam4kau4 aa3 ho2?*
Michael like hit basketball PRT PRT
'Michael likes to play basketball, right?'

d. *Michael zung1ji3 daa2 laam4kau4 me1?*
Michael like hit basketball PRT
'Michael doesn't like to play basketball, does he?'

(17) a. Neutral: *Kitty ge3 baa4baa1 maa4maa1 soeng2 maai5 syut3gou1 bei2 Kitty keoi5dei6 soeng2 zi1 Kitty wui5 gaan2 mat1je5 mei6.*
'Kitty's parents are buying her ice cream, and they are wondering which flavor she would like to have.'

b. Positive bias: *Kitty ge3 maa4maa1 ji5wai4 Kitty wui5 gaan2 wan-6nei1laa2 mei6 daan6hai6 keoi5 ge3 baa4baa1 waa6 Kitty soeng2 jiu3 zyu1gu1lik1 mei6 syut3gou1 so2ji5 maa4maa1 man6 haa5 Kitty wui5 gaan2 mat1je5 mei6.*
'Kitty's mother thinks Kitty prefers vanilla flavored, but her father says Kitty wants chocolate-flavored ice cream. So the mother asks Kitty for confirmation.'

c. Negative bias: *Kitty ge3 maa4maa1 ji5wai4 Kitty m4 soeng2 jiu3 wan6nei1laa2 mei6 syut3gou1 daan6hai6 Kitty ge3 baa4baa1 gin-3dou2 Kitty mong6zyu6 wan6nei1laa2 mei6 syut3gou1 maa4maa1 hou2ging1ngaa5 zau6 man6.*

'Kitty's mother thinks Kitty doesn't want vanilla-flavored ice cream, but her father saw Kitty staring at it. The mother is surprised and asked:'

(18) a. *Kitty soeng2 m4 soeng2 jiu3 wan6nei1laa2 mei6?*
Kitty want not want should vanilla flavor
'Does Kitty want to have vanilla-flavored ice cream or not?'

b. *Kitty soeng2 jiu3 wan6nei1laa2 mei6 aa4?*
Kitty want should vanilla flavor PRT
'Does Kitty want to have vanilla-flavored ice cream?'

c. *Kitty soeng2 jiu3 wan6nei1laa2 mei6 aa3 ho2?*
Kitty want should vanilla flavor PRT PRT
'Kitty wants to have vanilla-flavored ice cream, right?'

d. *Kitty soeng2 jiu3 wan6nei1laa2 mei6 me1?*
Kitty want should vanilla flavor PRT
'Kitty doesn't want to have vanilla-flavored ice cream, does she?'

(19) a. Neutral: *A hou2 soeng2 zi1 bin1go3 hai6 gam1 gaai3 zeoi3 leng3 zung6 jau5gei1wui6 lo2dou2 hoeng1gong2siu2ze2 gun3gwan1.*
'A is wondering who is the prettiest and would win the 2015 Miss Hong Kong Pageant.'

b. Positive bias: *A gok3dak1 Louis Mak hai6 zeoi3 leng3 ge3 daan6hai6 B gok3dak1 Ada Pong sin1hai6 zeoi3 leng3 A soeng2 seoi3fuk6 B zau6 waa6:*
'A thinks Louis Mak is the prettiest, while B thinks Ada Pong is the most beautiful one. A says to B to convince him:'

c. Negative bias: *A gok3dak1 Ada Pong hai6 zeoi3 leng3 ge3 daan6hai6 B gok3dak1 Louis Mak sin1hai6 zeoi3 leng3 A soeng2 seoi3fuk6 B zau6 waa6:*
'A thinks Ada Pong is the prettiest, while he heard B saying Louis Mak is prettier. A says to B to convince him:'

(20) a. *Louis Mak hai6 m4 hai6 gam1 gaai3 zeoi3 leng3?*
Louis Mak is not is this session most beautiful
'Is Louis Mak the prettiest in 2015 Miss Hong Kong Pageant or not?'

b. *Louis Mak hai6 gam1 gaai3 zeoi3 leng3 aa4?*
Louis Mak is this session most beautiful PRT
'Is Louis Mak the prettiest in 2015 Miss Hong Kong Pageant?'

c. *Louis Mak hai6 gam1 gaai3 zeoi3 leng3 aa3 ho2?*
Louis Mak is this session most beautiful PRT PRT
'Louis Mak is the prettiest in 2015 Miss Hong Kong Pageant, right?'

d. *Louis Mak hai6 gam1 gaai3 zeoi3 leng3 me1?*
Louis Mak is this session most beautiful PRT
'Louis Mak isn't the prettiest in 2015 Miss Hong Kong Pageant, is she?'

(21) a. Neutral: *A tung4 B joek3zo2 gam1maan5 heoi3 sik6faan6 A m4 zi1 sik6 mat1je5 hou2.*
'A and B are having dinner tonight. A has no idea about what kind of food they are going to have.'

    b. Positive bias: *A lam2zyu6 keoi5dei6 gam1maan5 sik6 jat6bun2coi3 so2ji5 keoi5 man6 haa5 B hai6 m4 hai6.*
'A thinks they are going to have Japanese dishes tonight, so she asks B for confirmation.'

    c. Negative bias: *A lam2zyu6 keoi5dei6 sik6 ji3daai6lei6coi3 daan6hai6 keoi5 teng1dou2 B hai2 jat6bun2 caan1teng1 buk1zo2 toi2 A hou2 ging1ngaa5 zau6 man6:*
'A thinks they are going to have Italian dishes, but she heard B has reserved a table at Japanese restaurant. A is surprised and asked:'

(22) a. *ngo5dei6 heoi3 m4 heoi3 sik6 jat6bun2 coi3?*
we go not go eat Japanese vegetables
'Are we going to have Japanese cuisine or not?'

    b. *ngo5dei6 heoi3 sik6 jat6bun2 coi3 aa4?*
we go eat Japanese vegetables PRT
'Are we going to have Japanese cuisine?'

    c. *ngo5dei6 heoi3 sik6 jat6bun2 coi3 aa3 ho2?*
we go eat Japanese vegetables PRT PRT
'We are going to have Japanese cuisine, right?'

    d. *ngo5dei6 heoi3 sik6 jat6bun2 coi3 me1?*
we go eat Japanese vegetables PRT
'We aren't going to have Japanese cuisine, are we?'

Notes

1 **Acknowledgements:** The research is partly supported by City University of Hong Kong Strategic Research Grant (7004334) and by JSPS Kiban (C) (No. 18K00589). I would like to thank Peggy Pui Chi Cheng, Phoebe Cheuk Man Lam, Jerry Hok Ming So, and Agnes Nga Ting Tam for their assistance in conducting the experiments.

2 I assume with Matthews and Yip (1994) that (1) and (2) are all syntactically interrogatives. That is, A-not-A question is an interrogative construction which is analogous to English aubject-aux inversion, while HO2, ME1, and AA4 are question particles analogous to the Japanese question particle *ka*.

3 The numbers in Cantonese example sentences indicate lexical tones: 1 = high level; 2 = medium rising; 3 = medium level; 4 = low falling; 5 = low rising; 6 = low level.

4 There is also MAA3 particle, which is borrowed from Mandarin and somehow more formal (Matthews & Yip 1994).

5 See Lam (2014a) for other arguments.

6 See also Law *et al.* (2019), who analyze HO2 as a speech act modifier. According to Law *et al.* (2019), HO2 yields a high-level question act which inquires whether the embedded speech act can be felicitously performed by the addressee. The positive bias of an HO2 utterance is explained by the felicity condition of the embedded assertion act.

7 '+' is an update function. QUD(C) + *S* is a stack that is exactly like QUD(C), except that QUD(C) + *S* has *S* as the topmost member of the stack.

8 CG(C) + *p* is a context that is exactly like CG(C) except that CG(C) + *p* has *p*.
9 Our recent work, Yuan and Hara (2019a, 2019b, 2019c), offers a different solution. Hara and Yuan (2019, to appear) also discuss Mandarin A-not-A questions using a different version of inquisitive semantics.
10 See https://sites.google.com/site/inquisitivesemantics/ for details.
11 Groenendijk (2013) calls this secondary meaning "conventional implicature." The current chapter does not employ this term, since at least for Cantonese data, the secondary meanings which arise from biased questions do not conform the properties of conventional implicatures in the sense of Potts (2005).
12 Actually, Groenendijk (2013) uses a more recent version, called suppositional inquisitive semantics (InqS), that includes the third semantic relation, *dismissing a supposition*, $\sigma \models° p$ iff $\sigma = \varnothing$, which characterizes a denial of the antecedent of conditional sentences. For the purpose of the current chapter, a (non-suppositional) radical inquisitive semantics suffices, since we do not consider conditional sentences.
13 A reviewer suggests that AA4 questions could be ambiguous between neutral and biased questions, which have a meaning similar to a HO2 question. The reviewer's suggestion comes from the observation by Liu (1987) and Yuan (1993) that Mandarin *ma* questions, which are allegedly the Mandarin counterpart of AA4 questions, are ambiguous. The current chapter does not take this approach not only because the unambiguous lexical entry is more economic but also that the ambiguous approach makes wrong predictions. That is, it cannot explain why in (8), the AA4 question cannot be responded by, "You're right." If it had the same semantics as an HO2 question, it would indicate an expectation toward *p*.
14 See Appendix A for the rest of the stimuli.
15 Qualtrics is a web-based system that conducts online surveys. Version 45634 of the Qualtrics Research Suite. Copyright©2018 Qualtrics. Qualtrics and all other Qualtrics product or service names are registered trademarks or trademarks of Qualtrics, Provo, UT, USA. www.qualtrics.com.
16 A reviewer pointed out that in Mandarin, an A-not-A question can be used when the speaker apparently has a strong belief toward the positive proposition, as in (ia). (ib) is a Cantonese translation of (ia).

(i) a. *Wo ai ma, nin shuo wo yuanwang bu yuanwang?*
I receive reprimand, you say I wronged not wronged
'I received a reprimand, don't you think I was accused wrongly?' (Mandarin A-not-A)
     b. *ngo5 bei2 yan4 naau6 nei5 wa6 ngo5 yun1 m4 yun1-wong2?*
I receive someone reprimand, you say I wronged not wronged
'I received a reprimand, don't you think I was accused wrongly?' (Cantonese A-not-A)

I speculate that at least part of the bias toward the positive answer in (i) comes from *nin shuo/nei5 wa6* 'you say' and not from the A-not-A construction. Indeed, both of my Mandarin and Cantonese consultants report that if *nin shuo/nei5 wa6* is removed, the whole discourse becomes unnatural or expresses much weaker bias. The Mandarin consultant further notes that if the subject is changed to a third person, as in (ii), the speaker can be either biased or neutral. Thus, the A-not-A construction is not the source of the speaker's bias.

(ii) *Ta ai ma, ta yuanwang bu yuanwang?*

he receive reprimand, he wronged not wronged
'He received a reprimand, was he accused wrongly?' (A-not-A (Mandarin))

References

Aher, Martin. 2012. Free choice in deontic inquisitive semantics. In M. Aloni, V. Kimmelmann, F. Roelofsen, G.W. Sassoon, K. Schulz & M. Westera (eds.), *Logic, language and meaning, 18th Amsterdam Colloquium, Amsterdam*, 22–31. Lecture Notes in Computer Science. Springer.

Asher, Nicholas & Brian Reese. 2005. Negative bias in polar questions. In E. Maier, C. Bary & J. Huitink (eds.), *Proceedings of SuB9*, 30–43.

Baayen, Harald R. 2008. *Analyzing linguistic data: A practical introduction to statistics using R*. Cambridge: Cambridge University Press.

Baayen, Harald R., Doug J. Davidson & Douglas. M. Bates. 2008. Mixed-effects modeling with crossed random effects for subjects and items. *Journal of Memory and Language* 59. 390–412.

Baayen, R.H. 2013. *Languager: Data sets and functions with "analyzing linguistic data: A practical introduction to statistics"*. http://CRAN.R-project.org/package=languageR. R package version 1.4.1.

Bartels, Christine. 1997. *Towards a Compositional Interpretation of English Statement and Question Intonation*: University of Massachusetts dissertation.

Bates, Douglas. 2005. Fitting linear mixed models in R. *R News* 5. 27–30.

Bates, Douglas, Martin Mächler, Ben Bolker & Steve Walker. 2015. Fitting linear mixed-effects models using lme4. *Journal of Statistical Software* 67(1). 1–48. doi:10.18637/jss.v067.i01.

Ciardelli, Ivano. 2009. *Inquisitive semantics and intermediate logics*. University of Amsterdam MA thesis. Master Thesis.

Ciardelli, Ivano, Jeroen Groenendijk & Floris Roelofsen. 2013. Inquisitive semantics: A new notion of meaning. *Language and Linguistics Compass* 7(9). 459–476.

Ciardelli, Ivano & Floris Roelofsen. 2011. Inquisitive logic. *Journal of Philosophical Logic*.

Groenendijk, Jeroen. 2013. *TOCH and TOCH? in Dutch*. Presented at the Questions in Discourse Workshop, December 2013, Amsterdam.

Groenendijk, Jeroen & Floris Roelofsen. 2009. *Inquisitive Semantics and Pragmatics*. Presented at the Workshop on Language, Communication, and Rational Agency at Stanford, May.

Groenendijk, Jeroen & Floris Roelofsen. 2010. *Radical Inquisitive Semantics*. ILLC/Department of Philosophy University of Amsterdam.

Groenendijk, Jeroen & Floris Roelofsen. 2013. *Suppositional Inquisitive Semantics*. Workshop on Inquisitive Logic and Dependence Logic, ILLC, Amsterdam, June 17.

Gunlogson, Christine. 2003. *True to form: Rising and falling declaratives as questions in English*. New York: Routledge.

Hamblin, C.L. 1958. Questions. *Australasian Journal of Philosophy* 36. 159–168.

Hara, Yurie & Mengxi Yuan. 2019. Semantic universals of intonation and particles. In: *Proceedings of the 22nd Amsterdam Colloquium*, 465–474. ILLC: Amsterdam

Hara, Yurie & Mengxi Yuan. To appear. Even more varieties of conventional implicatures: Paratactically associating intonation, particles and questions. In *New frontiers in artificial Intelligence: JSAI-isAI 2019 Workshops Lecture Notes in Computer Science*, Springer: Berlin.

Heim, Irene. 1982. *The semantics of definite and indefinite noun phrases*: University of Massachussets, Amherst dissertation. [Distributed by GLSA].

Huang, C.-T. James. 1991. Modularity and Chinese A-not-A questions. In Carol Georgopolous & Robert Ishihara (eds.), *Interdisciplinary approaches to language*, 305–322. Dordrecht: Kluwer.

Kuznetsova, Alexandra, Per Bruun Brockhoff & Rune Haubo Bojesen Christensen. 2016. Lmertest: Tests in linear mixed effects models. https://CRAN.R-project. org/package=lmerTest. R package version 2.0–33.

Lam, Zoe Wai-Man. 2014a. A complex ForceP for speaker- and addressee-oriented discourse particles in Cantonese. *Studies in Chinese Linguistics* 35(2). 61–80.

Lam, Zoe Wai-Man. 2014b. A unified account for biased and non-biased questions in Cantonese. Slides presented at Workshop on Innovations in Cantonese Linguistics 2 at University of Chicago, March 7.

Law, Jess H.-K., Haoze Li & Diti Bhadra. 2019. Questioning speech acts. *Proceedings of Sinn und Bedeutung* 22(2). 53–70. doi:10.18148/sub/2018.v22i2.70. https:// ojs.ub.uni-konstanz.de/sub/index.php/sub/article/view/70.

Liu, Yuehua. 1987. A comparison of yes/no questions with ma and a-not-a questions. In: *Essays on Chinese grammar, Xiandai Chubanshe*, 209–232. Beijing.

Matthews, Stephen & Virginia Yip. 1994. *Cantonese: A comprehensive grammar*. Routledge.

Nelder, John & Robert Wedderburn. 1972. Generalized linear models. *Journal of the Royal Statistical Society. Series A (General) (Blackwell Publishing)* 135(3). 370–384.

Potts, Christopher. 2005. *The Logic of Conventional Implicatures Oxford Studies in Theoretical Linguistics*. Oxford: Oxford University Press. [Revised 2003 UC Santa Cruz PhD thesis].

R Core Team. 2017. *R:* A language and environment for statistical computing. R Foundation for Statistical Computing Vienna, Austria. www.R-project.org/.

Roberts, Craige. 1996. Information structure: Towards an integrated formal theory of pragmatics. In: Jae Hak Yoon & Andreas Kathol (eds.), *OSU working papers in linguistics*, vol. 49, 91–136. Columbus, OH: The Ohio State University Department of Linguistics. Revised 1998.

Sano, Katsuhiko. 2015. Avoiding impossibility theorems in radical inquisitive semantics. In: S. Ju, H. Liu & H. Ono (eds.), *Modality, semantics and interpretations*, Berlin, Heidelberg: Springer.

Stalnaker, Robert. 1978. Assertion. *Syntax and Semantics* 9. 315–332.

Yuan, Mengxi. 2015. *Mandarin discourse adverbs as presupposition triggers*. City University of Hong Kong dissertation.

Yuan, Mengxi & Yurie Hara. 2013. Questioning and asserting at the same time: The L% tone in A-not-A questions. In Maria Aloni, Michael Franke & Floris Roelofsen (eds.), *Proceedings of the 19th Amsterdam Colloquium*, 265–272.

Yuan, Mengxi & Yurie Hara. 2014. The semantics of the two kinds of questions in Mandarin: a case study of discourse adverbs. In: Jyoti Iyer & Leland Kusmer (eds.), *Proceedings of the 44th meeting of the north east linguistic society (nels44)*, vol. 2, 279–290. Amherst: GLSA.

Yuan, Mengxi & Yurie Hara. 2019a. Different ways of deriving Hamblin alternatives: Mandarin *ma* questions and A-not-A questions. In *Proceedings of CSSP 2019 the 13th Syntax and Semantics Conference in Paris*.

Yuan, Mengxi & Yurie Hara. 2019b. Mandarin polar questions: Their answers, contextual requirements andintonation. In *Proceedings of the 12th Generative Linguistics in the Old World & the 21st Seoul International Conference on Generative Grammar*, 585–594.

Yuan, Mengxi & Yurie Hara. 2019c. The semantic distinction between Chinese *ma* questions and A-not-A questions. *Contemporary Linguistics*.

Yuan, Yulin. 1993. A-not-A questions and their typological parameters. *Zhongguo Yuwen* 133. 103–111.

6 Softness, assertiveness and their expression via Cantonese sentence-final particles

Grégoire Winterstein, Regine Lai, and Zoe Pei-sui Luk

1 Introduction

In this chapter, we examine the notions of *assertiveness* and *softness* by looking at a set of Cantonese sentence-final particles (SFP) that have been described as conveying either assertiveness or softness.

The concepts of assertiveness and softness are frequently part of the discussions around *gendered discourse*: the study of the differences and similitudes between discourses produced by members of different genders. A typical claim is that softness is characteristic of female speech, whereas assertiveness is more male-oriented (see, for example, Lakoff 1975 for early examples). This has, however, been disputed: different authors showed that, depending on variables like context or the social status of the participants in the discourse, female participants can exhibit assertive characteristics and male speakers might be prone to softness (see, for example, Eckert & McConnell-Ginet 2013 for a critical discussion). Nevertheless, and rather unsurprisingly, it seems that subordinate groups (and, therefore, female speakers in many contexts) tend to opt for softness more often than dominating groups, while groups that hold power (such as male speakers) are more easily assertive.

On the other hand, softness and assertiveness are also part of the inventory of semantic primitives used to describe the contribution of natural language items, typically of discourse markers, in a variety of languages (e.g. English, Japanese, Chinese languages, or Thai). In this perspective, particles of softness are related to a form of politeness: they are described as "smoothing" relationships between the speaker and addressee, making an utterance sound more natural or less imposing on the addressee. Examples of particles described in this way include the Japanese particle *no* (especially in feminine speech, see McGloin 1986; Cook 1990, pace Rieser 2017), or Mandarin *a/ya* in questions (Li & Thompson 1989). Assertiveness, on the other hand, conveys a form of strong commitment or belief of the speaker regarding the content they are uttering. Again, such particles are frequently found in many languages, such as English *man* (McCready 2008, 2012) or Japanese *yo* (Davis 2009; McCready 2012).

The picture painted here raises several Issues about the status of softness and assertiveness in natural language. First, one needs to explicitly relate the

DOI: 10.4324/9781351057837-7

description of discourses (e.g., feminine or masculine discourse) as being soft or assertive, with the description of particles conveying these notions. A simple answer is that a discourse is made to be soft or assertive by the very markers used in that discourse, for example, a speaker is being soft if they use a softening marker. This is probably too simplificatory, for several reasons. For one, a discourse can be made soft or assertive in many (possibly infinite) ways that depend on the situational contexts, that is, there are factors beyond lexical choice that affect the soft/assertive dimension of a discourse.

Another issue is that there is no *a priori* reason to assume that particles are inherently soft or assertive. This is the main issue of the chapter: that of knowing whether assertiveness and softness are best considered as semantic primitives that are encoded by certain markers, or rather as side effects that arise due to the use of the markers in question in specific contexts. Though much of the literature that uses softness and assertiveness as descriptors of the meaning of discourse markers might seem to opt for the former option, nothing prevents us from seeing these notions as practical proxies for more decomposable atomic meaning postulates. This is the approach we will adopt here, showing how the formal description of our SFP accounts for how contextual and social factors trigger or impede the soft and assertive readings of these particles. Thus, the soft/assertive nature of a discourse cannot be tied to the use of markers. Rather, it is mostly contextual matters that will determine the soft or assertive reading of some discourse elements.

A last issue has to do with the compatibility of the two notions under study. Intuitively, assertiveness and softness appear mutually exclusive, since the former involves a degree of force that the latter precisely seeks to avoid or mitigate, at least according to most descriptions of the notion of softness. However, data show that what are described as assertive and softening markers can be used in combination, suggesting one of three options: (i) the notions are compatible (which would exclude the possibility that these markers bear on a single dimension with mutually exclusive readings), (ii) one notion is stronger than the other and supersedes it in case of conflict, or (iii) the soft/ assertive nature of an utterance is conversational and inferentially based on the elements present in an utterance in a given context. We will argue for that latter option.

To investigate these different issues, we focus on a subset of Cantonese SFP, namely, the particles *ge3* (嘅), *aa3* (呀/啊), and *gaa3* (㗎), which is considered to be the fusion of the first two. This is done for several reasons. First, we choose SFP because these elements scope over whole utterances and thus only bear on utterance-level properties rather than on sentence-internal elements, which somewhat simplifies the study of their meaning. Second, these particles are typically described as being either assertive or softening and thus embody the notions we are interested in. Finally, these elements have interesting combinatorial properties which show how the two notions can interact (or not).

The outline of the chapter is as follows. Section 2 gives a short overview of Cantonese, with a focus on SFP and the type of sentence types they modify, with a focus on the particles of interest and their treatment in the literature. In Section 3, we argue for a dialogical treatment of the softness particle *aa3*, based on the idea that the particle encodes a symmetry between the speaker's commitment and the call on addressee. Section 4 deals with the assertive particle *ge3* and analyzes it in a way similar to how the Japanese particle *yo* is analyzed and then show how it combines with the particle *aa3*. The semantics of *gaa3* is then laid out in order to account for the assertive nature of *ge3*. We conclude in Section 5.

2   Empirical domain and literature review

We begin this section by introducing Cantonese SFP and their general distribution and properties. In order to discuss and clarify the description of the semantic import of Cantonese SFP, we provide a summary overview of Cantonese sentence types and discuss whether SFP can modify the type of their host sentence. This section also serves to introduce some of the theoretical concepts we will use to formalize the meaning of the particles at hand. We then introduce the three particles of interest in this chapter: *aa3*, *ge3*, and *gaa3*.

2.1   *Cantonese sentence-final particles*

Like most Chinese languages, Cantonese has a number of elements called sentence-final particles that appear in the right periphery of discourse units (called sentences or utterances, depending on authors, cf. Luke 1990) and whose functions range over a great number of semantic and pragmatic dimensions. In Cantonese, the inventory of SFP is unusually large, with between 30 and 40 distinct monosyllabic elements being typically described (see a.o. Kwok 1984 or Matthews & Yip 2011). Besides their great number, another peculiar aspect of Cantonese SFP is their tendency to combine in sentence-final clusters that routinely contain two or more distinct SFP. The order of SFP in those clusters is not free and rather constrained, with at least four slots in which certain SFP can appear (Matthews & Yip 2011).

Many SFP convey information about the participants of the discourse – their "mood," their assumed epistemic status, etc. – and it is commonplace to classify SFP in terms of their meaning, for example, distinguishing SFP that are evidential, those that are exclamatory or affective, etc. (Matthews & Yip 2011), though classifications based on the type of sentence they appear in have been proposed (Kwok 1984). Out of these, the SFP of most interest to us, and expanded upon in the following, are the particle *aa3*, often described as a softener, and the particle *ge3*, described as assertive.

Another cogent reason to group some particles together is their segmental similarities and distributional patterns. Law (1990) observed that some SFP that share their onset consonant also seem to share part of their meaning, and that such SFP cannot appear together in clusters. Later, Fung (2000) and

Sybesma and Li (2007) refined and further formalized this analysis, decomposing a larger set of SFP by trying to characterize the semantic contribution of all the segmental information contained in a given SFP (i.e., onset, vowel, coda, and tone) and claiming that these elements are compositional and account for all the meaning space covered by SFP. For example, the particles *ge2* and *gaa2* share their *g-* onset with the assertive SFP *ge3*, and the previous authors identify the root of the assertiveness component of *ge3* in that particular onset, meaning, that it is also shared by all *g*-particles. Differences in how that component is conveyed by the three SFP thus depend on the meanings conveyed by the tone and rhyme of each particular SFP (which might, for example, mitigate and tone down the assertiveness). We will not discuss the well-foundedness of these claims, though we will occasionally refer to them when discussing differences between our SFP of interest and SFP that share some of their segmental characteristics (and thus, allegedly, part of their meaning).

2.2   *Cantonese sentence types*

Syntactically, Cantonese SFP attach to whole sentences. Some authors have argued that their precise sites of attachment differ between SFP (Law 2002), though these differences have little bearing on our discussions. Since SFP scope over full sentences, the semantic type of their argument thus corresponds to those of sentences. In most approaches to grammar, it is customary to distinguish between at least four main different sentence (or clause) types: declaratives, interrogatives (closed and open), imperatives, and exclamatives. There is, however, less consensus on how to define each type in a stable cross-linguistic manner. On one hand, these types have distinguishing syntactic features in languages like English, suggesting a syntactic characterization of these types (see, for example, Huddleston 2002 for characterizations of each type). On the other hand, and on a rather intuitive level, these types can also be defined in terms of their meaning and the illocutionary acts they allow. Thus, declaratives are used to convey assertions, interrogatives are used to ask questions, etc.

The overall picture is, however, more complex. First, sentence types cannot be defined on their syntactic properties alone. For example, interrogatives vary wildly in terms of their syntactic properties (Huddleston 2002) but seem unified on a semantic basis, that is, it would make little sense to bundle them up based on their sole syntactic profile, but the type of message they send is stable. Second, there is no one-to-one correspondence between illocutionary types and syntactic types. Thus, it is not true that all declarative sentences convey assertion, just like all questions are not necessarily conveyed using an interrogative sentence. This is the "Speech Act Assignment Problem," discussed by Sadock (1974) and Gazdar (1981) and in the literature they generated.

One way to clarify the matter is to follow authors like Ginzburg and Sag (2000) and assume that a sentence type is a *construction* that associates a family of syntactic types with a meaning of a certain type: a *message* that can be a proposition, a question, a fact, or an outcome (in the typology of Ginzburg & Sag 2000). This helps preserve the idea that interrogatives have a semantic unity and a syntactic disparity (though they remain related at higher level of abstraction; see Ginzburg and Sag 2000 for extensive discussion). The assignment of the illocutionary force is yet another distinct matter, partly driven by the construction at hand (which naturally allows some illocutionary acts) and the use of markers that affect the illocutionary force (see infra for details).

In Cantonese, the situation is made somehow more difficult by the fact that there are less clear-cut criteria to distinguish between syntactic sentence types. While it is straightforward to characterize the declarative and interrogative types in syntactic terms or by the presence of lexical terms (e.g., *wh*-words), the imperative and exclamative types are not distinguished in this way. There exists some constructions which can be argued to denote some particular instances of these two types, for example, the locution *m4hou2* "don't," which marks negative imperatives, (Yang 2010), or some constructions that arguably have an exclamative character (see Zhu 1994 for Mandarin), but there is no general criterion which would mark a sentence as being of either type.

Since the point of this chapter is not to establish a list of tests and characteristics of Cantonese sentence types, we will only briefly consider sentence types in relation with sentence-final particles. The question we want to answer here is whether an SFP can change the message conveyed by its host (i.e., change its sentence type) or only act on its illocutionary force. In many cases, SFPs do not appear to affect the message anyway and only add information to it, but some particles can, for example, turn declarative clauses into queries. For these latter SFPs, the question is relevant, and answering it is also relevant to the SFPs that are able to attach to different sentence types (without necessarily modifying them), because these could either shift all their compatible sentence types to a unique target type or leave all of them unchanged.

Here, we will only consider data relative to polar questions and show that SFP that mark polar questions cannot be treated as shifters of the sentence type of their host to an interrogative type. Instead, they take declarative sentences as their arguments and affect their illocutionary potential rather than change the nature of the message conveyed by the sentence. Our focus on polar questions is for several reasons:

1. Polar questions can be conveyed by both a syntactically marked interrogative sentence type pattern and through the use of SFP.
2. The question SFP we look at (*aa4*) is similar to the softening SFP we deal with here, the only difference being one of tone (and of course meaning, but the analyses we mentioned earlier suggest that they should thus have much in common).

In Cantonese, polar questions can typically be conveyed by using the so-called *A-not-A* interrogative construction, where *A* is the first syllable of the main predicate of the clause (1).

(1) *nei5 zung1 m4 zung1ji3 ngo5 aa3?*
    you   like   NEG   like   me   SFP?
    'Do you like me?'

Another way to convey a polar question is by the use of specific particles (see Hara, this volume, for details about the range of possible SFP and their semantic differences). Among the available options, the SFP *aa4* is the most neutral one in that it does not necessarily convey any bias toward an answer (though it is compatible with situations that do) and thus attaches to a declarative of content *p*, and the resulting utterance ends up conveying a polar question *?p*:

(2) *zi3ming4 jau5 fu6ceot1 gwo3 si4gaan3 aa4?*
    Jimmy   have   devote   ASP   time   SFP
    'Has Jimmy spent time (on the project)?'

In spite of their illocutionary similarities, we will show that only questions as in (1) can be treated as interrogatives, and that a question as in (2) is best treated as a questioning declarative, meaning, that its message type is a proposition. We use two observations to support this claim.

The first one is coordination, which is a routine test to show that two sentences share their types (or at least have compatible types). For example, *A-not-A* questions can easily be coordinated together (3), or with *wh*-questions, in either direction (4), showing their type of compatibility.

(3) *keoi5*   *leng3-m4-leng3*   *tung4maai4* *jau5-mou5*
    they.SG   good.looking-NEG-good.looking   and   have-have.NEG
    cin2   *aa3?*
    money   SFP
    'Are they pretty, and do they have money?'

(4) a. *bin1go3 wui5 lai4 tung4maai4 keoi5dei6 wui5-m4-wui5*
       who   will   come   and   they.PL   will-NEG-will
      sik6zo2faan6 aa3?
      eaten   SFP
      'Who will come, and will they have eaten?'

    b. *nei5 baau2-m4-baau2 tung4maai4 nei5 gan1zyu6 soeng2 heoi3*
      you   full-NEG-full   and   you   next   want   go
      bin1dou6 aa3?
      where   SFP
      'Are you full, and where do you want to go next?'

Similarly, questions with the *aa4* SFP can also be coordinated together (5).

(5) keoi5 leng3   aa4 tung4maai4 jau5 cin2 aa4?
they.SG good.looking SFP and   have money SFP
'They're good-looking? and they have money?'

An utterance of (5) is made up of two discourse units, as indicated by the use of an SFP in each unit, but the conjunction *tung4maai4* ('and') imposes the usual similarity constraints on its two arguments. Indeed, questions with the *aa4* SFP cannot be coordinated with either *A-not-A* or *wh*-questions (6), suggesting they are of different types.

(6) a. *nei5 m4hoi1sam1 aa4 tung4maai4 ji4gaa1 jiu3 zou6 mat1je5?
  you unhappy sSFP and   now want do what
  (int.) 'You're unhappy? and what do you want to do?'
 b. *zi3ming4 wui5 lai4 aa4 tung4maai4 keoi5 wui5m4wui5
  Jimmy will come SFP and they.SG will-not-will
  sik6zo2je5?
  eaten
  (int.) 'Jimmy will come? and will he have eaten?'
 c. *bin1go3 wui5 lai4 tung4maai4 ngo5dei6 wui5 zeon2si4
  who will come and we will on-time
  hoi1ci2 aa4?
  start SFP
  (int.) 'Who will come and we will start on time?'
 d. *keoi5 leng3-m4-leng3   tung4maai4 jau5
  they.SG good.looking-SG-good.looking and have
  cin2 aa4?
  money SFP
  (int.) 'Are they pretty and they are rich?'

Note that the degraded nature of the preceding examples cannot be attributed to the lack of an SFP in the first conjunct. This can be seen with example (7), in which the SFP *aa3* has been added to the first conjunct without improvement to the acceptability of the resulting utterance.

(7) *keoi5 leng3-m4-leng3   aa3 tung4maai4 jau5
they.SG good.looking-SG-good.looking SFP and have
cin2 aa4?
money SFP
(int.) 'Are they pretty and they are rich?'

Another test that distinguishes *A-not-A* questions from their *aa4* counterparts is their licensing of negative polarity items (NPI). One such element in Cantonese is the expression *jam6ho4jan4* 'anyone,' which we will consider close to its Mandarin counterpart *renhe* 'any' (Wang & Hsieh 1996). As shown in (8), the use of *jam6ho4jan4* is felicitous with *A-not-A* questions (8a), but not in *aa4* questions (8b), again pointing at a difference in the type of the two sentences.

(8) a. *jau5-mou5*   *jam6ho4jan4* *bong1dou2* *ngo5dei6?*
       have-have.NEG anyone   help   us
       'Is there anyone who can help us?'
    b. *#jau5* *jam6ho4jan4* *bong1dou2* *ngo5dei6* *aa4?*
       have   anyone   help   us   SFP
       'There's anyone who can help us?'

   Therefore, we will consider that SFPs like *aa4* do not change the semantic type of their host. Rather, they convey additional material that affects the illocutionary value of their host in a way comparable to, for example, question tags in English. We elaborate on the nature of this additional material when discussing the semantics of the particle *aa3* in the following. We now turn to this particle and the particle *ge3*.

2.3   *The softness particle* aa3

The SFP *aa3* appears to be the most frequent SFP of all. In the Hong Kong Cantonese Corpus (HKCanCor, Luke & Wong 2015), that sole particle accounts for nearly 27% of all the SFP tokens in the corpus and appears in about 25% of all the utterances in the corpus. This last figure jumps to nearly 37% if one adds to it the occurrences of the particle *gaa3* (which is analyzed as the combination of *aa3* and *ge3*).

   The following data show the use of *aa3* in a declarative (9), interrogative (10), and imperative sentences (11).

(9) *cin4min6*   *jau5* *hou2do1* *jan4*   *aa3.*
     in-front   have a-lot   person   SFP
     'There are lots of people in front.' (Fung 2000)
(10) *nei5* *hoi1-m4-hoi1sam1*   *aa3?*
     you   happy-NEG-happy   SFP
     'Are you happy?'
(11) *m4hou2* *jam2* *piu3baak6seoi2* *aa3.*
     don't   drink bleach   SFP
     'Don't drink bleach!'

In all these cases, the use of *aa3* does not seem to drastically affect the message conveyed by its host utterance, and the general intuition is that it adds a sense of "naturalness" to all examples.

   Possibly because of its high frequency and elusive meaning, *aa3* has often been described as an element without any contribution in terms of meaning.

Thus, Kwok (1984:45–46) claims that "*aa3* does not appear to carry much semantic content" and that its function is "to make the sentence sound less abrupt," noting that it can attach to declaratives, interrogatives, and imperatives. Similarly, Matthews and Yip (2011:398) mention that *aa3* can be used in questions if no other SFP is present and that it "softens" the force of statements and confirmations. Law (1990:4.2.2.3) echoes Kwok (1984) in considering that *aa3* lacks semantic content and that its main function is "to make an utterance sound more natural."

Sybesma and Li (2007) choose a slightly different route and describe it as conveying a value of "smooth alert," by which they mean that *aa3* "makes the utterance fit more smoothly in the conversation," though they never elaborate on how it manages to do so. The same authors also note the versatility of *aa3*, which can combine with all sentence types.[1]

There thus seems to be few constraints on the use of *aa3*, be it in terms of the type of message it can affect or in the semantic effects it conveys. Nevertheless, *aa3* cannot be taken as a semantically vacuous SFP. Example (12) shows a clear case in which the use of *aa3* is anomalous (under the most probable interpretation) and where the particle *ge3* is instead preferred.

(12) a: *m4hou2   ci4dou3*
      don't   late
      'Don't be late!'
   b: *hai6   ge3/#   aa3.*
      COP   SFP
      'I understand./# Yeah, right?'

In (12), B's acknowledgment of A's command cannot be expressed by using *aa3*. Using *aa3* there would convey a sort of cheekiness and detachment regarding the order, in a way very similar to what the use of a question tag would in English (as reflected in the choice of translation). If *aa3* was all about helping fit its host in the conversation, one would expect it to be felicitous in (12), where B offers the preferred sort of reply to an order, that is, acknowledgment. We deal with this case and the semantic import of *aa3* in Section 3.

2.4 *The assertive particle* ge3

Compared to *aa3*, the SFP *ge3* is much less frequent, being ranked as the 16th most frequent SFP in HKCanCor and appearing in slightly more than 1% of the utterances. That number increases to 12.3% if one adds the occurrences of the SFP *gaa3* in the picture (which comes as the fusion of *ge3* and *aa3*). A common description of *ge3* is as a marker of the epistemic status of the speaker, used when the speaker is fully committed to the content of their utterance. For example, *ge3* in B's answer in (13) is consistent with the assumption that the speaker is maximally sure of their place of birth.

(13) a. *nei5   hai2   bin1dou6   ceot1sai3   gaa3?*
      you   at   where   born   SFP
      'Where were you born?'
   b. *ngo5   hai2   hoeng1gong2   ceot1sai3   ge3.*
      I   in   Hong   Kong   born   SFP
      'I was born in Hong Kong.'

Thus, Kwok (1984:42–43) described *ge3* as expressing "certainty" and "determination," along the same lines as the Chinese Mandarin particle *de/的*.[2] She further characterizes *ge3* by asserting that "the [host] sentence is a factual statement expressing what the speaker regards as true. It is used to strengthen the force of the assertion, and is like prefacing the sentence with 'It is a fact,'" a description that is later adopted by Law (1990).

This "factuality" of *ge3* and its similarities with some English *it*-clefts are frequently noted in the literature. For example, Matthews and Yip (2011:401) note that *ge3* is used for assertions of facts, often marking focus or emphasis, then observe that *ge3* enters the emphatic construction *hai6 . . . ge3*, where *hai6* is the Cantonese copula.

Similarly, Fung (2000) argues that *ge3*'s major function is to "mark a high level of commitment on the part of the speaker to the proposition conveyed by the utterance, asserting the certainty of the proposition without any doubts." To back up this claim, Fung uses the incompatibility of *ge3* with epistemic markers expressing values below certainty, such as *daai6koi3* ('probably') cf. (14) (her (31')), where *daai6koi3* contrasts with the felicitous *jat1ding6* ('surely/definitely').

(14) *aa3-ji6 suk1   jat1ding6/?daai6koi3   wui3   luk6zuk6*
     second-uncle   sure/probably   will   continue
     gei3-faan1lei4   ge3.
     mail-back   SFP
     'Second uncle surely/?probably will continue to send (them to us).'

Later, Sybesma and Li (2007: fn. 12) summarize several descriptions of *ge3* and describe it as an "actuality marker," that is, as "asserting that the statement to which it is added is highly relevant to the current conversation." They continue by stating that the factuality of *ge3* "seem[s] to us to be side-effects," though they remain silent about how these are actually derived, or about how relevance is to be defined.

In terms of compatibility with sentence types, *ge3* appears to be more restricted than *aa3* and is mostly considered in declaratives, as in (13). However, beyond declaratives, *ge3* is also compatible with wh-interrogatives, as in (15).

(15) *bin1go3   se2   ge3?*
     who   write   SFP
     'Who wrote that?'

The contribution of *ge3* in interrogatives is again difficult to characterize precisely. Its function appears to indicate a form of assertiveness about the question having a (true) resolving answer, for example, excluding that the answer to (15) is "nobody" (rather than being assertive about a particular answer which would amount to a form of biased question).

While intuitive enough, these descriptions of the semantics of *ge3* are problematic on several accounts.

First, contrary to the claim of Fung (2000), *ge3* cannot be seen as an epistemic marker, or at least not one bearing on the same dimension as epistemic adverbs. To see it, we observe that in Fung's example, the allegedly problematic epistemic adverb *daai6koi3* can be replaced by either *ho2nang4* or *waak6ze2*, which both express epistemic uncertainty and are felicitous with *ge3* (16).

(16) *aa3-ji6 suk1   waak6ze2/ho2nang4   wui3   luk6zuk6   gei3-faan1lei4   ge3.*
       second-uncle   maybe/probably   will   continue   mail-back   SFP
       'Second uncle might continue to send (them to us).'

The most prominent reading of (16) is that the speaker is certain that there is a possibility of receiving mail from their second uncle. Under that reading, the use of *daai6koi3* is actually also judged natural.

Second, the description of *ge3* as indicating factivity is potentially misleading. Typical treatments of factivity treat it as the (usually presupposed) indication that a piece of information is true in all possible worlds and cannot thus be otherwise. Factive information is therefore not open to refutation (see, inter alia, the case of factive verbs that trigger presuppositions: Karttunen 2016; or that of exclamatives, Zanuttini & Portner 2003). For example, if one replies *no* to (17), they are refuting the regrets of Cameron, not the oversleeping (which is the factive part of the utterance).

(17) Cameron regrets oversleeping.

The information conveyed in a *ge3* declarative can, however, easily be refuted, as in (18), where B's reply directly targets the content of *ge3*'s prejacent, suggesting that labelling *ge3* as a factive element, or comparing it to the English construction "It is a fact that . . ." is ill-advised.

(18) a: *keoi5   hai2   hoeng1gong2   ceot1sai3   ge3.*
          they.SG   in   Hong-Kong   born   SFP
          'They were born in Hong Kong.'
      b: *m4   hai6   aak3.*
          NEG   COP   SFP
          'No they were not.'

Another piece of data is the fact that *ge3* can be used in the antecedent of conditionals (19).

(19) *jyu4gwo2   jau5   jan4   sung3   tiu4   hou2   gwai3   ge3*
      if   there.is person give   CL   very   expensive GEN
      kwan4   bei2   nei5,   daan6hai6   tiu4   kwan4   hou2   wat6dat6   ge3,
      dress   DAT   you   but   CL   dress   very   ugly   SFP
      gam2   nei5   jiu3m4jiu3   aa3?
      then   you   want.NEG.want   SFP
      'If someone gave you an expensive dress but the dress is ugly, will you
          still want it?'

If *ge3* did convey factivity about its prejacent in the way presupposition triggers do, one would expect that contribution to actually clash with the semantics of the conditional which precisely indicate that its antecedent is not true in
all possible worlds (Heim 1983). However, in an example like (19), there is no
such sense of factivity that comes with the use of *ge3*, or one of contradiction
with the conditional construction. Note that in (19), whatever contribution
ge3 is having is modalized: the intuitive understanding is that the speaker is
being forceful about the ugliness of the putative dress in the fictional world
introduced by the conditional. Therefore, a non-factive description of it seems
warranted, though it has to be one that salvages the intuition that *ge3* indicates
a form of assertiveness of the speaker.

Finally, Sybesma and Li's claim about *ge3* as a marker of relevance needs
to be made more precise. Example (20) shows that *ge3* is compatible with
gong2hoi1jau6gong2 ('by the way'), which is routinely taken to indicate that
the speaker is introducing an element which is not relevant to the current
conversation.

(20) *gong2hoi1jau6gong2   ngo5   hai4   m4tung4ji3   keoi5   ge3*
      by-the-way   I   am   disagree   them.SG   SFP
      'By the way, I disagree with them.'

Thus, if relevance is to be the key notion behind *ge3*, we need a precise description of what it is exactly that makes the host of *ge3* relevant. This will be
the topic of Section 4, where we show that a notion of relevance borrowed
from analyses of Japanese *yo* is applicable to the case of *ge3* and accounts for
the way it indicates the authority of the speaker.

2.5   *The merged particle* gaa3

As previously mentioned, the SFP *gaa3* combines *ge3* and *aa3* together in a single particle. The main reasons for this claim are that the sequence of *ge3* and *aa3*
is never observed in Cantonese and that particle merging is a rather-common
phenomenon (Matthews & Yip 2011); *gaa3* is the second most common SFP in
HKCanCor (after *aa3*) and appears in 11.24% of all the utterances in the corpus.

The merged status of *gaa3* partly explains that unlike *aa3* and *ge3*, its meaning is not discussed in all the works dealing with Cantonese SFP. The particle

is not discussed by Kwok (1984) or by Law (1990), Fung (2000), or Matthews and Yip (2011), who all mostly list it as the combination of *ge3* and *aa3*, without discussing the semantics of the combination in details (or at all).

Sybesma and Li (2007) discuss *gaa3* to a greater extent since in their account *gaa3* does not come as the fusion of two distinct SFPs but as the combination of more basic elements that are also found in *ge3* and *aa3*. This is summarized in Table 6.1, where one can see that all the meaningful elements in *gaa3* (i.e., those that are neither defaults nor empty) are the sum of those in *ge3* and *aa3*.

Table 6.1 The structure of *aa3*, *ge3*, and *gaa3* according to Sybesma and Li (2007)

SFP	Onset	Vowel	Coda	Tone
aa3	Ø	/a/	Ø	3 (default)
ge3	/k/	/ɛ/ or /ə/ (default)	Ø	3 (default)
gaa3	/k/	/a/	Ø	3 (default)

Sybesma and Li describe *gaa3* as

essentially the same as *ge3*; it may be seen as softening *ge3* a bit in the sense that by using *gaa3*, the speaker says 'it is a relevant fact that . . . but I don't mind that you don't know or forgot.'

Again, while the description might have some intuitive weight, the details of its formal implementation are not crystal clear.

The case of *gaa3* also shows that it felicitously combines the values of *ge3* and *aa3*. This means that the two SFPs are anything but incompatible (given the frequency of *gaa3*, they are even the two SFPs that combine the most frequently). This rules out simple descriptions of *aa3* as downtoning a conversational move and *ge3* as strengthening it. There is thus a need for a more precise description of the effects of *ge3* and *aa3* that allows both to coexist while conveying seemingly antagonist conversational contributions.

2.6 *Taking stock*

The preceding overview of the particles shows that even though these elements have received some attention on the syntactic level, the precise description of their meaning remains an open issue. On one hand, the conversational softness conveyed by *aa3* has to be qualified in a way that makes it compatible with all sentence types and accounts for the fact that in certain contexts, using *aa3* is not interpreted as indicating softness. On the other hand, the case of *ge3* requires the identification of the dimension on which *ge3* bears. As we have seen, this is probably not a scale of epistemic certainty, and if it marks relevance, this notion has to be properly defined. Finally, we need to ensure that each of the descriptions we come up with is compatible with each other to account for the semantics of *gaa3*, and have to describe the ways in which all these elements convey softness or assertiveness.

3   Softness from symmetry: the SFP *aa3*

3.1   *Theoretical background: dialogue*

To account for the semantic contribution of *aa3*, we will adopt a dialogical perspective, inspired, among others, by the KoS[3] model proposed by Ginzburg (2012) (whose elements can all be traced to earlier work in different perspectives). Specifically, we will distinguish the effect of an utterance in terms of *speaker's commitment* (SC) and *call on addressee* (CoA). These elements are the constituents of *conversational moves* which explicate the illocutionary force of an utterance.

To represent the content of SC and CoA (and deal with other phenomena), KoS uses a structured dialogue game board (DGB) for each conversation participant. Each participant keeps track of their and other participant's conversational moves on their DGB, for example, by incrementing the set of propositions shared with other participants (the shared ground, dubbed FACTS in KoS), the list of questions under discussion (QUD), the last question that was asked, the formal properties of the last utterance in the conversation, etc. A conversational move is then analyzed in terms of its effects on the DGB of all the participants in the conversation. For example, in the case of cooperative querying between two participants, the following protocol is proposed by Ginzburg (2012) (with the horizontal dimension representing temporal succession for A and B, meaning, that the moves that appear in parallel lines are temporally aligned).

```
LatestMove.Cont = Ask(A,q): IllocProp
A: push q onto QUD; release turn
B: push q onto QUD; take turn; make q-specific utterance
```

This is to be read as meaning that if the latest conversational move was a case of participant *A* asking a question *q* (an element of the type IllocProp), then both *A* and *B* are expected to push *q* on their QUD stack, which will be followed by *A* releasing the floor, which will be taken by participant *B*, who will then make some utterance related to *q* (thus instantiating a general conversational constraint stating that if *q* is the QUD-maximal element, then any participant can make a move relevant to *q*). That protocol is not binding: participants can choose to ignore it and, for example, reject or ignore the question instead of addressing it. That will, however, correspond to a different, non-cooperative protocol.

In general, there seems to be a default for having a match between the SC and the CoA (Stalnaker 1978), which is visible in the earlier script: both speaker and addressee are expected to treat the content of the latest move in the same way, in that case by pushing it on their QUD stack.

The case of assertion is given a more complex treatment, which might come as surprising, given how assertion is often thought as the most basic discourse move. This is linked to the observation that, from a dialogic point of view, assertions need to be *grounded* before they can enter the shared ground between speaker and addressee (Clark 1996). This is captured by considering that an assertion of a content p by a speaker A first opens an issue about whether p is the case, which is pushed on all participants' QUD stacks. After taking the floor, the other participant B then has the option of either discussing the issue or accepting it.

```
LatestMove.Cont = Assert(A, p): IllocProp
A: push p? onto QUD, release turn
B: push p? onto QUD, take turn;    Option 1: Discuss p?,
                                   Option 2: Accept p
```

Should B decide to accept the content p, the corresponding script states that p is added to all participants' FACTS set and that the question $?p$ is removed from their QUD stacks, effectively *grounding* the content p.

```
LatestMove.Cont = Accept(B, p): IllocProp
B: increment FACTS with p; pop p? from QUD;
A: increment FACTS with p; pop p? from QUD;
```

These scripts are exemplified in (21), where A's move is analyzed as involving a script which puts a question p? = *Has Cameron left for Thailand?* On both A's and B's QUD, and expecting B's to take the turn with either a discussion about the content of p? or indicate their acceptance of p (which B does with their assertion, thus grounding the content between A and B).

(21) a: *Cameron has left for Thailand.*
       b: *Yeah.*

We have given a rough presentation of how various interactions proceed in dialogue, described in terms of their import on the participants' DGB and general constraints on the elements of these DGB.

Another piece of the puzzle we need to consider is how these conversational moves are tied to the linguistic structure and content of the utterances used to perform these moves. As mentioned earlier, while there is no simple solution to this so-called speech act assignment problem, it has been argued that the conversational moves allowed by an utterance (partly) come from a combination of the semantic type of the message it denotes and the presence of some markers that signal specific moves.

One example is the case of English question tags, which explicitly signal a request for confirmation, which is then analyzed as a check move that forces a response about the issue, rather than a tacit acceptance. This is what accounts for the difference in (22), where *I see* indicates acceptance rather than explicit confirmation (and is thus infelicitous after a check-move).

(22) a. A: *Bo is leaving. B: I see.*
     b. A: *Bo is leaving, isn't he?* B: #*I see.*

3.2   aa3: *a marker of dialogical symmetry*

In Section 2.3, we showed how the SFP *aa3* is seemingly compatible with all sentence types and seems to have a very elusive semantic contribution. Here, we analyze it as a marker of conversational move. Precisely, we argue that *aa3* enforces the symmetry of the moves on the speaker and addressee's DGB.

We have mentioned earlier that this symmetry requirement has been considered to be a default in human communication (Stalnaker 1978). However, it can be, and is often, overridden by specific markers. For example, Beyssade and Marandin (2006) analyze rising declaratives as utterances that involve a mismatch between the SC and the CoA. Specifically, the speaker of a rising declarative adds the content of their assertion to the set of their publicly shared beliefs but asks their addressee to add an issue about that content to their QUD stack instead. The corresponding script is thus one where only the addressee is adding (and then resolving) a question to their QUD.

Rather than indicating a mismatch, we argue that the role of *aa3* is to signal that the speaker expects the addressee to deal with the content they uttered in the same way as they do. Roughly, this means the following for assertions, questions, and imperatives[4] (Beyssade & Marandin 2006):

- Committing to discussing or accepting a proposition in the case of the assertion of a content *p*. Formally speaking, this means that the speaker signals that they wish the addressee to follow the standard script for assertion described earlier (i.e., first adding an issue ?*p* to the QUD before either grounding it or discussing it, where grounding is the preferred and expected option).
- Committing to a question in the case of an interrogative of content *q*, which formally means adding *q* to the QUD stack.
- Committing to an outcome *o* in the case imperatives, that is, to the future actualization of some situation, possibly carried out by an agent. While we do not go in the details of how to formally represent outcomes, we will follow Beyssade and Marandin 2006 and assume a to-do-list (TDL) component in the DGB which is a set that keeps track of the outcomes. So adding *o* to the TDL means that the speaker considers that *o* will happen in the future, under the responsibility of the addressee. The use of *aa3* then explicitly asks the addressee to commit to that same future actualization.

Our proposal explains the versatility of *aa3* with different sentence types: it marks the symmetry of what the speaker and addressee are doing but is not tied to any peculiarity of the type of message. It also helps to account for the fact that the particle is, by far, the most frequent, since it seems reasonable that interrogatives are mostly used for questions, declaratives for assertions, etc.

One can wonder about the need for an SFP that enforces what appears to be a conversational default. We can think of several reasons for which such an SFP might exist. First, discourse particles that semantically mark conversational defaults are routinely found in all languages. For example, the English adverb *then* indicates temporal succession, which is a conversational default that, for example, can be inferred on the basis of Gricean maxims Grice (1989). Second, and somehow more speculatively, we have seen that Cantonese has less clear-cut syntactic criteria that define sentence types and that SFP seem to carry a lot of the information that constrains the conversational move associated with an utterance. Therefore, it does not seem that outlandish to have an element which semantically enforces that the conversational import of an utterance matches its type. Finally, the existence of other options, namely, other SFP that enter into competition with *aa3*, makes it look even more plausible to have a particle that marks the default interpretation and strengthens the norm. This also helps to explain some of the pragmatic effects that come with the use of competitors, as we shall discuss in the following.

3.3 Applications

We now show how our proposal applies to two different cases in which *aa3* is either not licensed or clashes with other information present in the utterance. As we already mentioned, such observations are unexpected if one assumes, with most of the existing literature, that *aa3* is semantically vacuous or simply serves to make things more natural.

The first case is the impossibility of using *aa3* in rising declaratives. Cantonese does allow the use of prosody to indicate questioning, as in many other languages, cf. (23) (where the use of a question mark indicates the rising intonation).

(23) *keoi5   lai4?*
      they.   sg come
      'They're coming?'

While (23) is possible without an SFP, adding *aa3* to it makes it infelicitous with a question reading (24).

(24) **keoi5   lai4   aa3?*
      they.sg   come   sfp
      'They're coming?'

Rising declaratives can be analyzed as involving a mismatch between the SC and CoA (Beyssade & Marandin 2006). These constructions involve a declarative sentence type, meaning, that the speaker commitment is to a proposition p (via the prototypical script of assertion). But the effect of the rising declaratives is to ask the addressee to commit to a question instead, which involves a different script than that of assertion. Therefore, we explain the infelicity of *aa3*: its symmetric semantic clashes with the asymmetric one of the rising declarative. Similarly, *aa3* is not compatible with rhetorical questions, as in (25) (adapted from Ginzburg 2012).

(25) a: *gam1maan1   gin3-m4-dou2   lou5sai3   ge3?*
        tonight   see-NEG-PRT   boss   SFP
        'I can't see the boss here tonight.'
   b: *nei5   gok3dak1   keoi3   hai2   bin1   aa1 (#aa3)?*
        you   think   they.SG   at   where   SFP
        'Where do you think he is?'
   a: *zing3   puk1gaai1*
        exactly   jerk
        'What a jerk.'

A case like (25) is analyzed as a reassertion (Ginzburg 2012), that is, as an interrogative that already has a resolving answer in the FACTS set. Here, the situation is, in a way, opposite to that of rising declaratives: the speaker's commitment is to a question, but the CoA is to add (or activate) a proposition in the shared ground that resolves the question. This asymmetry prevents the felicitous use of *aa3*.

The second case is that of (12), already introduced in Section 2.3, where *aa3* appears incompatible with a response acknowledging a command, unlike the SFP *ge3*, or a simple mark of acceptance such as *o4* 'right/I see.'[5]

(12) a: *m4hou2   ci4dou3*
        don't   late
        'Don't be late!'
   b: *hai6   (ge3/#aa3)/   o4.*
        COP   SFP   fine
        'I understand./# Yeah, right?/Right.'

To account for what happens in the previous example, we need some measure of understanding of how commands work from a dialogical perspective and of the contribution of the copula *hai6*.

Starting with the latter, we argue that *hai6* is best seen as a marker of confirmation. This can be seen in a simple interaction, as in (26).

(26) a: *Aa3-Mei5   kam4jat6   heoi3zo2   jat6bun2.*
        A-Mei   yesterday go:PFV   Japan
        'A-Mei left for Japan yesterday.'

b: *hai6   aa3.*
   COP   SFP
'Yes, she did.'

Though felicitous, B's reply in (26) does not convey mere acceptance but indicates that B is already aware of the information stated by A and wishes to confirm it. If the news of A-Mei leaving for Japan were new to B, the reply in question would be infelicitous. Thus *hai6* conveys a confirmation by B, and adding *aa3* to it basically entails the expectation that A will mirror B's contribution, namely, register that the information was known to B.

Turning now to the case of commands, we can see why replying to a command with a confirmation in the form of *hai6 aa3* is infelicitous. The use of *hai6* in the reply by B basically mimics the content of A's command, which means that B wishes to signal either that they add the outcome *o*, denoted by A's command to their TDL, or that *o* is already in their TDL. Thus, should B use *aa3* in their reply, they would trigger a mirror CoA on A to have *o* in their TDL. Thus, the utterance is problematic for two reasons. First, asking A to add *o* to their TDL matches the SC of A's own move when giving the order and is thus dialogically redundant (and the likely source of the "cheekiness" and detachment associated with the reply). Second, signaling that *o* is already in B's TDL would clash with the felicity conditions of directives that typically state that the person receiving the order should not be expected to act as indicated in the order if that order had not been given (Austin 1962). However, as we will argue in Section 4.2, when the same move is performed with the SFP *ge3*, no symmetry requirement is involved, and the import of the confirmation solely bears on B's DGB, which explains why it felicitously functions as a signal for accepting the command.

3.4   aa3 *and softness*

To conclude about *aa3*, we can now retrace the root of its "soft" nature. It is essentially tied to the fact that instead of inflicting content on the addressee, it is an explicit signal by the speaker to the addressee that they desire the addressee to act according to the script of normal conversation. In doing so, the speaker ensures that their contribution will be integrated in conversation as they intend, with the explicit approval of the addressee. That desire of approval by the addressee thus minimizes the potential for conflict, which we argue is precisely at the core of the notion of softness.

Note that this soft reading of *aa3* is tied to the conversational rules at play at a given point in a dialogue and is thus an inference rather than part of the semantics of the SFP. When the dialogical setting forbids a symmetry of moves between speaker and addressee (as in (12)), *aa3* cannot be used to add softness to a conversational move.

To go even further, in certain circumstances, using *aa3* will even convey aspects at odds with the notion of softness. For example, in the case of assertions, we claimed that *aa3* encodes the standard script for assertion. Because that script involves putting the prejacent *p* of *aa3* as a polar question ?*p* in the QUD, it also entails that *p* is presented as not being part of the facts shared by the discourse participants, and that the addressee is expected to explicitly endorse *p*. Thus, using *aa3* for potentially offensive or unpleasant content for the addressee can give rise to situations in which the content pushed by the speaker might not smoothly be validated by the other party.[6] Consider the dialogue in (27).

(27) a: | *dim2gaai2* | *nei5* | *m4* | *tung4* | *ngo5* | *ceot1gaai1* | *aa3?* |
| --- | --- | --- | --- | --- | --- | --- |
| why | you | NEG | with | me | go.out | SFP |

   'Why won't you go out with me?'

   b: | *jan1wai6* | *nei5* | *taai3* | *joeng2seoi1* | *aa3.* |
| --- | --- | --- | --- | --- |
| because | you | too.much | ugly | SFP |

   'Because you're too ugly.'

In (27), the use of *aa3* in B's answer is understood to mean that the ugliness of A is the objective, real reason for which B does not wish to go out with A. That information is presented as new by B, and A is explicitly asked to endorse it as such, which A might, in turn, find unpleasant. A somewhat more natural version of B's answer would rely on the SFP *lo1* ( ) instead of *aa3*. The SFP *lo1* has been analyzed as indicating information that is expected by all parties (Hara & McCready 2017), which means that using *lo1* will not require the addressee to explicitly endorse that information as with *aa3*. Thus, in a somewhat paradoxical way, presenting unpleasant information as information that is expected by all parties is less threatening than using a marker that indicates prototypical assertion.

4   Assertiveness from relevance: the SFP *ge3*

In Section 2.4, we rejected previous claims that the SFP *ge3* bears on a dimension of epistemicity, indicating a maximally high belief of the speaker in the content of their utterance. Furthermore, we also observed that *ge3* is compatible with interrogative utterances calling for a more abstract description of its content than one only involving matters of truth and belief. In this section, we first review proposals made to describe the particle *yo* in Japanese, which appears similar to *ge3* in many respects, notably about its alleged assertive character. We then show how to apply these insights to the case *ge3* in a way that combines with our proposal for *aa3* in order to yield the meaning of the SFP *gaa3*.

4.1   *Another assertive SFP: Japanese* yo

At first sight, the Japanese SFP *yo* seems to bear great resemblance to *ge3*: both are intuitively described as assertive markers that convey a form of certainty of the speaker. McCready (2012) summarizes two trends of approaches to *yo* that treat it either as a speech act strengthening operator, analogous to English sentence-final *man* (McCready 2008), or as a marker of Gricean relevance (Davis 2009). The first analysis basically entails that any sentence used with the SFP *yo* updates the shared ground with its prejacent, possibly discarding previously established information that is not compatible with that prejacent. The second one strips *yo* of its assertive nature, instead analyzing it as indicating that its prejacent is relevant (in a Gricean sense), because it resolves a contextually salient problem. Davis argues that the strengthening force of *yo* is a matter of intonation: *yo* is assertive only when uttered with falling intonation. With a rising intonation, *yo* still conveys relevance, but without that assertive component. In that regard, one could imagine that Davis's proposal is a formal implementation of how Sybesma and Li (2007) describe the content of *ge3* (cf. Section 2.4).

A first piece of data, and one that supports the analysis of *yo* as a marker of "strong assertion," involves explicit denials, as in (28).[7] Note that in that example, *yo* is uttered with falling intonation (indicated with ↓).

(28) (Japanese)
    a: *saki*   *Jon-ga*   *kaetta.*
       just.now John-NOM   went.home
       'John just went home.'
    b: *uso!*
       lie
       'No way!'
    a: *kaetta*   **yo**↓.
       went.home SFP
       'He DID go home.'

An example like (29) shows how *yo* can indicate a resolution to a salient decision problem (in that case, deciding which sushi to get). In (29), the intonation on *yo* is rising (indicated with ↑), and its contribution is not felt to be as forceful as in (28).

(29) (Japanese)
    a: *dono*   *sushi-ni*   *shi-yoo*   *kana?*
       which   sushi-DAT   do-HORT   PRT
       'Which sushi should I get?'
    b: *koko-no*   *maguro-wa*   *umai*   **yo**↑.
       here-DAT   tuna-TOP   good   SFP
       'The tuna here is good.'

To account for these examples, Davis (2009) proposes to tease apart the contribution of *yo* and intonation. Thus, in (28), the forcefulness of A's denial in their second utterance is a consequence of the falling intonation on *yo*, which conveys that the speaker requires some information to be downdated before updating the shared ground with the prejacent of *yo* (pretty much along the lines of what McCready 2012 proposes for *yo*). This accounts for the fact that using a falling intonation on *yo* in (29) would be odd, unless one assumes some extra reasons for the speakers to be in conflict.

To account for the contribution of *yo*, Davis then proposes to rely on the existence of a salient decision problem associated with the conversation. Such a problem can be related to the motivation behind QUD approaches to discourse structure (Roberts 1996), and also to the goal the speaker is arguing for in their discourse (Winterstein & Schaden 2011), meaning, it represents an important part of what makes up the interpretation of a discourse. It thus makes sense that some natural language items would refer to it. Minimally, a decision problem can be conceived as involving a set of possible actions, with some related payoffs for the discourse participants. The payoffs do not solely depend on the actions, but also on which world the participants are. So for example, in (29), the decision problem is which sushi to get, the related actions are picking up salmon, tuna, etc., and the payoffs for these actions depend on the actual quality of each fish at that particular tuna place. The role of *yo* is to indicate that grounding its prejacent (which might entail different actions, depending on the nature of the prejacent) will single out one action associated with the decision problem as being optimal. Thus, in (29), by mentioning that the tuna is good, the speaker singles out one particular action (choosing tuna) as yielding a good (and guaranteed) outcome.

4.2   *ge3 and relevance*

The various contexts of use we exemplified for *yo* do not all license *ge3*, but the two SFPs enjoy a degree of similarity, which we show in this section. This supports an analysis of *ge3* along the same lines as that of *yo*, that is, as a marker of relevance, where relevance is defined relative to a decision problem.

To begin, contexts that involve a denial, as in the dialogue (28), do license *ge3* in Cantonese, though to maximize its felicity, *ge3* should be followed by the SFP *laa3* (30).

(30) a: *Aa3-Mei5   faan1zo2   uk1kei2.*
       A-Mei   back-PFV home
       'A-Mei went home.'
   b: *m4hai6   maa5.*
       NEG-COP   SFP
       'No way.'
   a: *keoi5   hai6   faan1zo2 uk1kei2 **ge3**   laa3.*
       they.SG   COP   back   PFV   home   SFP   SFP
       'She DID.'

Furthermore, in scenarios such as (29), while the use of *ge3* is not licensed on its own, using *gaa3* is felicitous (31).

(31) a: *ngaai3 matlje5 sik6   hou2 le1?*
  order what eat   good SFP
  'What should I/we order?'
 b: *nildou6 ge3 gullouljuk6 hou2 hou2sik6 (gaa3/# ge3).*
  here GEN sweet.sour.pork very good.eat SFP
  'The sweet and sour pork here is delicious.'

In sum, the sort of examples that justify an analysis of *yo* also license *ge3*, though they usually require the use of some other SFP.

Therefore, we will argue that the semantics of *ge3* is basically the same as that of *yo*. The observations about the need for extra SFP come from external factors, which in Japanese are regulated by intonation but in Cantonese mostly come from the use of other SFP.

Specifically, the use of *aa3* can be likened to that of rising intonation in Japanese. Though we did not analyze *aa3* in the same way as Davis analyzes rising intonation, their general effects are comparable: both entail grounding information in the standard way associated with the type of their prejacent. Thus, the natural character of *gaa3* in (31) follows along the same lines as that of *yo* with rising intonation in (29).

Why, then, is the use of bare *ge3* degraded in (31)? Our discussion of example (12) earlier suggested that when *ge3* is used, there is no CoA that comes along with it. And indeed, when used on its own, *ge3* does not seem to allow the speaker to call on the addressee, for example, *ge3* is not felicitous in refusals, or more generally in dispreferred replies (which typically involve calling on the addressee to endorse one's unexpected move):

(32) a: *ngo5 gamlmaan5 daklhaan4. ngo5dei6 hou2m4hou2*
  I   tonight   free   we   good.NEG.good
  ceotlheoi3 haang4haa5?
  go.out   walk.a.bit
  'I'm free tonight, should we go out?'
 b: *nei5 gamlmaan5 jiu3 zou6je5 gaa3/? ge3.*
  you tonight   need work SFP
  'You have to work tonight.'

However, we do not want to directly put a constraint of "no CoA" in the semantics of *ge3*, since the existence of the SFP *gaa3* shows that the content of *ge3* is compatible with the symmetry constraint of *aa3* (which, in turn, can entail a CoA). Rather, we propose that this feature of *ge3* is an effect of Gricean-like pragmatic blocking. Because there exists a form that is equally complex (and even more frequent) as *ge3* that encodes the same thing as *ge3* plus an explicit CoA (namely, the SFP *gaa3*), then the use of *ge3* can be taken as a signal that the hearer does not wish to use *gaa3*, which in turn means that the speaker does not wish to call on the addressee.[8] So in a case like (32), if the speaker uses *ge3*, the most likely explanation for their choice is that they did not want to use *gaa3*. Since the only difference between the two is the contribution of *aa3*, the inference is that they do not have particular expectations of the addressee to add the content of their utterance to the common ground which clashes with the content of the discourse move.

Explaining the preference for adding *laa3* in (30) would require a proper analysis of the SFP *laa3*, which is beyond the aims of the present work. The SFP *laa3* is often introduced as indicating some change of state (Kwok 1984; Fung 2000; Sybesma & Li 2007) which does not directly account for its meaning in (30). Other authors mention that *laa3* can have an "adhortative/directive" reading (Fang 2003, cited by Sybesma and Li), which might more closely match its effect in (30). Whatever that effect, it comes as an addition to the contribution of *ge3*; just like in the case of *gaa3*, the effect of *aa3* is added to that of *ge3*.

A last point about *ge3* has to do with its role in questions. As already mentioned, *ge3* is felicitous in questions, as in (15), where its addition suggests that the speaker considers that their question does have a true resolving answer.

(15) *bin1go3   se2   ge3?*
     who   write SFP
     'Who wrote that?'

First, our description of *ge3* does not prevent it from being used in questions. This is because one question can help resolve another one (see discussions in Merin 1999, among others). Using the concepts introduced earlier, a question q addresses a decision problem d if answering q helps pick out an optimal action in d. This means that the set of answers to q must be such that for any particular answer in q, there is an associated optimal action in d. If the question has no resolving answer, then the relevance condition of *ge3* is not met. This, we argue, is what gives rise to its interpretation in questions.

Thus, in the case of (15), *ge3* entails that somebody did write "that" and that their identity can be recovered. A context that would make this question felicitous is one in which a teacher sees some offensive writing on a board and wishes to punish the author. Asking (15) indicates that the teacher assumes the culprit is in the room, and identifying them will help the teacher solve their decision problem, for example, identifying who should be punished.

4.3   *ge3 and assertiveness*

Having laid out the semantics of *ge3*, we can see how to account for its alleged assertive nature. The explanation has already been outlined in the discussion about *gaa3*. We argue that the assertive character of *ge3* corresponds to the Gricean inference that comes with its competition with *gaa3*. In the case of assertions, and in a context that would have licensed *gaa3*, using *ge3* instead can be interpreted as a signal that the speaker is not explicitly asking the addressee to indicate their acceptance of the assertion of the speaker. A very likely explanation for this is to assume the speaker is maximally certain of their claim and not presenting as susceptible to refutation. This predicts that the assertiveness inference disappears in contexts that disallow the use of a marker like *aa3*, which is precisely what we observed for examples such as (12).

5 Conclusion

Our study of Cantonese SFP shows that we can do away with semantic primitives like softness and assertiveness and instead treat them as derived effects based on the conversational and dialogical properties of SFP. An utterance is thus assertive or soft based not on the presence of either assertive or soft markers but because of the inferences one can draw based on the choice of certain lexical items in a given dialogical setting. In that, our treatment of the semantics of SFP matches that advocated by Luke (1990), who defends an approach to SFP that is conversational in nature. Our analysis therefore predicts that the SFPs we study are not necessarily soft or assertive. Accordingly, we showed examples of *aa3* that are not soft and examples of *ge3* that are not particularly assertive.

Another aspect of our core SFP, not mentioned in this study, is their relation with the gender of the speaker. As reported by Winterstein *et al.* (2018), there are significant gender differences in their usage. While all SFPs are used by all speakers, corpus data shows that *aa3* has a stronger tendency to be used by female speakers and *ge3* by male speakers (in casual conversations). The usual route to account for that situation would be to consider that the use of such particles is somehow gendered, for example, because they explicitly indicate a feminine register that is socially required to be softer (see a.o. Erbaugh 1985; Chan 2000; Yueh 2016).

Our analysis suggests another explanation for these gender differences. Instead of seeing them as signals that are compatible with the stereotypes associated with a certain gender, their conversational content suggests that the speaker can use them strategically to achieve certain ends. For example, the use of *aa3* explicitly involves the addressee in the grounding process of an information. In doing so, it also "borrows" the authority of the addressee to ground the information, which can help overcome various forms of epistemic injustice which minimize the authority of a speaker (for example, because they are female; Fricker 2007; McCready & Winterstein 2018). The details of these proposal shall form the body of future work.

Notes

1 Sybesma and Li (2007) actually claim that *aa3* attaches to exclamatives and imperatives, but all their examples are restricted to declarative and interrogative sentences. This is most likely because there is no clear exclamative sentence type in Cantonese and because, clearly, imperative sentence types in Cantonese are scarce (cf. our earlier discussion).

2 This parallel between Mandarin *de* and Cantonese *ge3* is often noted, and probably not accidental, given how both also work as genitive markers and enter parallel constructions involving the copula. We will not investigate these issues.

3 Note that KoS is a name rather than an acronym and does not stand for any particular phrase.

4 We omit the case of exclamatives whose status is unclear in Cantonese and whose formal treatment is also unclear.

5 Note that if the order is issued to a third person C, different from B, B's contribution with *aa3* in (12) is felicitous and signals the endorsement by B of the command to C.

6 We thank a reviewer for suggesting this possibility.

7 All Japanese examples are quoted from McCready (2012).

8 A reviewer suggests that this competition could be addressed via the *Maximize Presupposition!* (MP!) principle due to Heim (1990). Involving MP! might indeed be a good solution but would necessitate to show that the difference between *ge3* and *gaa3* is presuppositional in nature. Precisely, this would mean showing that the adherence to norm marked by *aa3* is a presupposition. Proving it is not straightforward, since most of the usual tests for presupposition (such as projection) cannot really apply to the content of SFP. We thus wish to remain noncommittal about that particular issue, simply noting that MP! might indeed end up being relevant to the matter.

References

Austin, John L. 1962. *How to do things with words William James lectures*. Cambridge: Harvard University Press.

Beyssade, Claire & Jean-Marie Marandin. 2006. The speech act assignment problem revisited: Disentangling speaker's commitment from speaker's call on addressee. In Olivier Bonami & Patricia Cabredo Hofherr (eds.), *Empirical issues in syntax and semantics*, vol. 6, 37–68. CNRS.

Chan, Marjorie K.M. 2000. Gender, society and the Chinese language. In Baozhang He & Wenze Hu (eds.), *Proceedings of the eleventh North American conference on Chinese linguistics (NACCL-11)*. Cambridge, MA: Harvard University.

Clark, Herbert H. 1996. *Using language*. Cambridge: Cambridge University Press.

Cook, Haruko Minegishi. 1990. An indexical account of the Japanese sentence-final particle no. *Discourse Processes* 13(4). 401–439. doi:10.1080/01638539009544768.

Davis, Christopher. 2009. Decisions, dynamics and the Japanese particle yo. *Journal of Semantics* 26. 329–366.

Eckert, Penelope & Sally McConnell-Ginet. 2013. *Language and gender*, 2nd edition. Cambridge: Cambridge University Press.

Erbaugh, Mary S. 1985. Sentence final particles as an Asian areal feature. In Scott De Lancey & Russell S. Tomlin (eds.), *Proceedings of the first annual meeting of the pacific linguistics conference*, 84–96. Eugene, Oregon: University of Oregon.

Fang, Xiaoyan. 2003. *Guangzhou fangyan jumo yuqi zhuci [Sentence final modal particles in the Guangzhou dialect]*. Guangzhou: Jinan University Press.

Fricker, Miranda. 2007. *Epistemic injustice: Power and the ethics of knowing*. Oxford: Oxford University Press.

Fung, Roxana Suk-Yee. 2000. *Final Particles in Standard Cantonese: Semantic Extension and Pragmatic Inference*: The Ohio State University dissertation.

Gazdar, Gerald. 1981. Speech act assignment. In Aravind Joshi, Bonnie Webber & Ivan A. Sag (eds.), *Elements of discourse understanding*, 64–83. Cambridge: Cambridge University Press.

Ginzburg, J. 2012. *The interactive stance: Meaning for conversation*. Oxford: Oxford University Press.

Ginzburg, J. & Ivan A. Sag. 2000. *Interrogative investigations: The form, meaning and use of English interrogatives*, vol. 123 CSLI Lecture Notes. Stanford, CA: CSLI Publications.

Grice, Herbert Paul. 1989. *Studies in the way of words*. Cambridge: Harvard University Press.

Hara, Yurie & Elin McCready. 2017. Particles of (Un)expectedness: Cantonese Wo and Lo. In M. Otake, S. Kurahashi, Y. Ota, K. Satoh & D. Bekki (eds.), *New frontiers in artificial intelligence: JSAI-isAI 2015: Lecture notes in computer science*, vol. 10091, 27–40. Berlin: Springer. doi:10.1007/978-3-319-50953-2_3

Heim, Irene. 1983. On the projection problem for presuppositions. *Proceedings of WCCFL* 2. 114–125.

Heim, Irene. 1990. Artikel und Definitheit. In A. V. Stechow & D. Wunderlich (eds.), *Handbuch der Semantik*, 487–535. Berlin: de Gruyter.

Huddleston, Rodney. 2002. Clause type and illocutionary force. In Rodney Huddleston & Geoffrey K. Pullum (eds.), *The Cambridge grammar of the English language*, 851–945. Cambridge: Cambridge University Press.

Karttunen, Lauri. 2016. Presupposition: What went wrong? *Proceedings of SALT* 26. 705–731.

Kwok, Helen. 1984. *Sentence particles in Cantonese*. Center of Asian Studies, University of Hong Kong.

Lakoff, Robin Tolmach. 1975. *Language and women's place*. New York: NY: Harper and Row.

Law, Ann. 2002. Cantonese sentence-final particles and the CP domain. In Ad Neeleman & Reiko Vermeulen (eds.), *UCL working papers in linguistics*, vol. 14, 375–398. UCL.

Law, Sam-Po. 1990. *The Syntax and Phonology of Cantonese Sentence-Final Particles*. Boston University dissertation.

Li, Charles, N. & Sandra A. Thompson. 1989. *Mandarin Chinese: A functional reference grammar*. Berkeley: University of California Press.

Luke, Kang Kwong. 1990. *Utterance particles in Cantonese conversation*. Amsterdam, Philadelphia: John Benjamins Publishing Company.

Luke, Kang Kwong & May L.Y. Wong. 2015. The Hong Kong Cantonese corpus: Design and uses. *Journal of Chinese Linguistics* 25. 312–333.

Matthews, Stephen & Virginia Yip. 2011. *Cantonese: A comprehensive grammar*, 2nd edition. Abingdon, UK: Routledge. doi:10.4324/9780203835012.

McCready, Elin. 2008. What man does. *Linguistics and Philosophy* 31. 671–724. doi:10.1007/ s10988-009-9052-7.

McCready, Elin. 2012. Formal approaches to particle meaning. *Language and Linguistics Compass* 6(12). 777–795. doi:10.1002/lnc3.360.

McCready, Elin & Grégoire Winterstein. 2018. Testing epistemic injustice. *Investigationes Linguisticae* 41. 86–104.

McGloin, Naomi Hanaoka. 1986. Feminine wa and no: Why do women use them? *The Journal of the Association of Teachers of Japanese* 20(1). 7–27. www.jstor.org/stable/489515.

Merin, Arthur. 1999. Information, relevance and social decision-making. In L.S. Moss, J. Ginzburg & M. de Rijke (eds.), *Logic, language, and computation*, vol. 2, 179–221. Stanford: CSLI Publications.

Rieser, Lukas. 2017. *Belief states and evidence in speech acts: The Japanese sentence final particle no*: Kyoto University dissertation.

Roberts, Craige. 1996. Information structure in discourse: Towards an integrated formal theory of pragmatics. OSU Working Papers in Linguistics, vol. 49: Papers in Semantics, 91–136. Jae Haek Yoon and Andreas Kathol.

Sadock, Jerrold M. 1974. *Towards a linguistic theory of speech acts*. New York: Academic Press.

Stalnaker, Robert C. 1978. Assertion. In P. Cole (ed.), *Pragmatics*, vol. 9 Syntax and Semantics, 315–322. New York: New York Academic Press.

Sybesma, Rint & Boya Li. 2007. The dissection and structural mapping of Cantonese sentence final particles. *Lingua* 117. 1739–1783.

Wang, Yu-Fang Flora & Miao-Ling Hsieh. 1996. A syntactic study of the Chinese negative polarity item renhe. *Cahiers de Linguistique Orientale* 25(1). 35–62. doi:10.3406/clao.1996.1491.

Winterstein, Grégoire, Regine Lai, Daniel Tsz-Hin Lee & Zoe Pei-sui Luk. 2018. From additivity to mirativity: The Cantonese sentence final particle *tim1*. *Glossa* 3(1:88). 1–38.

Winterstein, Grégoire & Gerhard Schaden. 2011. Relevance and utility in an argumentative framework: An application to the accommodation of discourse topics. In Alain Lecomte & Samuel Tronçon (eds.), *Ludics, dialogue and interaction*, 134–146. Berlin: Springer.

Yang, Pei Lin. 2010. *Imperatives in Chinese*. Taiwan National Chengchi University MA thesis.

Yueh, Hsin-I Sydney. 2016. *Identity politics and popular culture in Taiwan: A sajiao generation*. Lexington Books.

Zanuttini, R. & Paul Portner. 2003. Exclamative clauses: At the syntax-semantics interface. *Language* 79(1). 39–81.

Zhu, Xiaoya. 1994. xiàndài hànyǔ gǎntànjù chūtàn [Exploring the exclamative in modern Chinese]. *jiāngsū shīfàn dàxué xuébào : zhéxué shèhuìkē xuébǎn [Jiangsu Normal University Journal: Philosophy and Sociology]* 2. 124–127.

7 Formality weakening and the underspecified expressive *yo* in Korean

Soo-Hwan Lee

1 Introduction[1]

Potts (2005, 2007) discusses in detail the notion of expressives and how they denote something distinct from at-issue semantics. One defining property of expressives is repeatability: the iteration of an expressive signals a gradual heightening of one's emotional state. The Korean formality-denoting marker *si* nicely illustrates this point (Kim & Sells 2007):[2]

(1) pro *kong-ul   capa-po-ci   mos-ha-si-ess-ta.*
    3.SG ball-ACC catch-try-CI NEG-do-SI-PST-DECL
    '(S)he wasn't able to catch the ball.' ($\sim$ formal)

(2) pro *kong-ul   capa-po-si-ci   mos-ha-si-ess-ta.*
    3.SG ball-ACC catch-try-SI-CI NEG-do-SI-PST-DECL
    '(S)he wasn't able to catch the ball.' ($\sim$ more formal)

Choe (2004) notes that the increase of formality due to the repetition of *si* is an instance of formality strengthening. This is in tandem with the nature of repeatability.

Unlike ordinary formality-denoting expressives, however, the multiple realization of *yo* in Korean triggers the opposite effect of strengthening. (3)–(5) share the same descriptive content: 'Lee met Kim.' The presence of the sentence-final *yo* in (3) allows the speaker to convey a sense of formality to the addressee.[3] The addition of a sentence-medial *yo* in (4) weakens the level of the expressive content, and the addition of a secondary medial *yo* in (5) further undermines it. Note, however, that the cutback never amounts to zero, and a sense of formality is preserved even in (5).[4]

(3) *Lee-ka   Kim-ul   manna-ss-e-yo.*
    Lee-NOM Kim-ACC meet-PST-DECL-F.YO
    'Lee met Kim.' ($\sim$ formal)

(4) *Lee-ka   Kim-ul-yo   manna-ss-e-yo.*
    Lee-NOM Kim-ACC-M.YO meet-PST-DECL-F.YO
    'Lee met Kim.' ($\sim$ less formal)

DOI: 10.4324/9781351057837-8

(5)   *Lee-ka-yo*   *Kim-ul-yo*   *manna-ss-e-yo.*
      Lee-NOM-M.YO Kim-ACC-M.YO meet-PST-DECL-F.YO
      'Lee met Kim.' (∿ least formal)

Despite what is known about repeatability in the literature (Potts 2007; Mc-Cready 2019), the weakening effect induced by medial *yos* in Korean remains unexplored. To my knowledge, this phenomenon has not been analyzed with theoretical scrutiny (Lee & Park 1991; Yim & Dobashi 2016, 2018). Thus, I argue that (6) is an additional type of repeatability.

(6)   Weakening: each use of the expressive makes what it initially expresses weaker (example: medial *yo* in Korean).

Quite interestingly, medial *yos* can perform a weakening effect on a formality marker other than the final *yo*. (7)–(9) have the same descriptive content as (3)–(5): 'Lee met Kim.' The marker (*su*)*pni* triggers formality in (7). The realization of medial *yo*(s) in (8) and (9) triggers the weakening effect observed in (4) and (5). Note that the final *yo* is not realized in these examples:[5]

(7)   *Lee-ka*   *Kim-ul*   *manna-ss-supni-ta.*
      Lee-NOM Kim-ACC meet-PST-PNI-DECL
      'Lee met Kim.' (∿ very formal)

(8)   *Lee-ka*   *Kim-ul-yo*   *manna-ss-supni-ta.*
      Lee-NOM Kim-ACC-M.YO meet-PST-PNI-DECL
      'Lee met Kim.' (∿ less formal)

(9)   *Lee-ka-yo*   *Kim-ul-yo*   *manna-ss-supni-ta.*
      Lee-NOM-M.YO Kim-ACC-M.YO meet-PST-PNI-DECL
      'Lee met Kim.' (∿ least formal)

In the absence of the final *yo* or (*su*)*pni*, however, medial *yos* cannot be realized in the derivation. Hence, medial *yos* are dependent on other formality-denoting expressives:[6]

(10) **Lee-ka-yo*   *Kim-ul*   *manna-ss-e/ta.*
      Lee-NOM-M.YO Kim-ACC meet-PST-DECL
      Intended: 'Lee met Kim.'

Here, I argue that medial *yos* are underspecified in terms of their expressive content and therefore must be accompanied by another formality-denoting marker that can fill in the gap.[7] This work will address which information medial *yos* lack in particular and how this issue can be properly resolved.

The purpose of this work is twofold. First, I address a pattern of repeatability which has been understudied in the literature (Lee & Park 1991; Yim

2012): the iterative use of *yo* in Korean weakens the strength of formality. Second, I argue that not all expressives are fully specified in nature.

The organization of this work is as follows: Section 2 examines whether medial and final *yo*s qualify as expressives using Potts's (2007) diagnostics. Section 3 discusses a theoretical approach to handling the underspecificity and the weakening effect of medial *yo*s. Section 4 explores whether medial *yo*s display properties of indexicals. Section 5 concludes.

2   Medial and final *yo*s as expressives

In this section, I mainly show that medial and final *yo*s satisfy all the properties Potts (2007) assumes for expressives, except for one, namely, repeatability, which we focus much of our attention on throughout this work. In addition to the typological observation made by McCready (2019), I elaborate on why the weakening effect should be a subclass of repeatability.

2.1   Expressive properties

First, let us go over each of the expressive properties and examine whether they are compatible with medial and final *yo*s. Under Potts's (2007) scrutiny, expressives exhibit six major properties: (a) independence, (b) nondisplaceability, (c) perspective dependence, (d) descriptive ineffability, (e) immediacy, and (f) repeatability.

Independence shows that the descriptive meaning, which is truth-conditional, is separate from the expressive meaning, which is non-truth-conditional. To illustrate, (11) conveys two different sources of meaning which cannot be readily unified.

(11)   The honkies received all the credit.
- *Descriptive: The White people received all the credit.*
- Expressive: The speaker has a bad opinion about the White people.

The same can be said about (12). Its descriptive content and expressive content cannot be readily unified.

(12)   *Sonnim-i-yo   wa-ss-e-yo.*
       guest-NOM-M.YO come-PST-DECL-F.YO
- *Descriptive: The guest came.*
- Expressive: The speaker is being a bit formal to the addressee.

Nondisplaceability shows that expressives predicate something of an utterance situation (see also McCready 2019). Hence, expressives outscope operators internal to an utterance. To give a comparison, the non-expressive *despised White people* in (13a) cannot scope over the past-tense operator *yesterday*, and thus a contradiction is not observed. However, the expressive *honkies* in (13b) must scope over the past-tense operator *yesterday*, and thus a contradiction is observed in the second sentence:

(13) a. *The despised White people received all the credit yesterday. (But they are not despised today, because today they received no credit.)*
   b. *The honkies received all the credit yesterday. (#But they are not honkies today, because today they received no credit.)*

Medial and final *yo*s also display this property. That is, they scope over tense operators. (14) contains two sentences denoting events in two different time settings: (i) the first sentence denotes an event in the past, whereas (ii) the second sentence denotes an event in the present. If medial and final *yo*s in the first sentence display nondisplaceability and must scope over past-tense operators such as *ecey* 'yesterday,' the following sentence leads to a contradiction: the speaker is conveying formality but is, at the same time, conveying informality. This prediction is borne out:

(14) *Ecey   sonnim-i-yo wa-ss-e-yo.   (#cey-ka   cikum*
    yesterday guest-NOM come-PST-DECL-F.YO (1.SG-NOM now
    cokum mwulye-ha-key say-do-PST-NEY(-F.YO).)
    a.bit rude-ADJ-KEY *mal-hay-ss-ney(-yo))*
    • *Descriptive: The guest came yesterday. (I was being a bit rude/informal just now.)*
    • Expressive: The speaker is being a bit formal to the addressee. (#The speaker is a bit rude/informal to the addressee.)

The embedding of *yo* under an attitude verb also yields the same effect. (15) shows that medial *yo* realized inside the embedded clause scopes over the matrix attitude verb *think*.[8] This is consistent with the idea that the expressive content should be independent from the descriptive content. (16) is contradictory in that medial *yo* must scope over a direct-quoted embedded clause, which traps scope-taking elements within its domain.

(15) *John-i   ecey   sonnim-i-yo   wa-ss-ta-ko*
    John-NOM yesterday guest-NOM-M.YO come-PST-DECL-C
    sayngkak-hay-yo.
    think-do-F.YO
    • *Descriptive: John thinks that the guest came yesterday.*
    • Expressive: The speaker is being a bit formal to the addressee.

(16) *#John-i   ʿecey   sonnim-i-yo   wa-ss-taʾ-lako*
    John-NOM yesterday guest-NOM-M.YO come-PST-DECL-C
    sayngkak-hay-yo.
    think-do-F.YO
    • *Descriptive intended: John thinks 'the guest came yesterday.'*
    • Expressive intended: The speaker is being a bit formal to the addressee.

Expressives reflect the emotion or the attitude of a particular individual, which is subject to **perspective dependence**. The expressive in (17) conveys the speaker's emotion toward a particular group of individuals, namely, *the White people*. As noted earlier, the expressive content cannot convey the emotion of any random individual:

(17) *The honkies received all the credit.*
  • *Descriptive: The White people received all the credit.*
  • Expressive: The speaker(/#someone other than the speaker) has a bad opinion about the White people.

Medial and final *yo*s share this property. That is, they always reflect the speaker's attitude toward the addressee and no one else.

(18) *Sonnim-i-yo   wa-ss-e-yo.*
   guest-NOM-M.YO come-PST-DECL-F.YO
  • *Descriptive: The guest came.*
  • Expressive: The speaker(/#someone other than the speaker) is being formal to the addressee(/#someone other than the addressee).

Expressive contents cannot be adequately paraphrased in truth-conditional terms. This property is referred to as **descriptive ineffability**.[9] Instead of defining them in descriptive terms, Potts (2007) uses *expressive index*, which hosts a real-numbered interval (I):

(19) An *expressive index* is a triple *<a I b>*, where *a* and *b* are in the domain of entities and $I \subseteq [-1, 1]$.   (Potts 2007:177)

In *<a I b>*, *a* and *b* may be represented as the speaker and the addressee of a conversation or a referent that the two interlocutors have in mind. When $I \subseteq [0, 1]$, positivity is conveyed. When $I \subseteq [-1, 0]$, negativity is conveyed. As for $[-1, 1]$, no expressive contribution is available, as it encompasses all possible Is. With the expressive index, the semantics of the following sentences may be represented as (20) and (21) ($[referent]$[10] in (20) refers to *the White people*):

(20) *The honkies received all the credit.*
  • *Descriptive: The White people received all the credit.*
  • Expressive: <$[speaker][-1, 0][referent]$>

(21) *Ce salam-i   tangkun-ul an   mek-e-yo.*
   that person-NOM carrot-ACC NEG eat-DECL-F.YO
  • *Descriptive: That person doesn't eat carrots.*
  • Expressive: <$[speaker][0, 1][addressee]$>

Is are flexible enough to be overwritten by Is of other expressives. **Immediacy,** another property of expressives, ensures that the overwriting process cannot take away the content which has already been uttered. This is because the effect of an expressive is immediate and cannot be undone. However, it is possible to make the content more specific by overwriting **I**s *within* the range of their initial real-numbered figures (e.g., [0, 1] (initial **I**) ⇒ [.5, 1] ⇒ [.75, 1]).[11] Epithets and formality-denoting markers are no exceptions.

The final defining property of expressives is **repeatability**: the iteration of an expressive signals a gradual heightening of one's emotional state.

(22) Repeatability
    If a speaker repeatedly uses an expressive item, the effect is generally one of strengthening the emotive content, rather than one of redundancy.   (Potts 2007:167)

This property is observed when the overwriting process of **I** takes place possibly multiple times. Potts (2007) provides (23) as an example of repeatability. The multiple realization of *damn* induces the desired strengthening effect:

(23) a. Damn, I left my keys in the car.
     b. Damn, I left my damn keys in the car.
     c. Damn, I left my damn keys in the damn car.   (Potts 2007:182)

The multiple realization of *yo*, on the other hand, does not elevate the level of its expressive content (see also Choi 2021). Rather, the opposite effect holds. Recall that (3)–(5) showcase this effect. They are repeated in what follows:

(24) *Lee-ka   Kim-ul   manna-ss-e-yo.*
    Lee-NOM Kim-ACC meet-PST-DECL-F.YO
    'Lee met Kim.' (⁓ formal)

(25) *Lee-ka   Kim-ul-yo   manna-ss-e-yo.*
    Lee-NOM Kim-ACC-M.YO meet-PST-DECL-F.YO
    'Lee met Kim.' (⁓ less formal)

(26) *Lee-ka-yo   Kim-ul-yo   manna-ss-e-yo.*
    Lee-NOM-M.YO Kim-ACC-M.YO meet-PST-DECL-F.YO
    'Lee met Kim.' (⁓ least formal)

Little has been discussed in the literature on how the overwriting process works for non-strengthening effects. In the next subsection, I present one way of addressing the overwriting process for the weakening effect induced by medial *yos*.

2.2   *The weakening effect induced by medial yos*

In addition to the general mechanism discussed in Section 2.1, I introduce two key concepts for capturing the weakening effect displayed by medial *yos*. First is the double down-arrow ⇓, which indicates the decrease in the level of formality. Second is the operator $+n$, which indicates the actual number of iteration present in the derivation. Putting these two together, I represent the overwriting process as $\Downarrow_{+n}$:

(27) a. *Ce salam-i   tangkun-ul an mek-e-yo.*
        that person-NOM carrot-ACC NEG eat-DECL-F.YO
        • *Descriptive: That person doesn't eat carrots.*
        • Expressive: <[*speaker*][0, 1][*addressee*]>

   b. *Ce salam-i   tangkun-ul-yo   an mek-e-yo.*
        that person-NOM carrot-ACC-M.YO NEG eat-DECL-F.YO
        • *Descriptive: That person doesn't eat carrots.*
        • Expressive: <[*speaker*][0, 1]$\Downarrow_{+1}$[*addressee*]>

   c. *Ce salam-i-yo   tangkun-ul-yo   an   mek-e-yo.*
        that person-NOM-M.YO carrot-ACC-M.YO NEG eat-DECL-F.YO
        • *Descriptive: That person doesn't eat carrots.*
        • Expressive: <[*speaker*][0, 1]$\Downarrow_{+2}$[*addressee*]>

The mean value of the initial **I** is taken to be the maximum value of the overwritten **I**. Similarly, the mean value of the updated **I** is taken to be the maximum value of the next overwritten **I**. The process repeats itself each time a medial *yo* is added to the derivation. **I** takes into account that certain discourse cues may bias the outcome of **I**. Potts (2007:178) mentions that facial gestures, hand gestures, posture, tone, and pitch are some potential factors inducing these biases. He posits that **I** is designed to accommodate these uncertainties. **I** incorporate the variable β, which reflects any biases present in the context. When an instance of non-truth-conditional semantics is subject to repeatability, β adjusts **I** accordingly. That is, β, which can be a positive or a negative value, adds or subtracts the minimum or the maximum value in order to reflect the discourse situation. (28) illustrates how this mechanism works.

(28) The overwriting process of the weakening effect in **I** terms
     $[min_1+\varphi, max_1+\varphi] \Rightarrow [min_1+\varphi, max_2+\varphi] \Rightarrow [min_1+\varphi, max_3+\varphi] \ldots \Rightarrow$
     $[min_1+\varphi, max_n+\varphi]$
     ☞ $max_2 = (min_1+max_1)/2$
     ☞ $max_3 = (min_1+max_2)/2$
     . . .
     ☞ $max_n = (min_1+max_{n-1})/2$

Applying (28) to **I**$\Downarrow_{+n}$ in (27a)–(27c) yields (29a)–(29c). Here, I take φ to be 0 ($\varphi = 0$), as no discourse bias is specified.[12]

(29) a. (27a) **I**: [0, 1] (no overwriting process)
     b. (27b) **I**: [0, 1]$\Downarrow_{+1}$ = [0, (0+1)/2] = [0, .5]
     c. (27c) **I**: [0, 1]$\Downarrow_{+2}$ = [0, (0+1)/2]$\Downarrow_{+1}$ = [0, .5]$\Downarrow_{+1}$ = [0, (0+.5)/2] = [0, .25]

(29) captures three essential qualities of medial *yo*s. First, the minimum and the maximum values of an overwritten **I** are contained within their initial threshold (e.g., [0, 1] in the case of (27)). Contrast this with an unconstrained subtractive system which may produce non-existing values, such as *−100* and *−1,000*. Second, the overwriting process is, by and large, autonomous. That is, reference to external sources other than the number of iteration (i.e., *+n*) is unnecessary. Due to this autonomy, defining expressive contents can be simplified (see Section 3.2 for more discussion). The mechanism captures another significant characteristic of repeatability. That is, the *n*th round of iteration brings a greater impact to its expressive content than the *n*+1th round. Compare the drop of formality between (29a)–(29b) and (29b)–(29c). The gap between the two maximum values of the former is greater than that of the latter. Simply put, the decline in formality becomes subtler as more iterations are applied to the derivation.

While *yo* exhibits many of the properties defined in Potts (2007), repeatability seems to be one exception. In fact, McCready (2019) posits that Potts's definition of repeatability is not entirely adequate when data from Thai and Japanese are given consideration. I argue alongside McCready and assume that more needs to be articulated about the effect(s) of repeatability. McCready classifies repeatability into three subclasses. Here are some examples: (i) The multiple use of *damn* triggers a strengthening effect, as we saw in (23). (ii) The multiple use of *sensei* 'teacher' preserves its expressive content without strengthening it. McCready classifies this type of phenomenon as 'reinforcement.' (iii) The expression *good morning* is not considered to be repeatable by virtue of its meaning: one can only greet once. McCready assumes that a single use of the expression is enough to convey the full potential of its content, and thus, iteration is by no means necessary in an ordinary setting.

(30) (McCready 2019:134)
  a. *Strengthening: each use of the expressive makes what it expresses stronger.* (example: *damn* in English)
  b. Reinforcing: each use of the expressive keeps what it expresses salient. (example: *sensei* in Japanese)
  c. Unrepeatable: repetition induces infelicity. (example: *good morning* in English)

Despite McCready's typological survey, the weakening effect induced by medial *yo*s has not been reported. Hence, I propose (31), which is repeated from (6), as a new subclass of repeatability.

(31) Weakening: each use of the expressive makes what it initially expresses weaker (example: medial *yo* in Korean).

In the next section, I explore theoretical ways of defining medial and final *yo*s and examine the nature of the weakening effect in greater detail.

3   Lexical entries and the analysis

In this section, I introduce McCready's (2019) analysis on defining formality-denoting expressives. McCready's approach is most suitable for analyzing Thai and Japanese discourse markers, but it can also be used to characterize the roles of Korean expressives, including medial and final *yo*s. Based on Mc-Cready's assumption, I provide details on how the weakening effect in Korean may be represented in lexical entry terms.

3.1   Thai formality markers khá and khráp

McCready (2019) provides lexical entries for various expressives in Thai and Japanese. Among these discourse particles, the formality-denoting markers *khá* and *khráp* in Thai closely resemble Korean final *yo* in three crucial ways: (i) they are vacuous in terms of descriptive content, (ii) they represent the speaker's attitude toward the addressee, and (iii) they are realized at the end of a sentence. Consider (32) and (33):

(32) *Fŏn dtòk khá*
      rain fall POL.PT
      • *Descriptive: It's raining*
      • Expressive: The feminine speaker is being formal to the addressee.
      (Thai, McCready 2019:45)

(33) *Mii   gaaf..khráp*
      exists coffee POL.PT
      • *Descriptive: There is coffee.*
      • Expressive: The masculine speaker is being formal to the addressee.
      (Thai, McCready 2019:47)

Type specification of expressive contents differs from that of descriptive contents (Potts 2005, 2007; McCready 2019). Type-theoretically, this is to separate the composition of the two, since they are not semantically composable. Mc-Cready (2019) labels the descriptive type as σ^a and the expressive type as σ^s (σ is a metavariable).[13] A language-specific feature of Thai that relates to our discussion is gender specification. Quite interestingly, *khá* is used to express femininity, whereas its counterpart, *khráp*, is used to express masculinity. McCready specifies the former as $fem(s_C)$, denoting a feminine speaker of the context, and the latter as $mas(s_C)$, referring to a masculine speaker of the context. Under this system, the semantics of *khá* and *khráp* are represented as (34) and (35), respectively:

(34) Lexical entry for *khá* in Thai
      $[\![khá]\!]^C = (Hon = [.6, 1] \wedge fem(s_C)): t^s$ (McCready 2019:46)

(35) Lexical entry for *khráp* in Thai[14]
      $[\![khá]\!]^C = (Hon = [.6, .9] \wedge masc(s_C)): t^s$ (McCready 2019:46)

For derivational clarity, I provide semantic trees with type specifications for (32) and (33):

(36) Tree derivation for (32)

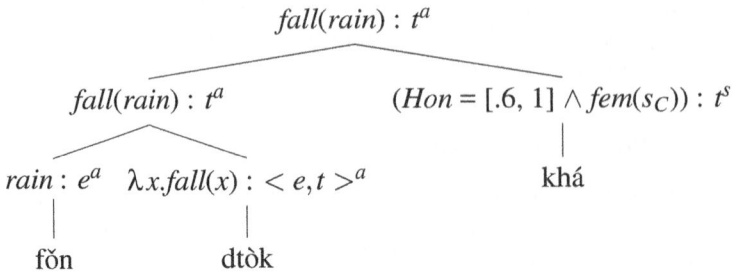

(37) Tree derivation for (33)

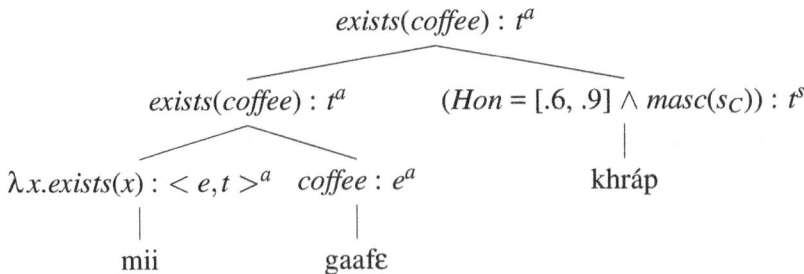

Note that t^a and t^s do not compose. In other words, they do not interact. Hence, the output semantics given in (38) and (39) represents the descriptive content and the expressive content on separate grounds:

(38) Output semantics of (32)
    <*fall*(*rain*), {*Hon* = [.6, 1], *fem*(s_C)}>   (McCready 2019:47)

(39) Output semantics of (33)
    <*exists*(*coffee*), {*Hon* = [.6, .9], *masc*(s_C)}>   (McCready 2019:47)

The expressive semantics for (38) is valid if a feminine speaker is conveying formality to the addressee and **I** is defined as [.6, 1]. The expressive semantics for (39) is valid if a masculine speaker is conveying formality to the addressee and **I** is defined as [.6, .9].

   McCready introduces additional apparatuses for handling lexical items conveying both expressive and descriptive contents, referred to as mixed contents. Japanese honorific copulas such as *desu* and *gozar* fall under this category (McCready 2019:49).[15] Further elaboration on mixed contents, however, need not be introduced in this work, since the weakening effect of formality in Korean only applies to items that are purely non-descriptive (e.g., *yos* and (*su*)*pni*).

Hence, I adopt McCready's core analysis on expressive contents, leaving out much of the discussion on mixed contents.

3.2 Korean formality markers

Adopting McCready's general analysis on *khá* and *khráp*, I provide (40) and (41) as the lexical entries for final and medial *yo*s, respectively.[16] Here, I specify the interlocutors, namely, the speaker and the addressee, in order to better represent the *expressive index* given in Section 2.1. *F* labeled above **I** refers to formality:

(40) Lexical entry for final *yo*
$$[\![yo_{final}]\!] = ([speaker][0, 1]^F[addressee]): t^e$$

(41) Lexical entry for medial *yo* (☞ **I**^{F} is underspecified)
$$[\![yo_{medial}]\!] = ([speaker]\mathbf{I}^{F\Downarrow}_{+1}[addressee]): t^e$$

The lexical entry given in (40) can be applied to (42) and (43). They yield nearly the same output as (38) and (39) in part by aligning the expressive content next to the descriptive content:

(42) *pi-ka nayli-e-yo*
rain-NOM fall-DECL-F.YO
<*fall(rain)*, {[*speaker*][0, 1]^F[*addressee*]}>

(43) *khephi-ka iss-e-yo*
coffee-NOM exist-DECL-F.YO
<*exists(coffee)*, {[*speaker*][0, 1]^F[*addressee*]}>

In order to derive the weakening effect, more needs to be articulated. The lexical entry for medial *yo* given in (41) showcases this effect.[17] As mentioned in Section 2.2, $\Downarrow$ indicates the decrease in expressive strength, and +*n* indicates the number of iteration in the derivation. Crucially, note that **I**^{F} is underspecified for medial *yo*s, unlike final *yo*. The lexical entries (40) and (41) capture the fact that final and medial *yo*s take on different roles: Final *yo* generates formality, whereas medial *yo* takes away a portion of formality. The division of labor correctly predicts the weakening effect observed in (45) and (46) as well as the absence of the effect in (44).

(44) *Lee-ka Kim-ul manna-ss-e-yo.*
Lee-NOM Kim-ACC meet-PST-DECL-F.YO
'Lee met Kim.' (∿ formal)

(45) *Lee-ka Kim-ul-yo manna-ss-e-yo.*
Lee-NOM Kim-ACC-M.YO meet-PST-DECL-F.YO
'Lee met Kim.' (∿ less formal)

(46) *Lee-ka-yo Kim-ul-yo manna-ss-e-yo.*
Lee-NOM-M.YO Kim-ACC-M.YO meet-PST-DECL-F.YO
'Lee met Kim.' (∿ least formal)

For clarity, I provide a step-by-step derivation for (44)–(46).[18] I align the expressive content next to the descriptive content in each step of the derivation if there is one. [*speaker*] and [*addressee*] are abbreviated as [*s.*] and [*h.*], and the type specifications of the descriptive and expressive contents (e.g., σ^a and σ^e) are omitted for simplicity. Lastly, I provide the following rule to sum up the number of iterations used in a given derivation (see (50) on how this rule is applied to an actual example). The mother node adds up the operators $+n$ and $+m$ of its daughter nodes in a compositional fashion:[19]

(47) Compositional rule for iterative $\mathbf{I}^r$

$$\{...\mathbf{I}^\alpha\!\Downarrow_{+n+m}...\}$$

$$\{...\mathbf{I}^\alpha\!\Downarrow_{+n}...\} \quad \{...\mathbf{I}^\alpha\!\Downarrow_{+m}...\}$$

With (47), we are now in a position to flesh out the semantic details of the sentences hosting medial *yo*(s). The derivations for (44)–(46) are given in (48)–(50):

(48) Tree derivation for (44)

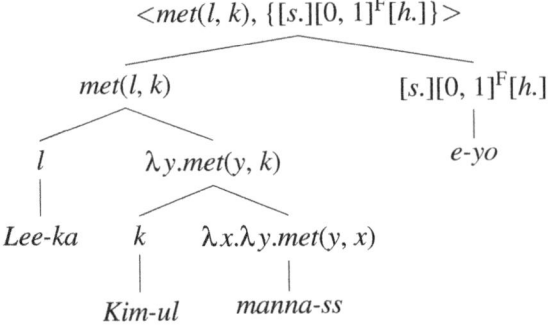

(49) Tree derivation for (45)

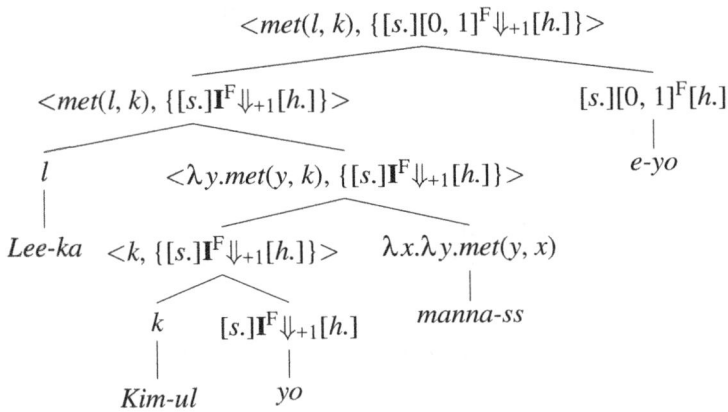

(50) Tree derivation for (46)

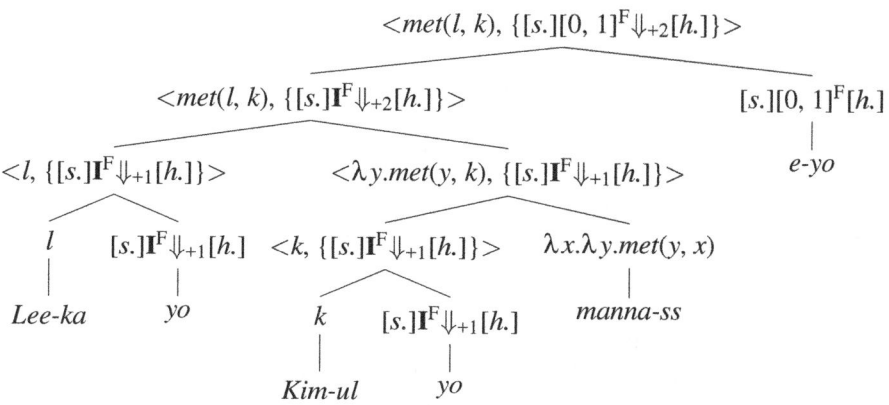

After the trees are built compositionally, the final step of the derivation involves applying (28) to (48)–(50). This yields the following results:

(51) [(48)] <*met*(*l*, *k*), {[*speaker*][0, 1]^F[*addressee*]}>
(52) [(49)] <*met*(*l*, *k*), {[*speaker*][0, .5]^F[*addressee*]}>
(53) [(50)] <*met*(*l*, *k*), {[*speaker*][0, .25]^F[*addressee*]}>

Similar results are derived even in the absence of final *yo*. (54)–(56), repeated from (7)–(9), host (*su*)*pni*, which conveys a higher degree of formality than final *yo*:

(54) *Lee-ka   Kim-ul   manna-ss-supni-ta.*
      Lee-NOM   Kim-ACC   meet-PST-PNI-DECL
      'Lee met Kim.' (∿ very formal)

(55) *Lee-ka   Kim-ul-yo   manna-ss-supni-ta.*
      Lee-NOM   Kim-ACC-M.YO   meet-PST-PNI-DECL
      'Lee met Kim.' (∿ less formal)

(56) *Lee-ka-yo   Kim-ul-yo   manna-ss-supni-ta.*
      Lee-NOM-M.YO   Kim-ACC-M.YO   meet-PST-PNI-DECL
      'Lee met Kim.' (∿ least formal)

In order to represent the varying degrees of formality, **I**s for final *yo* and (*su*)*pni* ought to differ. The lexical entry for (*su*)*pni* is provided in the following:

(57) Lexical entry for (*su*)*pni*
      [[(*su*)*pni*]] = ([*speaker*][.5, 1]^F[*addressee*]): t^s

(41) and (57) together yield the following interim output for (54)–(56):

(58) [(54)] <*met*(*l, k*), {[*speaker*][.5, 1]^F[*addressee*]}>
(59) [(55)] <*met*(*l, k*), {[*speaker*][.5, 1]$^{F\Downarrow}_{+1}$[*addressee*]}>
(60) [(56)] <*met*(*l, k*), {[*speaker*][.5, 1]$^{F\Downarrow}_{+2}$[*addressee*]}>

Applying (28) to (58)–(60) yields the following results:

(61) [(58)] <*met*(*l, k*), {[*speaker*][.5, 1]^F[*addressee*]}>
(62) [(59)] <*met*(*l, k*), {[*speaker*][.5, .75]^F[*addressee*]}>
(63) [(60)] <*met*(*l, k*), {[*speaker*][.5, .625]^F[*addressee*]}>

Unlike final *yo*, medial *yo*s are always reliant on another formality-denoting marker. The host need not be final *yo*, but rather *(su)pni* as in (54)–(56). Medial *yo*s cannot surface in the absence of final *yo* or *(su)pni*. No other discourse marker can rescue the derivation. This form of dependency suggests that medial *yo* is not an ordinary expressive:

(64) a. *Lee-ka-yo   Kim-ul   manna-ss-e*(-yo).*
        Lee-NOM-M.YO Kim-ACC meet-PST-DECL-F.YO
        'Lee met Kim.'
     b. *Lee-ka-yo   Kim-ul   manna-ss*(-supni)-ta.*
        Lee-NOM-M.YO Kim-ACC meet-PST-PNI-DECL
        'Lee met Kim.'

Although Choi (2021) correctly observes that medial *yo*s do not induce a strengthening effect, he is not able to account for the weakening effect of medial *yo*s. This is mainly because Choi assumes that both medial and final *yo*s are defined with the same **I** and that their **I**s are averaged when realized together. Additionally, the analysis is unable to capture the simple strengthening effect induced by *si* shown in (1) and (2). More needs to be articulated about this data point. Moreover, it does not provide an adequate explanation as to why medial *yo*s are always dependent on another expressive item whereas final *yo* is not.[20] Lee and Park (1991) and Yim (2012) also mention the dependency of medial *yo*s. Here, I argue that the dependency arises because medial *yo*s lack a fully specified **I**^{F} and must rely on a fully specified **I**^{F} elsewhere in the derivation. The lexical entry given in (41) yields this effect. It also predicts that medial *yo*s are flexible enough to be realized with formality markers hosting different levels of **I**^{F}, such as final *yo* ([0, 1]^F) and *(su)pni* ([.5, 1]^F). Here, I argue that the parasitic nature of medial *yo*s sheds light on an unexplored aspect of non-descriptive semantics. Under my analysis, medial *yo*s are underspecified, and the restriction imposed on their distribution suggests that not all expressives are unconstrained in nature (see also Lee & Kim 2018).

4   Indexicals and free indirect discourse (FID)

Before concluding, I would like to examine whether medial and final *yos*
can be viewed as indexicals rather than expressives. One way to test this
is to see if they can target the utterance level in free indirect discourse
(FID). FID, which appears in the form of an embedded clause, reflects the
speaker's perspective instead of the matrix subject's perspective by shifting the center of deixis. Only a small number of indexical pronouns are
able to display this effect. This is sometimes referred to as indexical shift.
A question arises as to whether *yos* are subject to indexical shift in FID.
My analysis predicts that *yos* will not display this effect, since they are not
indexicals.

In many cases, FID is attested by shifting personal pronouns (e.g., first-
person pronoun → third-person pronoun). The shifting of person pronouns
is closely tied with the alternation between direct discourse (DD) and FID.
One obvious difference between DD and FID is that the former employs direct quotations whereas the latter does not. An English example of shifting
personal pronouns (e.g., *I → he*) is given in (65). The first-person pronoun in
(65a) refers to *John* from the perspective of the matrix subject (DD), whereas
the third-person pronoun in (65b) refers to *John* from the perspective of the
speaker (FID):

(65) a. *"I$_1$ would buy some chocolate on my$_1$ way to work," John$_1$ said.* (☞ DD)
     b. *He$_1$ would buy some chocolate on his$_1$ way to work, John$_1$ said.* (☞ FID)

Note that embedding a medial *yo* under DD is not possible in Korean.
For one, DD should not be grammatically integrated with the matrix
clause. Also, medial *yos* do not reflect the matrix subject's perspective
but rather the speaker's. This is expected under the expressive account.
Consider the following example, where a medial *yo* cannot surface within
DD:

(66) *John$_1$-I*   *"nay$_1$(/#ku$_1$/#caki$_1$)-ka(#-yo)*   *wang-i-ta"-lako*
     John-NOM   1.SG(/#3.SG.D/#3.SG.L)-NOM(#-M.YO)   king-COP-DECL-C
     mal-hay-ss-e-yo.
     say-do-PST-DECL-F.YO
     • *Descriptive: "I$_1$ am the king," John$_1$ said.*
     • Expressive: The speaker (/#John) is being formal to the addressee.

(67) and (68) host Korean third-person pronouns *ku* (default) and *caki* (logo-
phoric). In both examples, the embedded medial *yo* projects out of FID and
targets the utterance-level discourse. This is possible because FID reflects the
speaker's perspective. Hence, formality is maintained between the speaker and
the addressee of the conversation.[21]

(67) *John₁-i   ku₁-ka-yo   tangshin-ul silhe-ha-n-tako mal-hay-ss-e-yo.*
John-NOM 3.SG.D-NOM-M.YO 2.SG-ACC dislike-do-PRES-C say-do-PST-DECL-
E.YO
- *Descriptive: He₁ dislikes you, John₁ said.*
- Expressive: The speaker (/#John) is being a bit formal to the addressee.

(68) *John₁-i   caki₁-ka-yo   tangshin-ul silhe-ha-n-tako mal-hay-ss-e-yo.*
John-NOM 3.SG.L-NOM-M.YO 2.SG-ACC dislike-do-PRES-C say-do-PST-DECL-
E.YO
- *Descriptive: He₁ dislikes you, John₁ said.*
- Expressive: The speaker (/#John) is being a bit formal to the addressee.

English expressives such as *honkies* can be used in FID. However, it is not entirely clear whether they always project out of an embedded clause. (69) differs from (67) and (68) in that the expressive content can either reflect the attitude of the speaker or the subject of the matrix sentence:

(69) *No, really, here he₁ didn't want to meet any honkies, John₁ said.*
- *Descriptive: He₁ didn't want to meet White people, John₁ said.*
- Expressive: The speaker (/John) has a bad opinion about White people.

Speas and Tenny (2003) also mention that epithets such as *damned* may reflect the attitude of the speaker or the matrix subject when the sentence is embedded under a predicate of speech:

(70) *John said he phoned his damned cousin.* (damned by the speaker, or the subject)

(Speas & Tenny 2003:328)

In fact, Harris and Potts (2009) report that non-speaker-oriented readings are possible for English expressives even if they are not syntactically embedded under a predicate. In such cases, a rich contextual cue is necessary.

Although examples such as (69) and (70) seem to require further scrutiny, I wish to emphasize that Korean medial *yo*s are always speaker-oriented. Simply put, they are always the widest scope-taking element in a given sentence. In fact, this is exactly the kind of result that one would expect from a non-descriptive (expressive) content.

5   Conclusion

The previous notion of repeatability requires further scrutiny. Unlike ordinary formality-denoting markers, sentence-medial *yo*s show an uncommon pattern of behavior: the more *yo*s you have within a sentence, the less sense of formality you get. Further, the distribution of medial *yo*s suggests that they are dependent on other expressives. I have put forward the claim that medial *yo*s are impoverished in terms of their expressive content. We have also seen that medial *yo*s do not behave like indexicals. The implication we derive from these findings is that there are restrictions on expressives which can be explained using previously established theoretical means. By exploring this particular aspect of Korean, I hope to have shed light on the weakening effect as well as the parasitic nature of medial *yo*s.

Abbreviations

1	first person	LOC	locative
2	second person	M.YO	medial *yo*
3	third person	NEG	negation, negative
ACC	accusative	NOM	nominative
ADJ	adjective	POL.PT	politeness particle
C	complementizer	PRES	present
COP	copula	PST	past
DECL	declarative	SG	singular
F.YO	final *yo*	TOP	topic

Notes

1 **Acknowledgements:** My greatest thanks go to Chris Barker, Philippe Schlenker, and WooJin Chung. This work would not have been possible without them. I would also like to thank Elin McCready, Hiroki Nomoto, and the audience at LSA 2021 for their valuable comments. All remaining errors are my own.
2 In Korean, various terms such as *politeness* and *honorifics* have been adopted to characterize formality. For present purposes, I wish not to make a fine-grained distinction among these terms.
3 I briefly note that sentence-final *yo* conveys less formality than many other formality-denoting markers in Korean. However, this does not mean that final *yo* is used in informal contexts: a sentence with final *yo* conveys more formality than the baseline sentence without a formality marker.

   (i) a. *Lee-ka   Kim-ul   manna-ss-e.*
        Lee-NOM Kim-ACC meet-PST-DECL
        'Lee met Kim.' (⤳ baseline: formality valued at 0)
      b. *Lee-ka   Kim-ul   manna-ss-e-yo.*
        Lee-NOM Kim-ACC meet-PST-DECL-F.YO
        'Lee met Kim.' (⤳ formal: formality valued above 0)

   All else being equal, final *yo* does trigger a sense of formality, although its effect may be subtle.
4 Medial and final *yo*s behave like clitics: (i) they can attach to various grammatical categories without actually changing the category, and (ii) they can attach to phrases instead of words (see Yim & Dobashi 2016, 2018):

   (i) [$_{XP}$ *Lee-wa *(-yo) Kim-i*]-*yo*   *wa-ss-e-yo.*
      [$_{XP}$ Lee-and   Kim-NOM]-M.YO come-PST-DECL-F.YO
      'Lee and Kim came.'

   Further, there may be a non-trivial correlation between formality weakening and the elevation of some other content, such as engagement or hesitation, when medial *yo*s are used in different discourse settings (see Lee & Park (1991) for an overview on these various discourse effects). While I recognize this form of dynamicity, the focus of this work is to provide an account for the formality-weakening effect displayed by medial *yo*s.

5 A naturally occurring sentence hosting a medial *yo* and (*su*)*pni* is provided in the following:

(i) *Sinmwun-un-yo*   *capdongs ani-ka ani-pni-ta.*
   newspaper-TOP-M.YO junk-NOM   NEG-PNI-DECL
   'Newspapers are not junk.' (Korean National Corpus; MBC 100 Minute Debate)

6 Medial *yo*s can only be licensed by formality markers that reflect the speaker's attitude toward the addressee.

   Formality markers other than final *yo* and (*su*)*pni* such as *nim* (nominalizer), *pwun* (classifier), *kkeyse* (nominative case), and *si* may reflect the speaker's attitude toward a referent who is not the addressee. These particles, along with other discourse markers, be it informal or non-formal, do not have a medial *yo* counterpart and thus cannot display the weakening effect.

7 Elin McCready (p.c.) mentions that this phenomenon could be viewed as a kind of presupposition failure at the expressive level. While this idea seems very interesting, I leave much of the discussion for future research.

8 Philippe Schlenker (p.c.) mentions that the impossibility of semantically embedding expressives under attitude verbs in English is at least debated.

9 Geurts (2007) mentions that descriptive ineffability is not a decisive property of expressives. For present purposes, I wish to emphasize that defining expressives without a descriptive content *is* possible. This does not necessarily imply that all expressives are descriptively undefined. I leave much of the broader discussion for future research.

10 In this work, I use square brackets to indicate expressive entities and real-numbered intervals (Is). Double square brackets indicate lexical entries (see Section 3.2).

11 I will discuss in detail how the overwriting process works for medial *yo*s in Section 2.2.

12 For convenience, β is set to 0 by default.

13 According to McCready (2019), type denotation itself (*a* or *s*) is not crucial. What is important, however, is the type distinction made between the descriptive and the non-descriptive contents.

14 The maximum value of *khráp* is capped off at .9 because there is a particle in Thai that conveys a higher level of formality, namely, *khrápphôm*.

15 Korean honorific nominalizer *nim* and honorific classifier *pwun* may also be viewed as mixed contents.

16 I leave out gender specification since final and medial *yo*s do not specify gender identity.

17 Yim and Dobashi (2018) also distinguish medial *yo* from final *yo*. They recognize the meaning difference between the two, but little is mentioned about the actual semantics of medial *yo*s. Here, I wish to fill in the gap.

18 Final *yo* is always the last element on the verb. It comes after the tense marker as well as the declarative and question particles. Following Choi (2016) and Yim (2012), I place final *yo* in a position structurally higher than the verb. Also, there are cases where the verb is followed by right dislocated constituents:

(i) a. *Ecey*   *Lee-ka*   *Kim-ul*   *manna-ss-e-yo.*
      yesterday Lee-NOM Kim-ACC meet-PST-DECL-F.YO
      'Lee met Kim yesterday.'
   b. *Ecey*   *Kim-ul*   *manna-ss-e-yo*   *Lee-ka.*
      yesterday Kim-ACC meet-PST-DECL-F.YO Lee-NOM
      'Lee met Kim yesterday.' (right dislocated subject)

   c. *Ecey   Lee-ka   manna-ss-e-yo   Kim-ul.*
      yesterday Lee-NOM meet-PST-DECL-F.YO Kim-ACC
      'Lee met Kim yesterday.' (right dislocated object)

   d. *Lee-ka   Kim-ul   manna-ss-e-yo   ecey.*
      Lee-NOM Kim-ACC meet-PST-DECL-F.YO yesterday
      'Lee met Kim yesterday.' (right dislocated adverb)

These constructions do not pose a challenge under my analysis, since syntactic movement to the right periphery of the matrix clause is done only after the final *yo* is introduced in the derivation.

19 Although the upper limits to the variables +*n* and +*m* are not mentioned in this work, I wish to emphasize that the variables should not be astronomical in number. Instead, they should be simple enough for linguistic computation. Further, the compositional rule given in (47) may potentially apply to degree modifiers (e.g., very very tall and slightly slightly tall). While this topic is relevant and worth pursuing, I leave much of the discussion for future research.

20 Reducing this issue to syntactic licensing such as agreement also does not seem to be desirable, since other types of expressives, such as epithets, do not require the same type of licensing.

21 Philippe Schlenker (p.c.) mentions that a similar effect is observed for French *tu/vous* in DD and FID:

(i) *J'ai fait un rêve étrange. Nous étions deux enfants dans la même classe, j'étais assis à vos côtés, et vous me disiez que vous aviez du mal avec votre exercice de maths.*
(Translation) I had a strange dream. The two of us were children in the same class, I was sitting next to you-formal, and you-formal told me that you-formal had trouble with your-formal math exercise.

   a. *"Je vis bien sûr t' aider," vous répondis-je.* (☞ DD)
      (Translation) "I am of course going to help you-familiar," I replied to you-formal.

   b. *?J' allais bien sûr t' aider, vous répondis-je.* (☞ FID)
      (Translation) I was of course going to help you-familiar, I replied to you-formal.

   c. *? "Je vais bien sûr vous aider," vous répondis-je.* (☞ DD)
      (Translation) "I am of course going to help you-formal," I replied to you-formal.

   d. *J'allais bien sûr vous aider, vous répondis-je.* (☞ FID)
      (Translation) I was of course going to help you-formal, I replied to you-formal.

References

Choe, Jae-Woong. 2004. Obligatory honorification and the honorific feature. *Studies in Generative Grammar* 14(4). 545–559.

Choi, Jaehoon. 2016. The discourse particle *-yo* in Korean: Its implications for the clausal architecture. *Rivista di Grammatica Generativa* 38. 65–73.

Choi, Jaehoon. 2021. An 'expressive' analysis of *-yo* in Korean. *The Journal of Linguistics Science* 98. 455–476.

Geurts, Bart. 2007. Really fucking brilliant [Commentary on Chrisopher Potts, the expressive dimension]. *Theoretical Linguistics* 33. 209–214.

Harris, Jesse & Christopher Potts. 2009. Perspective-shifting with appositive and expressives. *Linguistics and Philosophy* 32(6). 523–552.

Kim, Jong-Bok & Peter Sells. 2007. Korean honorification: A kind of expressive meaning. *Journal of East Asian Linguistics* 16(4). 303–336.

Lee, Chungmin & Sunghyun Park. 1991. *-Yo* ssuimuy kwucowa kinung [The structure and function of the mid-sentential *-yo* construction]. *Linguistic Journal of Korea* 16. 361–389.

Lee, Soo-Hwan & Minjung Kim. 2018. Suppletive allomorphy conditioned by humbleness in Korean. In *Proceedings of the 44th Annual Meeting of the Berkeley Linguistics Society*, 131–146.

McCready, Elin. 2019. *The semantics and pragmatics of honorification: Register and social meaning*. Oxford: Oxford University Press.

Potts, Christopher. 2005. *The logic of conventional implicature*. Oxford: Oxford University Press.

Potts, Christopher. 2007. The expressive dimension. *Theoretical Linguistics* 33(2). 165–197.

Speas, Peggy & Carol Tenny. 2003. Configurational properties of point of view roles. In Anna Maria Di Sciullo (ed.), *Asymmetry in grammar*, 315–344. Amsterdam: John Benjamins.

Yim, Changguk. 2012. Fragment answers containing *-yo* in Korean: New evidence for the PF deletion theory of ellipsis. *Linguistics Inquiry* 43(3). 514–518.

Yim, Changguk & Yoshihito Dobashi. 2016. A prosodic account of *-yo* attachment in Korean. *Journal of East Asian Linguistics* 25. 213–241.

Yim, Changguk & Yoshihito Dobashi. 2018. On the distribution of the discourse particles *-yo* in Korean and *-ne* in Japanese. In Kunio Nishiyama, Hideki Kishimoto & Edith Aldridge (eds.), *Topics in theoretical Asian linguistics: Studies in honor of John B. Whitman*, 125–138. John Benjamins.

Index

Printed and bound by CPI Group (UK) Ltd, Croydon, CR0 4YY

28/11/2024

01796647-0006